CITIZEN  ISLAM

CITIZEN
ISLAM

The Future of Muslim Integration in the West

ZEYNO BARAN

WITH EMMET TUOHY

continuum

2011
The Continuum International Publishing Group
80 Maiden Lane, New York, NY 10038
The Tower Building, 11 York Road, London SE1 7NX

www.continuumbooks.com

Library of Congress Cataloging-in-Publication Data
Baran, Zeyno
Citizen Islam : the future of Muslim integration in the West / Zeyno Baran.
    p. cm.
ISBN-13: 978-1-4411-0400-7 (hardcover : alk. paper)
ISBN-10: 1-4411-0400-3 (hardcover : alk. paper)
ISBN-13: 978-1-4411-1248-4 (pbk. : alk. paper)
ISBN-10: 1-4411-1248-0 (pbk. : alk. paper)
    1. Muslims—Europe—Politics and government. 2. Muslims—United States—Politics and government. 3. Islamic fundamentalism—Europe. 4. Islamic fundamentalism—United States. 5. Islam and politics—Europe. 6. Islam and politics—United States. I. Title.
    D1056.2.M87B36 2011
305.6'97091821—dc22   2011004343

Typeset by Pindar NZ, Auckland, New Zealand
Printed and bound in the United States of America

Contents

Preface

In the present volume, Zeyno Baran has managed to shed new light on a subject of timeless importance: the dynamic relationship between religion and the state. For millennia, politics and faith have in some societies been locked in cycles of bitter conflict, while in others they have coexisted in peaceful harmony. This same opposition can be found today between countries based on the secular principle of *laïcité*, on the one hand, and those based on fundamentalist interpretations of Islamic *sharia* law, on the other.

In the first group — found mostly in the West — the state is governed not according to religious dictates, but secular laws. Public order is maintained by these laws, leaving religion as a matter between individuals and God. The state does not ask anything from religious communities — which, in turn, ask nothing from the state.

By contrast, in many majority-Muslim countries, Islam has — as Baran demonstrates in these pages — developed into the *political* ideology of Islamism, which calls for *sharia* law to be applied both to individuals and to the state. Mixing the eternal teachings of a religion like Islam with the volatile, changing demands of politics is a recipe for creating chaos. Political Islamism damages not only political institutions, but Islam itself.

The dangers of mixing politics and religion were highlighted by Jean-Jacques Rousseau, who in 1792 wrote, "Whenever theological intolerance is allowed, it is impossible for it not to have some civil effect; and once it does, the sovereign no longer is sovereign, not even over temporal affairs. Thenceforward, priests are the true masters; kings are simply officers."

The best way to handle this tension is to place religion in a separate sphere of respect, and then conduct politics outside it. This is how the Republic of Turkey has proceeded since its founding in 1924. Although a majority of its citizens are Muslims, the Republic is based on the principles of secular law. The state and religion are separated; both work together in pursuit of the common goals of progress and growth. This is a very significant revolution. Of the 55 countries with majority-Muslim populations, Turkey is uniquely distinguished by the way in which it has combined democracy, secularism, Islam and modernity.

Certainly, these are still important topics of popular debate and discussion in Turkey and elsewhere, and they will long remain so. But with this work, Zeyno Baran has strengthened the case for separating religion and politics, thus making it possible for one to hope that this debate will lead to positive outcomes for governments and for faith communities all across the world.

Suleyman Demirel
9th President of Turkey

CHAPTER 1

Introduction

This book explores one of the most serious strategic threats confronting the United States and Europe today: the advance of Islamism. I define Islamism as a political-religious ideology asserting that Muslims are obligated to convince other Muslims to restructure their private lives and societal norms to reflect God's divine law, or sharia. Islamism shares the most fundamental aim of Islam and all religions — to bring the world closer to God. But Islamism is an ideology with a political agenda that differentiates it from the religion of Islam. While millions of Muslims around the world believe their religion is compatible with modern society, Islamists believe all societies must adapt to the legal and social norms of sharia, and they seek political power to achieve this global transformation. Islamists thus maintain that all forms of government, including secular democracies, must at some point be replaced by Islamic theocracies based on sharia. Islamists' ultimate goal is the establishment of a worldwide community of Muslims (*umma*) unified in a single Islamic state (caliphate) ruled by an Islamic leader (caliph). Islamism is therefore a utopian ideology that blends politics and religion.

Islamism is comprised of diverse strains that differ according to their adherents' patience for and tolerance of diverse interpretations of sharia. The most impatient and intolerant group of Islamists are terrorists like Osama bin Laden, who use violence to speed implementation of their draconian conception of sharia, which they insist is the only correct way

1

to interpret God's divine law. The next most extreme faction is the Salafis, a loose grouping of Sunni Muslims who seek to reestablish the legal and social norms of seventh-century Arabia in today's world. The Wahhabis of Saudi Arabia are the most influential sect under the Salafi umbrella. A Shiite group analogous to Salafism is Khomeinism in Iran.

On the more patient end of the spectrum are organizations like Hizb ut-Tahrir (HT), which officially reject violence and strive to gain political power through a step-by-step process they hope will culminate in theocratic states leading ultimately to the caliphate. More patient still is the Muslim Brotherhood, a global organization founded and headquartered in Egypt that has a vast network across Europe and the United States; this group aims to achieve political power through elections and then use that power to restructure society according to sharia's norms. At the most patient and tolerant end of the Islamist spectrum are activists like Tariq Ramadan, who use Western rhetoric on tolerance and religious freedom to allay Western concerns while consolidating Muslims in Europe and the United States into unified communities that coexist alongside mainstream society instead of integrating with it. Despite their differing tactics and levels of tolerance, all of these various types of Islamists share the same ultimate goal: to replace secular governments and the rule of secular law with sharia.

Since September 11, 2001, Western leaders have failed to differentiate *Islamism*, the ideology, from *Islam*, the religion. They have learned through trial and error that referring to "Islamic terrorism" is highly offensive to Muslims around the world, and have therefore avoided exploring how religion and politics fuse when Muslims commit terrorism. But terrorism, or violence in pursuit of political objectives, continues to be committed in the name of Islam. It is the ideology of Islamism that defines the terrorists' political goals; they are therefore *Islamist* rather than *Islamic* terrorists. Condemning Islamist terrorism thus does not equate with attacking Islam. On the contrary, Western leaders need to make clear that they are natural partners for the vast majority of the world's non-Islamist Muslims, who also oppose Islamist terrorism and seek to prevent Islamists from hijacking Islam in pursuit of their utopian political vision.

A great debate rages today over whether to work with nonviolent Islamists to deter impatient Islamists from committing terrorism. The fundamental argument of this book is that the West should avoid this Faustian bargain. The West's true partners are Muslim moderates who not only reject violence but also believe in the compatibility of Islam with democracy and universal human rights. Such a partnership is essential to blunting Islamists' efforts to undercut the core values of modern society. Moreover, the "root causes" of terrorism can never be eradicated as long as Islamist ideology continues to thrive and motivate terrorists.

For the past several decades, Islamists have misrepresented their extremist ideology in the West as mainstream Islamic thinking. Their efforts have been boosted by billions of dollars from the governments and private citizens of Saudi Arabia and several other Gulf states. This support has allowed Islamists to found a wide range of institutions aimed at establishing their political interpretation of Islam as the dominant Muslim discourse in the United States and Europe. These include imam training centers, elementary and secondary schools, youth clubs, and civic action groups. Islamist movements seek to use such institutions to advance their utopian social engineering project: to "Islamize" the world through a gradual, bottom-up process.

The initial step in the Islamists' grand strategy is to transform individuals into "true Muslims," meaning people who seek to restructure their lives according to sharia. Over time, individuals are supposed to incorporate aspects of sharia into their lives. From the non-Islamist perspective, some of these aspects are positive (such as surrendering to God's will and helping other members of the Muslim community with everyday problems) while others are negative (such as treating women unequally and showing hostility toward non-Muslims). As these Islamizing Muslims' lives are increasingly based on sharia, they gradually reject Western norms of political pluralism, tolerance of ethnic and religious differences, individual rights, and the rule of secular law. The next steps in the Islamization process are the adoption of sharia norms by family members and the refocusing of their identities toward their Muslim community rather than their country of citizenship. Islamists expect that, as other families undergo this transformation, they will eventually coalesce into a single Muslim community that conceives of itself as a society existing in parallel with mainstream society and owing primary allegiance to Islam rather than to a nation-state. As that Muslim community grows in size and clout, Islamists anticipate it will apply political pressure for sharia norms to be introduced into mainstream society. As its influence grows, Islamists believe, the Muslim community will eventually secure political power and transform preexisting secular states into theocracies governed by sharia.

The ultimate step is for Islamists to gain political control of governments around the world, and unify all countries into the caliphate. Those who refuse to convert to Islam in the final stages of the world's Islamization will face a stark choice: either abide by sharia or die. While the vast majority of Islamists prefer to Islamize the world by peaceful means, they accept the potential need for violence to counter resistance to the final unification of the *umma* and the establishment of the caliphate.

To a non-Muslim reader this thesis may sound alarmist. But the devastating impact of Islamist rule on society has already been demonstrated in Afghanistan, where the Taliban regime violently implemented gender apartheid during the 1990s. Moreover, as Chapter 5 will show, Islamist activists are already demanding and securing the introduction of sharia norms into mainstream society in several European countries. To a Muslim like myself, raised in a democratic country, it is self-evident that Islamism threatens to undermine the fundamental liberties Muslims enjoy in modern societies. I reached this conclusion not because of any personal political conviction or ideological agenda, but because of my experience growing up as a Muslim in Turkey.

I was raised to believe, like most of Turkey's 70 million Muslims, that Islam and democracy can and must coexist; that there are a myriad of ways to interpret Islam; that I can be both a pious Muslim and a modern woman; and that the center of my religion is my personal relationship with God. But not all Turkish Muslims are as secure in their identities as I am. I witnessed firsthand how Islamist recruiters manipulate young Turkish Muslims, who are struggling to understand their identity as both Muslims and citizens of a secular and democratic society, by offering clear-cut answers to perplexing questions. Several of my acquaintances during high school followed the Islamist path of radicalization, withdrawing from their circle of friends, then rejecting their families' Islamic traditions, and finally adopting elements of sharia in their daily lives.

I was resistant to Islamist recruiters because of my upbringing, which was relatively typical for a Turkish child in the 1970s and 80s. My family's geographic origins were diverse, as were the ways in which its members practiced Islam. On my father's side, my great-grandfather was born into a Muslim family in Macedonia and settled near Ankara, the heart of secular Turkey, where he and my great-grandmother led a highly secular life. On my mother's side, my great-grandmother came from Bulgaria and settled in Konya, the center of religious Turkey. Konya is also where one of the greatest Islamic mystics, Mevlana Celaleddin Rumi, lived out his life and is buried. My great-grandmother was a Sufi (Islamic mystic) and a follower of Rumi's teachings of love and compassion, although she lived an outwardly secular lifestyle. Like her and millions of other Turks, I was raised to treat religion as a private matter between God and myself. I was taught that those who make their religion public do so not for God, but for themselves, either to improve their personal reputation or to make a political statement against the secular order.

I spent most of my summers in the Princes' Islands, an archipelago in the Sea of Marmara that is part of Istanbul, where Turks, Greeks, Jews, and Armenians have lived harmoniously for centuries. The imam of the mosque I attended never emphasized religious differences among these diverse communities, but instead highlighted our commonalities. His teachings were about being a good *human being*, not about being a good *Muslim*. Neither he nor anyone around me ever taught that gender segregation or female covering were essential aspects of Islam. "What matters most is not what is on your head but what is in your heart" was the teaching I best remember. My family's way of understanding Islam was typical of Turkish people; until the spread of Islamism in the 1970s and 80s, it was the norm in many other Muslim-majority countries as well.

I was alarmed as a high school student in the mid-1980s when I noticed a different form of Islamic understanding encroaching on Turkey in the wake of Iran's Islamist revolution in 1979. For the first time in my life, interpretations of Islam that felt alien and repressive, especially for women, were gaining traction in Turkey. My family, friends, and I were shocked when a small number of Turkish citizens publicly expressed hope for a revolution in Turkey similar to Iran's, which would eliminate the democratic and social freedoms that defined our lives as Turkish Muslims.

My best friend and I found Islamist ideas so difficult to comprehend that, in order to get a sense of what the life of a woman adhering to Islamist norms might be like, we devised a small experiment. We donned the full black Islamic veil (chador) for several days. At that time, few women in Turkey wore this ultraconservative attire; even the most pious women would wear only headscarves. My friend and I were curious. We wanted to find out how we would feel while wearing the chador, and how various segments of Turkish society would react to us. From the moment we put on the full veil, we felt restricted in our actions, as we constantly had to ensure none of our inner clothing or body would be exposed. Only our hands and eyes could be visible. We experienced two diametrically opposed reactions from Turkish society. In modern parts of Istanbul, we were kicked out of Western stores, ridiculed for being "penguins," and cursed by women wearing miniskirts. The moment we entered a McDonald's restaurant, all diners froze in silence and stared at us as if we were total aliens. Istanbul's secular mainstream reacted with hostility because they viewed us as propagandist tools of Iranian and other Islamist radicals who sought to spread sharia norms to Turkey. In more conservative sections of Istanbul, we experienced the opposite reaction. Women and men showed us respect and made us feel welcome, even though our dress was more conservative than the norm in their neighborhoods. Our most memorable experience was on a public bus: instead of the usual sexual harassment Turkish women often endure on buses, male passengers immediately offered us seats and referred to us as "sisters."

Whatever the smaller lessons of the experiment — for instance, that some women might welcome the chador as a way to avoid sexual harassment — the larger lesson was clear: Turkish society was becoming torn between those who feared the growth of Islamism as a threat to their way of life, and those who wanted to live according to conservative interpretations of Islamic norms.

When I came to the United States in 1990 to attend college, I was surprised to find elements of Islamism taking hold at my campus in northern California. During my first year, I initially socialized with members of the Muslim student organization, searching for a reassuring sense of cultural familiarity in a distant land. But I was taken aback by the association's overwhelming focus on the Arab world, the Israeli–Palestinian dispute, and the application of sharia to the West. I was disappointed by Arab graduate students who spent all their free time with other Muslims and left the United States without learning much about Americans or American culture. I worried they would bring their distorted views of the United States and the West back to their countries in the Middle East, and fuel tensions between tolerant Muslims and Islamists. These tensions increased during the 1990s, and finally exploded, literally, into the world's consciousness with the terror attacks of September 11, 2001.

On that day, I once again experienced in a deeply personal way how Islamists were fusing religion and politics. That tragic morning, I had just entered an internet café in London when the first plane hit the World Trade Center. I heard raucous cheers from several young men of South Asian descent gathered around a computer. As I approached their computer to see why they were making such a racket, I saw the second plane hit. At first I thought I was observing a computer game, and was shocked when I heard one of the men rejoice: "Yeah, they deserved it!" Others joined in, adding comments such as "It's about time." Then I heard more jubilant cheers as it was reported that another airplane had hit the Pentagon and that others were about to hit the White House and the US Capitol. I felt sick to my stomach, knowing that my fiancé would at that time be in his office at the National Security Council within the White House complex.

Although I didn't understand it at the time, the terror attacks of September 11 were part of a long-term violent Islamist political strategy Osama bin Laden had been pursuing for several years. Bin Laden had issued a declaration of war on America on August 23, 1996, ostensibly in protest of the US military presence in Saudi Arabia, the site of Islam's most sacred shrines.[1] In February 1998, bin Laden created the World Islamic Front for Jihad against Jews and Crusaders to plan and conduct terrorist attacks with the goal of aggravating tension between Muslims and non-Muslims while undercutting secular governments. His underlying goal was to accelerate the coming of the *umma* and caliphate. In August 1998, al-Qaeda foot soldiers took a key step in implementing the plan, launching terror attacks on the US embassies in Kenya and Tanzania. Bin Laden's next move was the attack on the USS *Cole* in Yemen in 2000. Each of these acts helped lay the foundation for the attacks of September 11. In true Islamist style, bin Laden targeted the core symbols of American secular power: the US financial system, as symbolized by the World Trade Center; the US military's headquarters at the Pentagon; and the US political system, embodied by either the US Capitol or the White House — the targets of the fourth plane that, thanks to the heroism of its supremely courageous passengers, was brought down well before it reached Washington.

Bin Laden hoped the September 11 attacks would pull the United States and its Western allies into a military conflict he could portray as a "war against Islam." He anticipated that such a conflict would force people around the globe to choose between the West and the "Muslim world," thereby pushing Muslims into the struggle to replace secular law with sharia and to reestablish the caliphate. As al-Qaeda propagandist Saif al-Adl later remarked, the goal of the September 11 strikes was to provoke the United States to "lash out militarily against the *umma*" and thereby generate Muslim hostility toward the West. Al-Adl further noted, "The Americans took the bait . . . and fell into our trap."[2] Bin Laden's binary "us versus them" view had particular impact in the West: loyal Muslim citizens of the United States and of European countries felt new pressures from

---

1   The full title of bin Laden's statement was: "Message from Osama bin Laden to His Muslim Brothers in the Whole World and Especially in the Arabian Peninsula: Declaration of Jihad against the Americans Occupying the Land of the Two Holy Mosques (Saudi Arabia); Expel the Heretics from the Arabian Peninsula."

2   Fouad Hussein, "Al Zarqawi: The Second Generation of Al Qaeda — Seif al-Adl's Testament," part 9, *Al-Quds al-Arabi* (May 23, 2005), cited in Fawas A. Gerges, *The Far Enemy: Why Jihad Went Global* (Cambridge: Cambridge University Press, 2005), p. 322.

Islamist organizations to band together with other Muslims to protect against a coming assault from non-Muslims.

It was my research into the radical Islamist organization Hizb ut-Tahrir (HT) that fully opened my eyes to the gravity of Islamism's strategic threat to the West, and that enabled me to see that both bin Laden and nonviolent Islamist groups were in reality pursuing the same agenda. Since HT's founding in the 1950s in East Jerusalem as an offshoot of the Muslim Brotherhood, the outwardly nonviolent group has striven to unify Muslims into a single community and reestablish the caliphate. Though banned in Germany because of its harsh anti-Semitic rhetoric, HT has been able to operate with impunity in much of the West from its London headquarters. In my effort to understand HT's ideology and operations, I discovered how HT uses Western freedoms to catalyze Muslims' hatred of the United States, the West, and secular government in general. I found that HT is organized according to a secretive cell structure, patterned after that of the Bolshevik revolutionaries in early twentieth-century Russia. Its underlying (and unpublicized) aim is to establish centralized governing structures that would replace secular democracy with sharia rule. Moreover, despite HT's claims that it is not a violent organization, it has consistently instigated Islamist violence, thereby serving as a "conveyor belt" to terrorism.

My investigation of these worrisome aspects of HT was immeasurably helped by my experiences growing up in Turkey, where, since 1979, waves of Islamism threatening secular freedoms have ebbed and flowed. That other Muslim moderates shared my concerns became evident during a conference I organized on HT in February 2004. Conference participants from Muslim countries expressed serious and growing worry about the destructive power of HT's ideas; several noted that, despite HT's official renunciation of violence, the organization had attempted military coups in Jordan (1968), Syria (1969), and Egypt (1974). Most Muslim participants in the conference argued that Western governments should investigate and consider banning HT for its sedition, hate-mongering, and incitement to violence. In stark contrast, most participants from the United States and Europe opposed any action against HT because the organization had declared itself to be nonviolent. While Western participants expressed concern about HT's anti-Semitism, they were more focused on upholding Western values of freedom of speech and religion than on addressing HT's record of violence, its seditious political objectives, and its rejection of any alternative interpretation of Islam. As the conference ended, I was deeply dismayed that Western societies tolerated the intolerance of HT and other Islamist organizations, and that they did not see the commitment of these groups to political insurgency.

When I published a study of HT that compiled the above findings,[3] HT's leadership responded with an open letter condemning me for supposedly mischaracterizing their ideas and tactics. Yet despite this official condemnation, several former HT activists reached out to tell me I was in fact on track. One of them was Maajid Nawaz, HT's former number two in the United Kingdom. Born to a Pakistani family in Britain, Nawaz joined HT at age 16 and became a successful recruiter. He was sent to Pakistan, which as a nuclear power was viewed by HT as a potential seat for the future caliphate. Later, Nawaz operated in Denmark (where HT would play a significant role during the "cartoon crisis"[4] of 2005–2006). Nawaz eventually became disillusioned by HT's ideology and quit the group in 2007. We met in person in July 2008 at a hearing of the United States Senate Committee on Homeland Security entitled "The Roots of Violent Islamist Extremism and Efforts to Counter it," at which we both testified. Our presentations were almost identical in their characterization of the strategic threat confronting the West as Islamism in all its forms, not just "violent Islamist extremism." At the end of the hearing, Nawaz told me that my study of HT, in which I first spoke of the organization as a conveyor belt to terrorism, had hurt the organization. But, he added, "you were right."

I might never have reached these conclusions about HT and Islamism in general had I not been a Muslim moderate who was already concerned about Islamist ideology's encroachment on democracy. It was therefore understandable (though disappointing) that top leaders in the United States did not come to the same conclusions. Following September 11, American leaders were consumed with the urgency of stopping terrorist groups from carrying out any further terror attacks. They found it hard to accept that they were faced with a larger-scale threat of a political-religious movement that aimed to undermine secular democracy, as I myself witnessed in the Oval Office.

---

3   Zeyno Baran, *Hizb ut-Tahrir: Islam's Political Insurgency* (Washington, DC: The Nixon Center, 2004), available at: www.nixoncenter.org/Monographs/Hizbutahrir IslamsPoliticalInsurgency.pdf (accessed January 19, 2011).

4   On September 30, 2005, the Danish newspaper *Jyllands Posten* published a collection of cartoons depicting the prophet Muhammad, an act strictly forbidden according to most Islamic traditions. A wave of boycotts and protests — resulting in the deaths of approximately one hundred people — soon spread throughout the Islamic world, incited and exploited by Islamist groups.

I was privileged to be among a small group of academics who were asked to meet with President George W. Bush, along with Vice President Richard Cheney, National Security Advisor Stephen Hadley, Chief Political Advisor Karl Rove, and several other key national security officials, to explore how the United States could prevent further attacks and stop the spread of Islamic extremism. I told the president that the fundamental threat confronting the United States and its allies was not the tactic of terrorism but the strategic danger of Islamist ideology subverting democracy. I stressed the importance of differentiating between Islam, the religion, and Islamism, the political-religious ideology. I also called for the West to partner with Muslim moderates to counter Islamist extremists, who threaten Muslims and non-Muslims alike. Finally, I warned that unless Western leaders tackled the strategic threat of Islamist ideology, they would continue to lose the battle over the hearts and minds of this and the next generation of Muslims.

I did not expect that my brief presentation would generate any fundamental shifts in US policy. After all, the dominant thinking among US academics, policy analysts, Muslim activists, and Islamic scholars was (and still is) that neither ideology nor religion had anything to do with the terrorism of September 11. According to such conventional thinking, the United States could eradicate the "root causes" of terror not by confronting Islamist ideologues, but by "engaging" all nonviolent Muslims, regardless of their political agenda, in an effort to lessen their anti-Western hostility. According to this view, a key mechanism for reducing tension between Muslims and non-Muslims in the West is to further the integration of Muslims into mainstream society. To foster such integration, the United States and its allies in Western Europe have embraced Islamist organizations, which are the largest umbrella groups of Muslims. But Western leaders have failed to recognize that these same Islamist "partners" ultimately seek to undermine such integration in pursuit of the *umma* and caliphate.

US political leaders have been partnering with Islamist organizations for decades, inadvertently helping them to establish Islamist extremism as mainstream Islamic thought among American Muslims. In foreign policy, US officials have followed a similar pattern. For decades, Saudi Arabia has been one of America's most important allies, despite its promotion of Wahhabism, a draconian interpretation of Islam that seeks to restore and impose the legal and social norms of seventh-century Arabia — everywhere. Muslim moderates around the world have long understood the danger of partnering with Saudi Arabia on Islamic issues. After all, it is the moderates who most urgently feel the threat of Islamist ideologues and their efforts to silence them, often through violence. As one Moroccan government official told me in May 2007,

> [w]e are so confused. The U.S. wants us to fight al-Qaeda, but at the same time tells us we need to increase cooperation with Saudi Arabia, which gave us the problem [of Wahhabism] in the first place. What is America's real goal?

Similarly, a Muslim researching political Islam told me skeptically, "Your efforts to separate Islam and Islamism are nice but will go nowhere as long as the Americans remain so close to the Saudis, who promote the Wahhabis."

European officials have made many of the same mistakes as their American counterparts, as evidenced by their ongoing partnerships with Islamist groups like the Muslim Brotherhood. In my meetings with European government officials, law enforcement agencies, and experts working on Muslim integration and radicalization, I have found them reluctant to discuss how Islamism's political-religious ideology threatens their democratic institutions and core values. Accepting this reality would require fundamental and discomfiting changes in assumptions about terrorism, ideology, integration, and Islam that have become conventional wisdom throughout Europe. Rather than identifying and countering Islamist activists who seek to undermine European freedoms, many Europeans have chosen the politically correct path of blaming themselves and the Americans for Islamist terrorism, citing US foreign policy, social injustice, and Muslims' status outside the mainstream of Western society as the fundamental causes of "violent extremism" in the West.

Following September 11, and even more so after the bombings in Madrid in March 2004 and London in July 2005, Europeans seized on social integration as crucial to eliminating the root causes of terrorism at home. European countries generally adopted two approaches to integrating Muslims into mainstream society. The first of these approaches, *assimilation*, most prominently followed in France, seeks to forge a national identity based on common ideals regardless of religion or ethnicity, and insists such differences must melt away as immigrants blend into a single French identity. While this approach has enjoyed some success among educated Muslims, it has worked against social integration in the Muslim ghettos surrounding France's largest cities. The relatively less-educated and poorer French Muslims living in decaying suburbs feel that the French government is ignoring their specific grievances. Rather than listening to their concerns, the French government insists that all Muslims simply "become French." As a result, many young Muslims in France, those who are most susceptible to Islamist recruiters, feel even more alienated from mainstream French society.

The second approach, *multiculturalism*, the integration approach most prominently followed in the Netherlands and the UK, embraces the cultural distinctiveness of each ethnic and religious minority, but without discerning whether trends within these communities run contrary to society's mainstream values. Moreover, multiculturalism categorizes Muslims according to their families' religion and national origins, rather than accepting them as fully "Dutch" or "British." This leaves many Muslims in these countries feeling increasingly alienated, rather than integrated into the mainstream. As in the case of assimilation, multiculturalism thus creates openings for Islamist recruiters.

By averting their gaze from Islamists' ideology and their efforts to implement it, European leaders have cleared the way for Islamists to establish parallel societies among European Muslims. Islamists now provide a range of social services that duplicate those provided by the state, thereby emphasizing that Muslims should stick together as a single community while adjusting their lives to the norms of sharia.

Islamists thus seek to push Western societies toward sharia rule by aggravating Muslims' social alienation. Many of the most radical (and effective) Islamist recruiters go one step further by exploiting spiritual alienation. This is a condition that arises among many second- and third-generation Muslims in Europe as they search to understand their Muslim identity after having lost touch with their families' Islamic traditions. Islamist recruiters are ready to step in to fill this spiritual vacuum, providing straightforward, often simplistic answers to challenging questions of Muslim identity — answers that invariably reflect the radical fundamentalism of their ideology.

Most parents are unaware of the danger that Islamists pose to their children. Many are pleased if their sons and daughters choose to spend time at the mosque rather than with local gangs or in the alcohol-soaked club and bar scene. Even after their children begin to dress and act as prescribed by Islamists, parents often do not know what to do. They may be at a loss when their rebellious child dismisses their warnings about radicalism. Moreover, those families who want to intervene and "get their child back" may not know who to ask for help. Their community's mosque is often controlled by Islamists, and many families would never discuss matters of Islam outside their Muslim community.

Given their reluctance to discuss issues related to Islam (or to any religion), European governments have offered little help to parents struggling against Islamists' recruitment of their children. In fact, European leaders have generally turned a blind eye to the Islamist networks in their midst as long as these groups did not seem to pose a security threat to the homeland. Many European governments thus believed they were establishing an implicit "covenant of security," whereby Islamist radicals would oppose terrorism in Europe, and European governments would ignore Islamist activities. Those European officials who believed they had entered into such an agreement failed to understand that Islamist radicals were taking full advantage of the legal and social openness of Europe to consolidate their organizations and spread their ideas, and that some Islamists would break this supposed covenant at the time of their choosing — as occurred in Madrid in 2004 and London in 2005.

Since September 11, Western governments have legitimized and empowered "nonviolent Islamists" as representatives of Islam for all Muslims in the West. This approach has horrified Muslim moderates, who see Western officials as strengthening the very enemy that threatens the fundamental freedoms of all Westerners, including Muslims. My goal in writing this book is to help the West understand the dire implications of its approach. To this end, I provide an overview of the theology and history of Islam and show that violence and intolerance are not fundamental aspects of the religion — in other words, that Islamism is *not* synonymous with Islam (Chapter 2). I then explore in detail how Islamists were able to establish themselves so rapidly and effectively in Europe, and argue specifically that conditions within existing Muslim communities — in particular the social and spiritual alienation experienced by second- and third-generation immigrants — coupled with a kind of somnambulism on the part of European governments, created the perfect environment for Islamism's growth (Chapter 3). I also look at Islamism in the United States, and argue that America's own self-conception as a land of religious freedom has enabled Islamists to take over mainstream Islamic institutions and to use the rhetoric of democracy, diversity, and tolerance to advance their most intolerant ends (Chapter 4). Further, I suggest that countries on both sides of the Atlantic are finally beginning to recognize (albeit while remaining inconsistent in addressing) the threat posed by violent and nonviolent Islamists alike to democracy and other values they hold dear (Chapter 5). Finally, I outline steps that both Western leaders and Muslims themselves must take to strengthen moderate Islam and to counter the threat of Islamism, and speculate about how a Muslim "Reformation" might take place and about what it might entail (Chapter 6).

The good news is that there is much that Western governments can still do to reverse the spread of Islamism. But they must act quickly. The first step is to stop legitimizing Islamism. Until now, Western governments have protected the hateful and incendiary preaching of Islamist radicals under the legal safeguard of freedom of speech, rather than applying existing laws that prohibit sedition. Western government and civil society leaders have also legitimized Islamists by choosing them as partners in preventing terror and reducing social tension.[5] This has marginalized Muslim moderates, who share the Western objectives of preserving secular democracy and universal human rights but who are shouted down by Islamist activists. Second, Western governments need to expose Islamism for what it is: a political-religious ideology that seeks to replace secular governments around the world with sharia rule. This can lead to the discrediting of Islamism among the vast majority of Muslims in the West who are faithful to both their religion and countries. Third, Western leaders must deny Islamists their goal of separating Muslim communities from mainstream society. This will require more successful efforts to address Muslims' legitimate grievances in the West, which have laid the foundations for both social and spiritual alienation among Muslims. Fourth, Western leaders must partner and empower Muslim moderates who seek to provide a hopeful alternative to Islamist ideology by rejuvenating the rich and diverse traditions of Islamic culture around the world.

In the end, this struggle for the heart and soul of Islam must be waged by Muslims. Though the West has a vital interest in the triumph of Muslim moderates in the so-called war of ideas (which would be a triumph for religious pluralism, cultural diversity, democratic freedom, and universal human rights), the West can influence this struggle only on its margins. A decisive victory by Muslim moderates may require a renaissance within Islam itself.

---

5   As this book went to press, UK prime minister David Cameron unveiled a new strategy at a conference in Munich that, among other welcome measures, introduced a stringent ideological test for organizations seeking government cooperation and funding; time will tell if it can be successfully implemented (see David Cameron, "Speech at Munich Security Conference" (London: Prime Minister's Office, 2011), available at: http://www.number10.gov.uk/news/speeches-and-transcripts/2011/02/pms-speech-at-munich-security-conference-60293 (accessed February 13, 2011).

CHAPTER 2

Islam versus Islamism

For many people seeking to understand "Islamism," the term's first two syllables present a nearly insurmountable obstacle. The combined effect of Islamist pressure and political correctness in Western societies has deterred policymakers and observers in the West from linking radicalism to religious interpretation, despite the fact that Islamists have often publicly declared that religion motivates their actions. In the current political/cultural environment, those who comment publicly on *any* negative element associated with the word "Islam" are placing their livelihoods directly at risk; the charge of racism or Islamophobia can easily end one's career.[1] Consequently, any criticism of Islamism is wrongly portrayed as criticism of *Islam*; those who highlight problems with Islamism are branded as purveyors of "religious hatred."[2] In this climate of intimidation, few in the West are willing to contemplate — let alone acknowledge — the

---

1 Note that the use of the term "racist" as a synonym for "anti-Muslim" is rooted in the widespread conflation of the Middle East (which is overwhelmingly Arab and Muslim in population) and the "Muslim world" (in which Arabs themselves are only a minority). Islam is not a race; it is a religion whose followers can be found in every race and ethnic group.
2 When referring to terrorists or extremists, moreover, many Westerners have mistakenly used the word "Islamic" (which implies a problem with Islam) instead of "Islamist" (which, by analogy with "Fascist" or "Communist," implies an ideology). See Chapter 5, p. 142, for a more detailed account of how Islamists use accusations of Islamophobia in pursuit of their own ends.

distinction between Islam and the Islamists' political goals. Paradoxically, the West has thus allowed itself to be maneuvered by the Islamists into tolerating intolerance.

This Western hypersensitivity to political correctness is combined with the tendency (especially in the United States) to accept at face value any belief or practice framed as "part of my religion." Western officials are culturally disposed to accept individuals' self-declarations of religious identity at face value, thanks to the near-sacred status of the two concepts of freedom of religion and separation of church and state. In the United States, lawyers within government bureaucracies typically cite the establishment clause of the Constitution, which mandates the separation of church and state, as forbidding any critical discussion of religions. Moreover, this reluctance to address religious questions exists even in those European countries in which the state remains linked to a particular denomination (usually through the institution of the monarchy), such as in Denmark or the UK. For example, Prince Charles has indicated that as king he will adopt the generic title "Defender of Faith," rather than the traditional "Defender of *the* Faith," in order to emphasize the "importance" to the UK of non-Christian religions.[3] All in all, these efforts to sidestep the issue do little to foster a meaningful debate about the distinction between Islam and Islamism.

It is a major challenge for Western societies to respond to the demands of a religion with which they are fundamentally unfamiliar. While there was a significant Islamic presence in parts of Europe — notably the Iberian Peninsula and Sicily — up to the medieval period, this was a distant memory by the time of the great debates about secularism and religion in the nineteenth century. Since Westerners — particularly Europeans — are reluctant to upset the secular consensus that emerged from these debates, they tend to accept Islamists' demands without question. Accordingly, when Islamists' political goals and demands — for example, for separate sharia-based family court systems — are presented as religious obligations, Western governments are more likely to accommodate them as a gesture of tolerance and out of respect for religious freedom, rather than rejecting them as reflecting only a narrow interpretation of Islam.

Similarly, when Western governments seek to "engage Muslims" to reduce social tension, they do not question the religious credentials of

---

3 Andrew Pierce, "Prince Charles to be Known as Defender of Faith," *Telegraph* (November 13, 2008), available at: www.telegraph.co.uk/news/newstopics/theroyalfamily/3454271/Prince-Charles-to-be-known-as-Defender-of-Faith.html (accessed January 19, 2011).

those whom they engage, though many are Islamists.[4] Worse, because Islamists are so vocal in promoting their definition of what is "true Islam," their rigid criteria have filtered even into the mental frameworks of non-Muslim policymakers and analysts. Islamists who choose the "engagement" path to reach their ultimate objective — a society ruled by Islamic law — have been careful to avoid statements that would trigger suspicion among their interlocutors. Instead, these Islamists have emphasized "nonviolence" and repeated platitudes about "tolerance." These tactics are succeeding, with some Americans and many Europeans now echoing Islamists' claims that these fundamentalist religious doctrines are the norm for Islam.

This ideological straitjacket is hampering Western attempts to gain a more accurate understanding of Islam and to develop effective policy responses to Islamism. Like most of the world's religions, Islam has been a source of peace and justice as well as violence and hatred. Over the 14 centuries of Islamic history, the majority of Muslims lived and practiced Islam by emphasizing the positive ethics and principles of the religion, while ignoring or de-emphasizing the more militaristic and pharisaic elements. Today's Christians tend to do the same, emphasizing their religion's core messages of peace, love, justice, and forgiveness rather than the intolerance and zealotry that fueled the Crusades and other religious wars.

Even in Islam's earliest years, some religious scholars disagreed with the prevailing moderate interpretations of the Qur'an and the hadiths (literally, "tales" or "sayings"; these are narrations of the Prophet Muhammad's words and deeds collected by his associates). Instead, they used strict literalism to justify discrimination and violence against non-Muslims. Although these fundamentalists were in their time considered extremists or even heretics, Islamists now revere them as a key source of theological inspiration. Contemporary Islamists are thus fighting, with some success, to establish this once-discredited extremist theology as mainstream thinking in Islam.

With the adherents of this extreme theology, any real "engagement" is impossible. Their suffocating dogma allows no room for discussion — let alone modification — of their aim to replace the current world

---

4   The disproportionate presence of Islamists in these "engagement" efforts is not just due to Western ignorance; since Islamists by definition have political goals, they are naturally attracted to the political process. This is not true for Muslim moderates, who view their religion as personal, not political, in nature.

order with their vision of an Islamic utopia. For example, the European Commission's counterterrorism policy, several years in the making, was delayed by the French government because it bluntly described how Islam has inspired some to commit terrorist attacks. As European Union (EU) Counterterrorism Coordinator Gilles de Kerchove put it in 2008, some European countries "are extremely reluctant to be explicit about the link [of terrorism] with religion."[5] This reluctance is not limited to Europe; a US Department of State memorandum in March 2008 advised government personnel to avoid using not only confrontational terms like "Islamofascism," but even factual descriptions of al-Qaeda's theological affiliations such as "Wahhabi" and "Salafi."[6] Even "extremism" and "terrorism" are falling out of favor; in the UK, a ministerial order replaced them with "community resilience" and "anti-Islamic activity," respectively.[7] Moreover, the United States has left the "War on Terror" long behind it; as of 2009, its military is officially engaged in "Overseas Contingency Operations."[8] No matter how many different synonyms creative Western bureaucrats invent, however, the truth remains the same: Islamists are attempting to hijack Islam for political purposes.

While Islamist groups take different forms — from the "civil-rights organizations" sponsored in the West by the Muslim Brotherhood, to the paramilitary terrorists of al-Qaeda — most trace their theological origins back along an unbroken succession of literalist interpretations, from those of the eighteenth-century Arabian theologian Ibn Abd al-Wahhab, through the work of thirteenth-century religious scholar Ibn Taymiyyah, back to the strict interpretation of God's divine laws promoted by the Hanbali school of Islamic jurisprudence established in the ninth century, and finally to the literal truth of the text of the Qur'an. This "pedigree" thus denigrates modern interpretations of the words and actions of

---

5   Jason Burke, "Honesty Best Policy When Talking Militancy, Says EU Counter-Terrorism Chief," *Observer* (September 28, 2008), available at: www.guardian.co.uk/world/2008/sep/28/terrorism.eu (accessed January 19, 2011).

6   P. W. Singer and Elina Noor, "What Do You Call a Terror(Jihad)ist?" *New York Times* (June 2, 2008), available at: www.nytimes.com/2008/06/02/opinion/02singer.html?_r=1 (accessed January 19, 2011).

7   See Matthew Moore, "Political Correctness 'Hampering Battle Against Extremism,'" *Telegraph* (November 12, 2008), available at: www.telegraph.co.uk/news/uknews/3444674/Political-correctness-is-hampering-battle-against-extremism.html (accessed January 19, 2011).

8   Scott Wilson and Al Kamen, "'Global War on Terror' is Given New Name," *Washington Post* (March 25, 2009), available at: www.washingtonpost.com/wp-dyn/content/article/2009/03/24/AR2009032402818.html (accessed January 20, 2011).

Muhammad and his companions, and in effect holds up the norms of seventh-century Arabia — Muhammad's own time and place — as unassailable precedents that must be emulated.

Islamism dates only to the early twentieth century, when followers of Wahhab borrowed attacks on liberalism from the Communists and Fascists. The secretive and hierarchical structures of the Islamist groups most influential in the West — such as the Muslim Brotherhood and radical offshoots like HT — are patterned after those of revolutionary groups of the early twentieth century, like the Bolsheviks, which were similarly able to maintain organizational discipline and focus in the face of state repression. These organizational factors, coupled with massive financial support from the petro-states of the Persian Gulf, control over the holy sites of Mecca and Medina by Saudi Wahhabi authorities, postcolonial resentment of the West, and permissive legal environments in countries of Muslim immigration, have helped the Islamists establish their extreme interpretation of Islam as the mainstream in many countries over the last four decades. The Islamists are thus eroding the flexible, rational interpretation of Islam that was once the consensus view of the majority of Muslims throughout the world.

Today, despite their sharp theological differences, Islamist organizations such as al-Qaeda (Sunni), Hezbollah (Shiite), and the Caucasian Front of Chechnya (Sufi) are united by their political agenda. In turn, this agenda places them at sharp odds with the non-Islamists in each tradition, who do not necessarily adhere to a political ideology. Moreover, Islamist groups can and do disagree with one another on other matters, such as organizational structure and tactics. Some advocate violence; others adapt their tactics and strategies to their environment, sometimes concealing their true intentions (a religiously sanctioned practice known as *taqiyya*) to allay Western suspicions. Yet regardless of these distinctions, *all* Islamists are united by their support of the same objective: the creation of an Islamic state ruled by their vision of sharia. The fact that a group pursues this goal using nonviolent tactics does not make it "less Islamist" or "more moderate." As suggested in Chapter 1, groups of this kind serve as a "conveyor belt" by transforming non-Islamists into Islamist radicals — some of whom become terrorists.

Indeed, self-proclaimed nonviolent groups such as HT have often been *more* effective agents of the Islamist cause than have terrorists. Their denunciations of violence gain them legitimacy and public platforms (often publicly financed) to spread their extremist teachings in the West. Western efforts to mitigate extremism and the "root causes" of terrorism must therefore shift their current focus from countering extremist violence to preventing extremism from taking hold in the first place. Radicalizing an individual into an Islamist is a necessary step in the process of radicalizing an individual into a terrorist; once someone has accepted the goal of overthrowing the existing secular order and replacing it with a universal *umma* governed according to Islamic law, it simply becomes a question of which means will be used to pursue this objective. Preventing Muslims from becoming Islamists dries up the pool of potential terrorists by diminishing the number of extremist recruits.

Neutralizing the threats posed by Islamism therefore requires ideological countermeasures. At first glance, the West may seem ill-equipped to wage such an ideological struggle, given its reluctance to discuss theology, its ignorance of Islam, and its lack of credibility with Muslim audiences. In reality, the West has already demonstrated its ability to defeat the ideological challenge of a diverse popular movement organized in pursuit of a utopian goal; that is, Communism. However, it is precisely the victory in the struggle against Communism — which focused primarily on politics and economics — that has made it more difficult for policymakers to shift toward addressing matters of religion. Indeed, the Cold War precedent reinforces existing aversions to entering into religious debates or doing anything that could be interpreted as insulting Islam. But Western leaders must overcome these obstacles, since Islamism has replaced atheistic Communism as the most important threat to freedom, universal human rights, and physical security in the world today.

There is no Islamism without Islam, but neither is Islamism synonymous with Islam. This simple truth, which should guide any efforts to comprehend and combat the threat of Islamism, requires some basic understanding of the religion of Islam and the theological roots of Islamist ideology.[9] This chapter will show that Islamism reflects only one of the various competing strains in Islam, which until the twentieth century had always been a minor one. Islamists differ from other Muslims in several ways: in interpreting the Qur'an literally and in embracing the most anti-rational school of Islamic jurisprudence; in focusing on (and emulating) Muhammad as a "warrior Prophet"; in pointing to violence in the early years of Islam, specifically the struggles over the succession to Muhammad, in justifying violence today; and in viewing non-Muslims

---

9   Given that this is not a book devoted to Islamic theology or history, this discussion inevitably simplifies and generalizes issues that have been the source of passionate debate among Muslims for centuries.

as inferior and damned. This chapter will further show that Islamism as a political-religious ideology only really emerged in the early decades of the twentieth century; its values and tactics are thus similar to those of other totalitarian movements of the period.

The Qur'an and Sharia

Islamists' understanding of Islam's foundations — mainly the Qur'an, and also sharia — differs from that of other Muslims in important ways. Many Islamists believe that because the Qur'an conveys the precise words of God, all Muslims need to follow the literal text of the Qur'an as closely as possible. But many non-Islamists note the Qur'an also states that human beings need to use their own abilities to try to understand its universal and timeless message for themselves. Hence, according to non-Islamists, God's laws cannot be imposed on others, and all people have the right (and obligation) to establish their own relationship with God. They also point out that the Qur'an emphasizes the importance of the use of scientific methods and individual ability to discern the path to salvation.[10] The Qur'an is indeed rich with parables, symbolism, and metaphors; moreover, some of its verses seem contradictory. For these reasons, the holistic approach to interpreting the text of the Qur'an offers a more comprehensive understanding, one that — at least until the rise of Islamism — was generally shared by the majority of Muslims.

Non-Islamists emphasize the individual Muslim's obligation to use the power of reason to comprehend the deeper messages of the Qur'an. (The compatibility of reason and revelation within Islam is discussed in more detail below.) This is possible because Islam enables direct communication between God and humans, without the need for intermediaries such as priests to facilitate communion with the divine. Since there is no fixed hierarchy to create, disseminate, and maintain uniformity of belief in Islam, the discovery and understanding of divine wisdom can take place on an individual level. And since individuals' differing historical and cultural circumstances inevitably influence how passages from the

---

10   For example, "This is a Book, which We send down to you, full of blessings, so that they [people] may ponder its verses and that the people of discernment may reflect on it and be mindful" (Qur'an, 38:29). (Source: Ünal, Ali, *The Qur'an with Annotated Interpretation in Modern English* (Somerset, NJ: The Light, 2006). Unless noted otherwise, all passages from the Qur'an are taken from this translation.)

Qur'an are understood, individuals' interpretations of the Qur'an will differ — without any of them necessarily being erroneous.

Faced with the complexity of Qur'anic meaning — and with the difficult classical Arabic in which the Qur'an is written — most Muslims turn for guidance to the established schools of Islamic jurisprudence. Each of these schools has the same aim in interpreting the Qur'an: to discern God's instructions for how Muslims should structure their lives. These instructions — known collectively as sharia law — cover not only Muslims' personal relationships with God, but also the entirety of their interactions with the earthly world, including business dealings, politics, and family life. In Islam, the interpretation of sharia is known as Islamic jurisprudence (*fiqh*) and is the central focus of Islamic thought. By correctly interpreting sharia, a Muslim can understand God's directives in both the spiritual and temporal realms. Sharia thus defines a comprehensive set of religious morals and public ethics.

To understand the Islamists' approach to Qur'anic meaning and sharia, it is necessary to briefly go into further detail about the different schools of Islamic jurisprudence and their history. Four major Sunni *fiqh* schools had emerged in different centers of Islamic learning by the ninth century. Members of these schools engaged in a process called *ijtihad*, which is the independent interpretation of the Qur'an, the hadiths, and of the personal habits and practices of the Prophet, the sunnahs. The Hanafi school, founded by Imam Abu Hanifa in the middle of the eighth century, made use of logical deduction to derive new law in the settlement of cases not covered by existing law. Its main followings are in the Turkic-speaking lands as well as in the Indian subcontinent. The second *fiqh* school was founded at around the same time by Imam Malik; its core principle is to seek the true nature of sharia by following the traditional practices of Medina, the city that had nurtured the early Muslim community after it fled Mecca in the Hegira. The Maliki school has been strongest in North and West Africa. Imam Shafi'i, a student of both Hanifa and Malik, founded the third primary school of Islamic jurisprudence. The Shafi'i *fiqh* depended more on precedents defined by hadiths than on generating new case law through deductive reasoning. This school has a strong following in the Middle East, Egypt, southern India, and Indonesia. The fourth school, the Hanbali, was founded in the ninth century by Imam Ahmad ibn Hanbal, who stressed reliance on hadith over reason and believed in strictly literal interpretations of the Qur'an. The Hanbali *fiqh*, which took root in Arabia, is today followed by most Islamists.

By the end of the tenth century, disputes about how to interpret the

Qur'an and hadiths were intensifying. In particular, Sunni jurists argued over the issue of using deductive reasoning (as favored by the Hanafi school), and how much to rely on inductive reasoning to infer general elements of sharia from a literalist reading of the Qur'an and hadiths (as favored by the Hanbali school). In an effort to reverse the increased factionalization and prevent the disintegration of the caliphate, court jurists declared "the gates to *ijtihad* closed," meaning that all the important questions related to sharia had been answered by the four primary schools of Sunni jurisprudence.[11] From then on, all Muslims, whether juridical scholars or ordinary believers, would be constrained within the framework of these schools' teachings. Essentially, then, the development of mainstream Islamic thought was frozen in the tenth century.

The development of Islamist thought, by contrast, was just beginning. In the aftermath of the catastrophic mid-thirteenth-century Mongol invasion of Arabia, theologian Ibn Taymiyyah argued that the Arabs' defeat was caused by their failure to maintain and follow the traditions and values of Muhammad and the earliest Muslims. As a follower of the Hanbali school, Ibn Taymiyyah already had a strong preference for a strictly literal interpretation of the Qur'an; after the invasion, he combined this with a highly selective emphasis on those suras (chapters) that call for confrontation with non-Muslims.

Using the teachings of Ibn Taymiyyah as a starting point, the eighteenth-century Arab theologian Ibn Abd al-Wahhab argued that the Qur'an demanded the overthrow of existing political structures, the replacement of secular law with sharia, and the repression (by violence if necessary) of anyone who disagreed. In the early twentieth century, "Wahhabism" became the state ideology of Saudi Arabia, and now serves as the ideological foundation for almost all Islamists around the globe, sometimes even transcending sectarian differences among Sunnis and Shiites.

Though all four *fiqh* schools enjoyed equal recognition for centuries

---

11 For more on the closing of the gates of *ijtihad*, see: Karen Armstrong, *Islam: A Short History* (New York: Random House, 2002), p. 103; Abdullahi Ahmed An-Na'im, *Toward an Islamic Reformation: Civil Liberties, Human Rights, and International Law* (New York: Syracuse University Press, 1990), pp. 27–9; Hassan Abbas, "Ulema verus Ijtihad: Understanding the Nature of the Crisis in the Muslim World," *al Nakhlah* Fall 2004: 1–4 (3–4), available at: http://se2.isn.ch/serviceengine/Files/RESSpecNet/26152/ichaptersection_singledocument/03151DA2-4B5F-4EBF-AB74-312EB30174AD/en/1abbas_ulema+versus+ijitihad.pdf (accessed January 20, 2011); Wael B. Hallaq, "Was the Gate of Ijtihad Closed?" *International Journal of Middle East Studies* 16(1): 3–41.

after the shutting of the gates of *ijtihad*, Islamist thought emerged out of the Hanbali school. Wahhabis and other Salafis believe that Ibn Hanbal's strictly literalist interpretation of the Qur'an and hadiths provide precisely the right theological fuel to drive modern society toward adopting a form of governance based on medieval sharia norms. Some Islamists, such as the Muslim Brotherhood, do allow for a certain level of innovation in technology (such as production of automobiles, airplanes, and weapons) and in social organization (with less emphasis on tribe or clan), but these are cosmetic changes that do not change their underlying objective, which is shared by all Islamists. In this sense, both the strictly literalist Islamists and their ostensibly "moderate" counterparts strive toward the same utopian vision; as the experiences of Marxism–Leninism and National Socialism attest, the inevitable result of the pursuit of such a vision is totalitarianism.

Like in other examples of totalitarianism, there have been those who disagreed with the utopian vision and preferred to keep the gates *of ijtihad* open. The Shia, who follow the school of Islamic jurisprudence founded by Ja'far al-Sadiq in the eighth century, largely continue to practice *ijtihad*. Even within Sunnism, a dedicated minority have continued to innovate while insisting on understanding and adapting sharia according to their powers of reason and their spirituality. Spirituality has remained critical to understanding the Qur'an for the ascetic and mystic Sufis, who elevate the spiritual aspect of Islam above all else and believe that experiencing love for God is as important as strict adherence to sharia.[12] The Mu'tazili school of Islamic thought also rejected the literalism of the main *fiqh* schools, replacing it not with Sufi spirituality, but instead with human reason. Originating in Basra (in modern-day Iraq) in the eighth century, it embraced the power of deductive reasoning to reach the same divine truths obtained through revelation (e.g., by carefully reading the Qur'an and hadiths). The Mu'tazilis esteem the human mind as superior to scripture in unlocking God's key truths; hence Mu'tazilis interpret the Qur'an with greater intellectual freedom than other Muslims. A similar embrace of reason to uncover divine truth and a willingness to practice *ijtihad* characterize the school of Abu Mansur al-Maturidi, who lived and taught in Samarkand (modern-day Uzbekistan). Believing that God's divine truth

---

12   Many Sufis believe in the pursuit of moral excellence beyond the dictates of religious law, whereas others believe that once a certain level of spiritual enlightenment is reached, one can graduate from the norms of sharia. For many Sufis, there is no difference between Sunni and Shia, or Muslims and non-Muslims — all are God's creatures and for that reason alone are worthy of love. As a result, Sufis have been open to the incorporation of local customs and practices into their rituals.

was available through human intelligence, al-Maturidi and his followers employed their independent powers of reasoning to interpret sharia for themselves, in the context of the evolution of their societies.

Reason versus Revelation in al-Andalus: Ibn Sina, Ibn Tufayl, and Ibn Rushd

The embrace of reason by the Mu'tazilis and Maturidis was especially resonant in the Iberian kingdom of al-Andalus. There, Muslim scholars grappled with the theological problem posed by the rediscovery of Greek philosophy, particularly Aristotelian thought — that is, how could these concepts coexist with religious faith?[13] The central question for the Andalusian thinkers was how to reconcile reason with revelation. Until this time, most Muslims had largely relegated reason to the lesser role of applying to daily life the legal precedents for interpreting God's revelation to Muhammad. Most believed that because God is omnipotent and responsible for everything that is and ever was, there is no point attempting to understand God's actions; God obeys no laws but God's own. There are no "natural" laws; the sun rises in the east every day only because God wishes it. Consequently, the role of reason in understanding humanity's place in the universe is of far less importance than simple acceptance of the divine truths.[14]

Christianity also struggled to reconcile reason and revelation, often treading the same dialectical path as Islam. Particularly around the end of the first millennium, anti-rationalists such as Duns Scotus gained traction

---

13   Special thanks to Annemarie van Sandwijk for her research for this section.
14   The rejection of reason as a challenge to revelation was expounded by the early tenth-century Arab thinker Abu al-Hasan al-Ashari, founder of the Ashari school, in Basra. Al-Ashari held a deterministic view of God, maintaining that Allah created every moment in time and every particle of matter. His ideas were further developed in the following century by the Persian Abu Hamid al-Ghazali, who is considered by Muslims to be one of the most influential and most enlightened thinkers of classical times. Yet al-Ghazali attacked the reason of Aristotle, Plato, and Socrates as blasphemy, and argued that human beings are incapable of devising morality through reason. He believed that humans are overly influenced by their own self-interest and that morality and obligation can flow only from divine revelation. By this view, the Qur'an, hadiths, and sunnahs of Muhammad and his fellow early Muslims represent the sole appropriate sources of inspiration for how an individual should live — and for how a state should conduct its affairs. *Ijtihad* has little place in this scheme. Al-Ghazali further argued that cause and effect were determined entirely by God or God's angels.

in the populations of Christian Europe. Yet fideism (the theory that faith is both independent of and superior to reason) never predominated; led by the great thirteenth-century theologian St. Thomas Aquinas, Christendom eventually embraced reason as the natural counterpart of religion. What is less well known is the influence on Aquinas of Muslim scholars such as Ibn Sina (known in the West as Avicenna) of Persia, and Ibn Tufayl (known as Abubacer) and Ibn Rushd (known as Averroës) of Andalusia. Of the many philosophical and scientific works by Muslims acquired and translated by Europeans, perhaps none was more influential in shaping the intellectual character of the Continent, particularly its thinking on the relationship between reason and religion, than those of these three Muslim scholars. It is from Islam, then, that the rationalist stance of Christianity in part derives. This fact should remind us that much of Islamic thinking has seen reason and faith as compatible — and that the Islamists' rejection of reason is by no means shared by all Muslims.

To understand this important point fully, it is worth considering the views of these Muslim thinkers in greater detail.

Ibn Sina (Avicenna)

Avicenna (980–1037) was perhaps the most prominent Islamic thinker of his time. Born in present-day Uzbekistan, Avicenna was an avid student of ancient Greek and Roman physicians and is considered the father of modern medicine. He authored hundreds of works, with his fourteen-volume *Al-Qanun fi al-Tibb* (The Canon of Medicine) being the greatest. It was translated into Latin in the twelfth century, and continued to dominate the teaching of medicine in Europe up until the late sixteenth century. Avicenna was also a prominent Islamic theologian, astronomer, chemist, poet, psychologist, and philosopher. His work in all these fields would have a major impact on European thought during the Renaissance period, when it was translated into European languages. His seminal philosophical work was *Al-Shifa* (The Cure), which Avicenna hoped would both prove God's existence through rational thought and reform Aristotelian logic.[15]

---

15   Lenn E. Goodman, *Avicenna* (London: Routledge, 1992), pp. 4, 64; G. M. Wickens, "Some Aspects of Avicenna's Work," in Wickens, ed., *Avicenna, Scientist and Philosopher: A Millenary Symposium* (London: Luzac, 1952), pp. 49–65 (56).

Ibn Tufayl

Avicenna also influenced Ibn Tufayl (c. 1105–1185), who was born in Guadix in present-day Spain and served as vizier and royal physician in the court of Abu Ya'qub, an Almohad caliph. The Almohads were a Berber dynasty that had come to al-Andalus from North Africa and had imposed a restrictive and harsh interpretation of Islam. Yet Ibn Tufayl remained free to extol the power of reason in fields such as medicine, astronomy, poetry, and philosophy, even as the Almohad political leaders rejected reason. Unfortunately, few of Ibn Tufayl's writings survive. His most influential philosophical work was *Hayy ibn Yaqzan*, a novel that stresses reason as a crucial complement to revelation in understanding God's divine truth.[16]

The novel is a tale about Hayy Ibn Yaqzan (Alive, son of Awake), who washed ashore on an island as a newborn child and was raised by a gazelle, having no contact with human society. At an early age, Hayy's innate intellectual capabilities enable him to discover simple scientific truths by natural reason. For instance, when Hayy is seven, the gazelle dies and the young boy decides to open the corpse to conduct anatomical experiments. By continual observation and reflection — that is, by the development of his inductive (Aristotelian) intellect — Hayy gradually acquires knowledge of the physical universe. When he reaches manhood, he advances into exploring abstract philosophical truths and proves to himself the existence of a powerful Creator, with whom he seeks unification. After seven years of spiritual introspection, and without a prophet leading the way, he acquires divine truth. When Hayy is 50 years old, another person, Absal, arrives from a neighboring island, which contains a thriving civilization regulated by a conventional religion. Absal teaches Hayy language and informs him about the Qur'anic conceptions of God, which Hayy — by his self-developed intellect — immediately recognizes as truths. Hayy soon realizes that Absal's religion is merely the symbolic representation of the same philosophical truth that he had long ago discovered. Absal and Hayy become friends and Hayy decides to go to the people on the other island to offer them the benefits of his purely attained knowledge. Most people on the other island lack the desire and ability to grasp the higher truth Hayy has discerned, and are happier without it, as the teachings of the Qur'an are difficult enough to understand. To his regret, Hayy discovers that his exposition of the truth is beyond the

---

16   George Hourani, "The Principal Subject of Ibn Tufayl's *Hayy Ibn Yaqzan*," *Journal of Near Eastern Studies* 15(1): 40–6 (40).

intellectual capacity of average people, who are reflexively comfortable with the common elevation of "religion" over "reason."

In general, Ibn Tufayl supported the Almohad principle of withholding the teachings of philosophy from the masses, but he recognized that a small minority of intelligent and discerning minds could benefit from philosophy, as it could help them to understand divine truth. According to Ibn Tufayl, religion is simply a tool needed by unlearned people to grasp the same truth discerned by the gifted few through philosophy.[17]

Ibn Rushd (Averroës)

Ibn Tufayl was succeeded as royal physician by his younger colleague and friend Averroës (1126–1198). Born in Córdoba, Averroës became the key Islamic authority on Aristotle's writings; in Europe, he became known as "the Commentator," just as Aristotle was "the Philosopher." Averroës published numerous works on philosophy and medicine. His famous philosophical treatise *Tahafut al-Tahafut* (Incoherence of the Incoherence) was published in 1180 and refuted the anti-rationalist philosophy of Abu Hamid al-Ghazali. Like Ibn Tufayl, Averroës argued that religion and philosophy present different routes to the same truth: philosophy follows the theoretical route and involves rational arguments (demonstration); religion follows the practical route, meaning it involves arguments in defense of revelation and scripture (dialectics) that can be comprehended by common people.[18] Averroës argued that if the apparent meaning of scripture (derived by revelation) conflicts with demonstrative conclusions (derived by reason), then scripture must be interpreted metaphorically rather than literally. According to this view, it falls to philosophers to discover the less-apparent meanings within the Qur'an in order to carefully guide other members of the community beyond their acceptance of scripture as literal truth.

---

17   Hourani, "The Principal Subject of Ibn Tufayl's *Hayy Ibn Yaqzan*," 45–6.

18   Paul Kurtz, "Intellectual Freedom, Rationality, and Enlightenment: The Contributions of Avveroes," in Mourad Wahba and Mona Abousenna, eds., *Averroes and the Enlightenment* (Amherst, NY: Prometheus Books, 1996), pp. 29–40 (31); Ibn Rushd (Averroës), *The Attitude of Islam towards Science and Philosophy: A Translation of Ibn Rushd's (Averroës) Famous Treatise*, Faslul-al-Maqal, trans. Hamid Naseem Rafiabadi and Aadil Amin Kak (New Delhi: Sarup & Sons, 2003), pp. 135–72.

Impact on Europe

For its time, Averroës' endorsement of the Aristotelian belief that the world is a comprehensible place — and thus that there is no need to seek transcendental explanations for natural phenomena — was extremely radical. Averroës' works were banned at the University of Paris in 1210, and this was followed by religious condemnations elsewhere. Averroës' influence nevertheless rose in Europe, where he had a profound impact on Jewish and Latin scholars between 1200 and 1650, including Aquinas. Aquinas carefully distinguished between theology and philosophy, assigning each discipline to its own independent sphere of action. Echoing the thinking of Averroës, as well as that of Ibn Tufayl and Avicenna, Aquinas distinguished between natural truths, which anyone can acquire through analytical inquiry, and revealed truths, which can only be known through faith in God's revelation. Aquinas argued that theology and philosophy were often just two ways of looking at the same thing. He maintained that natural and revealed truths could not contradict each other because God was ultimately the source of both.

Through Aquinas, European thinkers became acquainted with the works of Avicenna, Ibn Tufayl, and Averroës, and the seeds for the intellectual flowerings of the Renaissance and the Enlightenment were planted. The seminal Western ideals of independent thought, universality, and secularism are thus connected to Muslim thinkers, and — as Chapter 6 suggests — may even provide the foundation for a potential Islamic Renaissance and Enlightenment. But these ideas were largely rejected by Averroës' Muslim contemporaries, and religious leaders ordered his books to be burned. This was the beginning of the end of a rationalist approach to religion in mainstream Islam. It was already paradoxical that Averroës and Ibn Tufayl had been able to write during the puritanical rule of the Almohads, who in 1145 had wrested control of al-Andalus from the Almoravid dynasty.

The fundamentalist approach of the Almohads was critical in closing off the mainstream of Islamic thinking to reason. Their anti-rationalism would soon be echoed in other Islamic lands, and the works of the great Muslim philosophers of the eleventh and twelfth centuries disappeared into the shadows — at least in the Islamic world.

Prophet Muhammad

The philosophical tension between revelation and reason has led Muslims to divergent interpretations of key aspects of Islam. While the sectarian split between Sunnism and Shiism emerged from a quasi-political dispute over who would succeed Muhammad as leader of the Muslim community, today's division between Islamists and Muslim moderates derives from a more basic philosophical difference over the theological validity of revelation versus reason. Islamists do not accept the exercise of independent reasoning to interpret Islam; moderates, however, rely on reason to help discern the deeper truths revealed by God to Muhammad.

A key starting point for understanding the practical impact of revelation and reason on today's ideological struggle between fundamentalist and moderate Muslims is an exploration of how Muslims interpret and seek to emulate the life of the Prophet Muhammad, who was a politician, military commander, husband, father, and businessman as well as a religious figure. All Muslims generally believe that Muhammad, like the prophets before him, was unhappy with the harshness and corruption of tribal life, where warfare between families and clans was common, and women and children (especially orphans) were often treated like slaves. All Muslims further recognize Mecca and Medina as critically important places in Muhammad's life, specifically to his receiving of divine revelation and to his struggle to establish a community of believers.[19]

Beyond such basic elements, there are fundamental disagreements among Muslims as to how to interpret the 62-year lifetime of Muhammad. These disagreements have been reflected in countless factional divisions, from sectarianism to *fiqh* schools to today's split between Islamists and non-Islamists. Many non-Islamists recognize that to understand the fullness of Muhammad's life and thus also to unlock God's profound messages hidden deep within the Qur'an, one must exercise independent reason to interpret the sunnahs as compiled in the hadiths. Sometimes hadiths and passages in the Qur'an contradict each other. For example, according to

---

19   Muhammad's father, Abdullah, died in Yathrib (the city later known as Medina). When Muhammad was six years old, he visited his father's grave in Medina with his mother and relatives; his mother passed away on their journey back to Mecca. His later years, especially after he began — as Muslims believe — to receive God's revelation in a cave on Mount Hira in 610, was divided between Mecca and Medina. The first Muslim community came into armed conflict with the people of Mecca in 622; the community's flight to Medina (known as the Hegira) marks the beginning of the Islamic calendar. After eight more years of fighting, they made a triumphant return to Mecca under Muhammad's leadership.

various sunnahs, like most people of his time the Prophet is believed to have been illiterate, but clearly Muslims trying to emulate the Prophet ought not to remain illiterate. Similarly, though Muhammad kept slaves (like many of his contemporaries), that does not mean Islam approves of slavery; on the contrary, Muhammad freed his slave, Zayd, and adopted him as his own son. Full appreciation of the meaning of Muhammad's sayings, deeds, and personal traits therefore requires the exercise of reason to place the sunnahs, hadiths, and scriptures in historical context. Given that the revelation is said to have unfolded over a 23-year period, there were of course many changes to the political and societal context in which Muhammad and his growing number of followers found themselves. To continue interpreting these revelations for the believers, Muhammad had to rely upon his own powers of reason to keep them relevant to changing contexts. Many non-Islamists believe in emulating Muhammad's example by exercising their own powers of reason to gain a deeper understanding of their religion in the context of the world around them.

For their part, Islamists reject the idea that Muhammad used his reason to interpret divine revelation, instead believing that he merely conveyed it to the believers word-for-word as he heard it. In this way, they restrict themselves to replicating the norms and customs of Muhammad's own time and place. As we will see, such selective interpretation of Muhammad's life is routine for Islamists. They take "the Warrior Prophet" as their role model, even though non-Islamist scholars plausibly argue that Muhammad's military activities were born only of necessity and were primarily *defensive* in nature. And they ignore the peaceful Muhammad of the Meccan period, who never urged his followers to fight back against ongoing harassment. Islamists point to Muhammad's wars to validate their own active opposition to the West as "just war" or "defensive war," based on their assertion that Islam is "under attack" by Western cultural, political, and military encroachment everywhere. Such Islamist distortions of Muhammad's life not only instigate violence against the West, they also harm Islam by teaching the West to understand it as a religion founded by a brutal, violent man. In all but one sura of the Qur'an, Allah is described as the "Most Merciful and Most Compassionate." No one would learn from the Islamists that in numerous cases, "Allah's last Prophet" showed himself to be merciful and compassionate as well.

The failure to take changing historical context into account when interpreting the Qur'an has led Islamists — as well as some non-Muslims — to misunderstand the relationship of religion to politics and to view Muhammad erroneously as the ruler of an Islamic "state." Although at the time of his death Muslim forces had conquered much of the territory of the Arabian Peninsula, the people living there had not been incorporated into anything resembling a state; the consolidation of Muslim-conquered lands into a caliphate came years later. The Prophet was acknowledged as the spokesperson of God, a judge, a moral referee, and even the leader of his community, but never as a king like David or Solomon. Muhammad's leadership role was instead more like that of Moses. Rather than appreciating how Islam's relationship with politics evolved over time, Islamists find it more convenient, given their global political objectives, to assert that Muhammad established an Islamic state in the seventh century, and that all Muslims must emulate the Prophet's example by recreating it.

Yet far from establishing a formal political structure, the Prophet did not even make arrangements for his succession; there was no "office" for a "successor" to assume. Even when the caliphate coalesced in the eighth century under the Umayyads, it was not a centralized institution; quite the contrary: the lands under the dominion of the caliphate effectively governed themselves even "while granting obligatory recognition to the autocratic ruling powers."[20] Modern theocracies like Saudi Arabia, Iran, or Taliban-run Afghanistan, as well as the utopias of groups such as HT, thus bear little resemblance to Islamic governments of the past.

Religion of Peace or Religion of Violence?

An exclusive focus on the militaristic Muhammad — whether a failure to see his acts in context or a lack of recognition that compassion and mercy were also part of his nature — distinguish Islamism from other strains of Islam. Together with the unwillingness to consider historical context and the tendency to glorify violence, this narrow focus is a key characteristic of Islamism in general.

Consider Islamists' understanding of the events that followed Muhammad's death in 632, when the issue of succession was paramount. The question of who would be Muhammad's caliph (literally "successor" as leader of the Muslim community) led to a fundamental split within Islam, that between Sunnism and Shiism.

This schism was both theological and political. On one side were

---

20   Hassan Mneimneh, "The Islamization of Arab Culture," *Current Trends in Islamist Ideology* 6: 48–65 (50), available at: www.currenttrends.org/research/detail/the-islamization-of-arab-culture (accessed January 21, 2011).

the Shiites, who believed that the Prophet bore special spiritual qualities, which allowed only him and his descendants to understand and interpret the inner meaning of Islam. Hence, only a member of the Prophet's family could exercise the spiritual authority that they saw as an inherent part of the caliph's role. The early Sunnis, on the other hand, viewed the caliph as the political leader of the community of Muslims, not a spiritual leader who enjoyed a special relationship with God. For the Sunnis, any Muslim could serve as caliph.[21]

In the absence of a formal structure for selecting a caliph, it proved virtually impossible to reach consensus decisions. The selection of the first caliph, Abu Bakr, a close friend of Muhammad and the first person outside the Prophet's family to convert to Islam, disappointed those who believed Muhammad should be succeeded by his son-in-law Ali. The resentment of the defeated Shiites continued to grow. The third caliph, Uthman, who was also selected amid considerable controversy, endured increasing unpopularity throughout his reign for favoring his fellow tribesmen; he was ultimately murdered by rebels. Uthman's murder finally cleared the way for Ali to become caliph. However, this did not settle the issue of succession, as the defeated Sunnis refused to recognize Ali's authority; the caliph was soon murdered by extremists. In turn, the emerging Shiite community refused to recognize the legitimacy of Muawiya, the caliph selected after Ali.

Ali's son (and Muhammad's grandson) Husayn raised an army to avenge Ali's death, but he and 72 companions were killed by the forces of Muawiya's successor, Yazid I, on the tenth day of the month of Muharram (now one of the holiest days in the Shiite calendar).[22]

The killing of Husayn sent shockwaves throughout the Islamic world. While Husayn's death consolidated Umayyad (that is, Sunni) control over the caliphate, it also helped consolidate the Umayyads' Shiite opponents who were outraged at what they viewed as the murder of Husayn, the grandson of the Prophet, by fellow Muslims. This strong sense of anger, present as it was during the formative years of Shi'ism, had a profound impact on the evolution of this branch of Islam. Shi'ism has since been associated with the oppressed and victimized; the Shia believe they must maintain strong reverence for martyrdom and for those who stand up to

---

21   Vali Nasr, *The Shia Revival: How Conflicts within Islam will Shape the Future* (New York: W. W. Norton, 2006), p. 35.
22   For the Shia, the number 72 has since symbolized martyrdom. It is interesting to note that suicide bombers often are told 72 virgins will greet them in heaven.

tyranny. At the same time, the killing of Husayn set a precedent for Sunni repression of Shiites. Many of today's Sunni Islamists continue to draw on this precedent. Today, Shiites are believed to comprise some 10–13 percent of the world's Muslim population.

The slaying of Husayn and the murder of Ali — like the military campaigns of Muhammad — suggest the violence that characterized the earliest days of Islam. For radical Islamists, these episodes are not remnants of an earlier period of human history when warfare was more common and various institutions to address conflict more peacefully had not yet evolved. They are instead seen as precedents for violent actions today.

Radical Islamists also emphasize violence in their view of the relative importance of suras revealed to Muhammad in Mecca versus those revealed in Medina. The debate over this issue has implications far beyond those for Islamic scholarship. Around three-quarters of the Qur'an's 114 suras date to the Meccan period — that is, the period from 610 to 622. These suras, which tend to be shorter than those of the Medinan period, emphasize eternal themes such as the unity of God and the necessity of faith, as well as the values, ethics, and principles of Islam. Despite the harassment inflicted upon Muhammad's followers by the Meccans, the Prophet never urged the first Muslims to strike back; this Meccan precedent stands in stark contrast with the bellicose precedents that violent Islamists choose to cite.

As harassment intensified in Mecca, Muhammad fled with his followers to Medina in 622. The suras revealed after Muhammad's flight to Medina are longer than those revealed in Mecca, and often discuss the establishment of legal and governing structures of an Islamic society. They also contain the most vitriolic verses of the Qur'an. Many of the radical Islamists believe that because the Medinan suras were revealed later, they correct, or abrogate, the Meccan suras. But even among the most learned Islamic scholars, there is no consensus about whether chronological abrogation is a valid concept. While some scholars insist on the greater validity of the later Medinan suras, many others argue that the Meccan verses are more timeless and universal in scope, and therefore enjoy precedence over the Medinan verses. They further argue that the Qur'an was not revealed by God according to a linear chronology; nor is the Qur'an organized sequentially. Even among those Muslims who do believe the Medinan suras abrogate the Meccan suras, there is significant controversy over *which* teachings are abrogated.

But Islamists who insist on a simple and literalist reading of the Meccan and Medinan verses often conclude that the messages received by

Muhammad in Mecca stressed cooperation and peace with non-Muslims only because the Muslims were a minority at that time. According to this logic, after the Muslim community fled to Medina and grew larger and more powerful, the Prophet received permission via new revelations to fight those who persecuted Muslims. Violent Islamists focus in particular on sura 9 ("Repentance"), revealed to Muhammad in Medina, to justify their violence against non-Muslims and those who disagree with them:

> Kill them [i.e., non-Muslims] wherever you may come upon them, and seize them, and confine them, and lie in wait for them at every conceivable place ... (9:5) Fight against those from among the People of the Book who do not believe in God and the Last Day ... and do not adopt and follow the religion of truth, until they pay the *jizya* [tax of protection and exemption from military service imposed on "unbelievers"] with a willing hand in a state of submission ... (Qur'an 9:29)[23]

Islamists who read these and similar lines out of context and in a literalist manner argue that they abrogate the Meccan suras, calling for coexistence with and tolerance of Jews, Christians, and other "unbelievers." Non-Islamist Muslims on the other hand are guided by the hundreds of other verses — both from the Meccan and Medinan periods — that preach the need for mutual respect between and peaceful coexistence of Muslims and non-Muslims.

The understanding of the word "jihad" provides one more example of radical Islamists' narrow focus on violent elements within Islam. While the meaning of the term is debated by Islamic scholars, who can find various suras and hadiths to support a range of interpretations, extremists favor those that suggest jihad is a never-ending struggle to exterminate infidels who oppose the spread of Islam. One hadith commonly used by terrorists to justify their violent actions states:

> The Prophet said: "...*jihad* will be performed continuously until the day the last member of my community will fight with the Dajjal [Antichrist]. The tyranny of any tyrant and the justice of any just (ruler) will not invalidate it. One must have faith in Divine decree."[24]

---

23   Sura 9 is also the only sura that does not begin by calling God "all-merciful." The most commonly accepted explanation for this omission is that this sura is an ultimatum to non-Muslims to stop breaking their agreements with Muslims.

24   *Sunan Abu Dawud*, book 14, no. 2526, narrated by Anas ibn Malik, translated by Ahmad

But scholars of classical Islam have noted that the Arabic word "jihad" means "to strive for some objective," without any necessary reference to fighting or violence. In the twelfth century, Averroës believed armed jihad to be only one of four different types of jihad, and stressed that it should be used only when other options have been exhausted (there are over a dozen conditions that must be fulfilled before engaging in a military jihad) or when Muslims and Islam are under attack.

Moreover, according to the hadiths most cited by moderates, the Prophet intended for armed jihad to be used only rarely. They point to Muhammad's statement, upon returning from a military battle, that "we have returned from the minor jihad to the major jihad," or from "armed battle to the peaceful battle for self-control and betterment."[25] These verses are interpreted to show that for Muhammad, jihad was not primarily an external struggle to exterminate the infidel, but rather an internal struggle for self-improvement.

Radical Islamist groups have chosen to ignore such classical Islamic scholarship and its focus on the elements of inward jihad that call for self-improvement. Instead, to support their view of jihad as a violent external struggle, they quote the first caliph, Abu Bakr, in a warning to his nemesis, Persian leader Kisra: "I have come to you with a people who love death as much as you love life."[26]

Islam's Relations with Other Faiths: Tolerance, Coexistence, or Superiority?

In keeping with their conception of jihad as an internal struggle for self-improvement, many non-Islamist scholars (especially Sufis) approach non-Muslims with a tolerant "live and let live" attitude. They derive their

---

Hasan, available at: http://www.usc.edu/schools/college/crcc/engagement/resources/texts/muslim/hadith/abudawud/014.sat.html (accessed February 11, 2011).

25 Although this hadith is not part of the most authoritative collections, it has had enormous influence in Islamic mysticism (Sufism). It can be found in many sources, including Ali ibn Uthman al-Hujwiri, *The Kashf al-Mahjub: The Oldest Persian Treatise on Sufism by Al-Hujwiri*, trans. Reynold A. Nicholson (London: Luzac, 1911), pp. 200–1.

26 Islamists often quote this passage in sermons and educational material. See, for example: Adam Pashut, *Dr. Azzam al-Tamimi: A Political-Ideological Brief*, The Middle East Media Research Institute (MEMRI) Inquiry and Analysis Series Report No. 163 (February 19, 2004), available at: www.memri.org/report/en/0/0/0/0/0/0/1066.htm (accessed January 21, 2011).

thinking from verses in the Qur'an such as: "You have your religion and I have my religion" (109:6) and "There is no compulsion in the Religion" (2:256). Under Muhammad, non-Muslims were generally offered two options short of armed conflict: either convert to Islam or pay a tax (*jizya*) to acquire dhimmi (protected) status. Most non-Muslims chose the *jizya*, which led to the development of a vast system of laws and statutes regarding the treatment of non-Muslims in a Muslim state. For centuries, non-Muslims (including Jews) often enjoyed greater security under Muslim political leaders because of their dhimmi status than did religious and ethnic minorities under European leaders.

But Islamists overlook this precedent. They focus on different suras and reach the conclusion that other "peoples of the book" (i.e., Jews and Christians) are inferior to Muslims, and are consigned to Hell unless they convert. Certainly, some suras seem to *compel* Muslims to wage war against unbelievers. Qur'an 2:216, for example:

> Prescribed for you is fighting, though it is disliked by you. It may well be that you dislike a thing but it is good for you, and it may well be that you like a thing but it is bad for you. God knows, and you do not know.

Qur'an 2:190 commands, "[f]ight in God's cause against those who fight against you" — and in fact many terrorists quote this verse while omitting the remainder, which continues, "but do not exceed the bounds, for surely God loves not those who exceed the bounds." Non-Islamists understand this and similar suras in the context of defensive and just war. Islamists, however, selectively quote such verses to justify violence by claiming that in a general sense, Islam is under attack by the West, and that all means are justified by the ends.[27]

---

27 Wahhabi/Salafi interpretations of such suras talk about military jihad as if it is one of Islam's pillars; a footnote for Qur'an 2:190 in a Wahhabi translation says:

> *Al-Jihâd* (holy fighting) in Allâh's Cause (with full force of numbers and weaponry) is given the utmost importance in Islâm and is one of its pillars (on which it stands). By *Jihâd* Islâm is established, Allâh's Word is made superior, . . . and His Religion (Islâm) is propagated. By abandoning *Jihâd* (may Allâh protect us from that) Islâm is destroyed and the Muslims fall into an inferior position; their honor is lost, their lands are stolen, their rule and authority vanish. *Jihâd* is an obligatory duty in Islâm on every Muslim, and he who tries to escape from this duty, or does not in his innermost heart wish to fulfill this duty, dies with one of the qualities of a hypocrite.

(King Fahd Complex for the Printing of the Holy Qur'an, trans., "Translations [of the

Islamists also seek to twist the meaning of dhimmi status to justify violence against Israel. According to Bat Ye'or, an Egyptian-born scholar living in the UK, the Islamist way of thinking leads Muslims to conclude that since Jews are necessarily dhimmis, they cannot enjoy political independence from Muslims or form an independent Jewish state; therefore, Muslim rule needs to be reestablished in place of the illegitimate state of Israel.[28] While this is not the view of non-Islamist Muslims, it is the thinking shared by the leadership of Hamas and by Iranian president Mahmoud Ahmadinejad. That dhimmi continues to be a concept at all meaningful to Islamists is evidence of an antique mindset, one that considers Muslims superior to non-Muslims and requires Muslims to maintain their own separate communities even while living within Western societies.

To buy time to prepare for their ultimate objective of Islamizing society, Islamists use two primary examples from Islam's earliest days to justify their position that Muslims can live among non-Muslims without integrating. The first example is the Muslim community's escape from Mecca to the Christian kingdom of Axum (modern-day Ethiopia) in 615 — rather than fight back at once, they fled and regrouped; and the second (and more important) is Muhammad's journey from Mecca to Medina, where the Prophet found sanctuary from the Meccans and set up the first Islamic community, in 622. Today, many Islamists — both violent and non-violent — cite these two precedents in their own migration to Europe, where they believe they are consolidating their strength to prepare for a push to reshape society, both in Europe and in their homelands, into Islamic states. The relevance of these precedents is evident in the name of the HT splinter group founded by radical Islamist Omar Bakri after he moved to the UK from Saudi Arabia; Bakri called it "Al-Muhajiroun," which means "the emigrants."[29]

Qur'an]," 2:190, fn. 1 [Medina: King Fahd Complex for the Printing of the Holy Qur'an, n.d.], available at: www.qurancomplex.org/Quran/Targama/Targama.asp?nSora=2&l=en g&nAya=190#2_190 [accessed January 21, 2011].)

28   Bat Ye'or, *Islam and Dhimmitude: Where Civilizations Collide* (Cranbury, NJ: Associated University Press, 2002), p. 216.

29   Today's Islamists also argue in favor of a temporary truce (*hudna*) with non-Muslims, which according to their interpretation is valid only until Muslims regain strength for the further spreading of Islam. Addressing this subject in the fourteenth century, Islamic scholar Ibn al-Naqib wrote:

> Truces are permissible, not obligatory . . . Interests that justify making a truce are such things as Muslim weakness because of lack of numbers or materiel, or the hope of an enemy becoming Muslim . . . If the Muslims are weak, a truce

Islamists also cite Qur'anic precedent for the use of deception to further the ends of Islam. The Qur'an and Qur'anic commentators allow for believers to protect themselves from aggression by non-Muslims by denying their faith, if need be. The concept of *taqiyya* permits believers to lie about their faith when necessary, and *kitman* advocates concealment of malevolent intentions. Both of these were historically used by Shiites who were persecuted in Sunni lands. The Islamists of today have elevated these practices of self-defense into almost an objective duty for Muslims, using them to infiltrate and overthrow secular regimes in Muslim lands. In Europe and the United States, Islamists routinely use *taqiyya* and *kitman*, employing Western-style rhetoric extolling the democratic principles and universal human rights they seek to replace with sharia-based rule.

In all these areas governing Muslims' relations with non-Muslims, non-Islamist Muslims differ significantly from Islamists. They follow classical Islamic teachings about the need for residents to follow the law of the land they live in and maintain peaceful relations with all members of society, regardless of their religion (or lack thereof). But Islamists' teachings threaten the freedom non-Islamists seek in their daily lives. Non-Islamists may need to become more active in theological debates to counter Islamist justifications of sedition and even violence by selectively citing the Qur'an and Islamic scholars. This task is particularly important regarding women's equality.

Women and Islamism

For Islamists, the primary factor shaping attitudes toward women is the cultural context of Muhammad's time and place of birth. In the Arabia of 570, women had few legal or social rights. Polygamy was practiced without limit; women could not receive inheritances or testify in legal proceedings; and infant girls were killed openly. Islam immediately brought improvement to the situation of women during Muhammad's

---

may be made for ten years if necessary, for the Prophet (may Allah bless him and give him peace) made a truce with the Quraysh for that long, as is related by Abu Dawud . . . The rulings of such a truce are inferable from those of the non-Muslim poll tax; namely, that when a valid truce has been effected, no harm may be done to non-Muslims until it expires.

(Ahmad ibn Lulu ibn al-Naqib, *Umdat al Salik* [Reliance of the Traveler], rev. ed. [Beltsville, MD: Amana, 1994], p. 605.)

lifetime. One of Islam's core messages is the equality of men and women before God; the Qur'an states: "[Your wives] are a garment for you, and you are a garment for them" (2:187), "Whether male or female, you are all on the same footing"[30], "Whether male or female, you are all one from the other" (3:195), and "[m]en and women are guardians, confidants, and helpers of one another" (9:71). In contrast to Christianity, Islam believes that woman was not created from man, but that both man and woman were created at the same time. Islam also rejects the notion that woman is responsible for original sin. In the Muslim telling of the story of the Garden of Eden, Adam and Eve were both tempted by Satan (2:36).

Perhaps because the full implications of this equality were not spelled out in the Qur'an, Islamists (and many Muslim men generally) today fail to respect the freedom and dignity of their wives and daughters, hearkening back to attitudes of pre-Muhammadan Arabia; they do not allow these women to work and insist on marrying young women because they believe this is what both the Qur'an and the life of the Prophet teach. With their penchant for selective interpretation, many Islamists ignore the suras and hadiths that call for men to treat women with respect and instead draw inspiration from al-Ghazali, the twelfth-century anti-rationalist Islamic scholar who wrote:

> Marriage is a form of slavery. The woman is man's slave and her duty therefore is absolute obedience to the husband in all that he asks of her person. A woman, who at the moment of death enjoys the full approval of her husband, will find her place in Paradise.[31]

Islamists hardly ever mention that Muhammad followed the Qur'an's instructions to treat women respectfully and as equals. His first wife, Khadija, was already an accomplished businesswoman and 15 years his elder when they married. In fact, Muhammad originally worked for her. The Prophet, then a 25-year-old already endowed with a reputation for trustworthiness, met Khadija when she hired him as a trader on her caravan route. Once Muhammad began preaching, Khadjia became the first person to convert to Islam. There are numerous other accounts of

---

30 Ali Quli Qara'i, *The Qur'an, with a Phrase-By-Phrase English Translation* (Elmhurst, NY: Tahrike Tarsile Qur'an, 2006).
31 Abu Hamid al-Ghazali, *Ihya' 'Uloum ed-Din*, vol. 2, bk. 2, *Kitab Adab al-Nikah* (Beirut: Dar al-Kotob al-'Ilmiyah, 2002), p. 64.

the Prophet's respectful treatment of Khadija, his other wives, and his daughter, Fatima.

Even with regard to polygamy, a case can be made for Muhammad's respectful treatment of women. Although polygamy was a common practice in his culture, Muhammad had no other wives during Khadija's lifetime (she died when he was 52), and was only persuaded to remarry two years after her death. His motivation in taking additional wives appears to have been to unite his tribal community and care for the needy. The only virgin Muhammad ever married was Aisha — whom he wed at the insistence of Aisha's father, Abu Bakr, who wanted to bring the two families together. Mainstream Muslim tradition says that Muhammad married nine other times, mostly elderly women who were socially vulnerable (widows whose husbands had died in battle, women with children, and divorcees). Muhammad expressed his general opposition to polygamy by forbidding his son-in-law, Ali (the fourth caliph), to practice it.

Islamists ignore these sunnahs, which demonstrate how Muhammad's view of polygamy differed from that of his contemporaries. Instead, they embrace the cultural norms of seventh-century Arabia that Muhammad himself disregarded. Islamic scripture actually does not condone the type of polygamy Islamists (and many other Muslim men) practice today. On the contrary, it is clear that the Qur'an regards marriage as a means of protecting women and ensuring that they are not mistreated (4:126). The Qur'an stipulates that a man may have up to four wives — *if* he can treat them all equally and with proper respect (4:3). But an earlier verse from the same sura says that a man will *never* be able to be fair and just with his wives, even if he wishes to be (4:129). Thus, the Qur'an's treatment of marriage is cloaked in indirection and is a response to the poor treatment and low status of women in its historical and cultural context. In effect, Islamists not only fail to emulate Muhammad's efforts to reform the treatment of women, they also seek to restore the norms that *predate* Islam's Prophet.

Islamists practice the same interpretive selectivity in regard to physical abuse of women. Often, one hears about imams who give advice on how to beat wives "properly," citing Qur'an 4:34: "As for those women from whose determined disobedience and breach of their marital obligations you have reason to fear, admonish them; then, remain apart from them in bed; then, beat [*daraba*] them." While wife-beating was common in Arabia during the lifetime of the Prophet, it is not clear that this passage actually condones beating, since the relevant Arabic word, *daraba*, can be translated in numerous ways: including "beat," "tap," "set a clear example," and "move away from." Even if the translation of *daraba* as "beat" is accurate, Qur'an 4:34 directs husbands to beat wives only as a last resort.

Moreover, the immediately preceding verse (4:33) instructs husbands, "If women are averse, then "talk to them [per]suasively; then leave them alone in bed (without molesting them); and go to bed with them (when they are willing). If they open up to you, do not seek an excuse for blaming them." This verse can be interpreted in the context of a key hadith in which the Prophet asks, "Could any of you beat your wife as he would a slave, and then lie with her in the evening?" Taken together, this hadith and Qur'an 4:33 suggest that Muhammad was instructing his male followers to alter the customs of the day and avoid the physical abuse of women. Indeed, there is not a single story in any hadith or oral account of any sunnah in which the Prophet beats or treats women harshly, and the final Qur'anic verse on male–female relationships regards men and women as each other's protecting friends and guardians who live together as partners (Qur'an 9:71).

In ignoring Muhammad's respectful treatment of women while selectively citing suras and hadiths that seem to condone polygamy and physical abuse of women, Islamists aim at more than simply justifying lifestyle choices. They have a deeper political objective — namely, to undercut gender equality and thereby to differentiate Muslim communities from mainstream Western societies. Such differentiation is a crucial first step in Islamizing Western society in an incremental way, through creeping Islamization, to avoid arousing Western suspicion and opposition.

Creeping Islamization also explains Islamists' insistence on covering Muslim women. In Muhammad's Arabia, the veil did not traditionally have religious connotations. Prior to the emergence of Islam, the veil was worn by upper-class Arab women in the Byzantine and Persian empires, who covered their hair as a symbol of status. More and more elite women began adopting the veil in the seventh century as a way to distinguish themselves from the lower classes. As Islam spread, the value of modesty — stipulated in the Qur'an for men as well as women — merged with the social customs of the upper class; thus the veil is associated with the Islamic faith, but it is not a religious requirement, as today's Islamists argue.[32]

---

32 Generally, Islamic religious scholars and Islamists cite two verses in the Qur'an to support their view that Muslim women should cover their hair. The first is 33:59, which is addressed to Muhammad and his family:

O Prophet! Tell your wives and your daughters, as well as the women of the

Islamists often demand that their wives and daughters cover at least their heads — and, in some cases, their entire bodies as well. But Islamists insist on covering their women for political, not religious, reasons. They generally begin the process of Islamization with those whom they view as the fundamental building block of any society: mothers and wives. The veil is the most dramatic way of communicating that Muslims are different from non-Muslims, and in particular from Western society. This explains why Iran's Islamist regime made wearing the veil mandatory in the immediate wake of the 1979 revolution. Similarly, the Taliban made the burqa mandatory for women immediately upon seizing power in Afghanistan in 1996. During Algeria's brutal civil war in the 1990s, radical Islamists killed unveiled women. In Gaza, Hamas has ordered schoolgirls to don the headscarf as the Islamist organization strives to restore medieval Arab norms to Palestinian territory.[33]

Precursors and Alternatives

Islamism as a religious-political movement did not emerge until the twentieth century. Under the tolerant Ottoman sultans, extremist Muslims remained on the margins; but the collapse of the Ottoman Empire and the abolition of the caliphate in 1923 provided a historic opportunity for the growth of theological utopianism and political rejectionism.

---

believers, to draw over themselves some part of their outer garments (when outside their homes). This is better and more convenient for them to be recognized (and respected for their decency) and not harassed.

The second passage is 24:31:

Tell the believing women that they should restrain their gaze (from looking at the men whom it is lawful for them to marry), and guard their private parts, and that they should not display their charms except that which is revealed of itself, and let them draw their veils over their bosoms.

These passages reinforce the social convention of Muhammad's time, which was for women to dress modestly. But as many mainstream theologians have argued over the centuries, these verses do not necessarily call for the covering of women's heads — and certainly not the veiling of their entire bodies; nor do these passages suggest that following the social custom of female veiling is a religious obligation. Neither are there are any hadiths where the Prophet instructs women to cover their hair as a religious obligation.

33 While many Muslim women genuinely choose to cover their hair out of personal conviction, many more are either indoctrinated by the Islamists into "choosing" to cover, or are outright forced to do so.

While Islamism itself may be of relatively recent origin, as an extremist movement it is not without precedent in Islamic history. Two important precursors are worth considering in further detail. One is the thirteenth-century Sunni scholar Taqi ad-Din Ahmad ibn Taymiyyah (1263–1328), who believed that the destruction of Baghdad and subsequent decline of the caliphate at the hands of the heathen Mongols had occurred only because Muslim leaders had strayed from the "true path" of Islam. He seized upon the legal-religious philosophy of Ibn Hanbal and developed it into a puritanical ideology. Even though the new Mongol rulers had converted to Islam, Ibn Taymiyyah denounced them as "insufficiently Muslim," pronouncing jihad against them and everyone else who disagreed with his interpretations of the Qur'an and hadiths. He was condemned by the religious authorities of his day and frequently imprisoned for his extremist views.

The second precursor is Muhammad ibn Abd al-Wahhab (1703–1792), who took his inspiration from Ibn Taymiyyah. The founder of Wahhabism, Ibn Abd al-Wahhab perceived the Islamic world to be in deep crisis, as the caliphate, in Ottoman hands since 1517, was beginning the protracted decline that would end with its abolishment in the early twentieth century. Like Ibn Taymiyyah, Ibn Abd al-Wahhab interpreted the failings of the caliphate as a sign that Muslim leaders were insufficiently devout. But Ibn Abd al-Wahhab went even further, arguing that any expression of reverence toward the Prophet was similar to the Christian treatment of Jesus and thus equivalent to polytheism. He forbade men from emulating the Prophet by trimming or shaving their beards. He condemned anything he viewed as innovation (*bid'a*) in Islam, meaning potentially anything not specifically mentioned in the Qur'an, including decoration in mosques, most books other than the Qur'an, and local festivals and "nontraditional" ceremonies. Ibn Abd al-Wahhab declared war on Shiites, Sufis, and anyone he considered an unbeliever, including Islamic rulers who would not follow his strict Hanbali interpretation of sharia. Killing any of these people was permissible in his view.

Indeed, like the Khawarij, the rebel sect that had murdered the fourth caliph Ali, Ibn Abd al-Wahhab considered jihad against perceived enemies of Islam as Islam's sixth pillar, a view that is at the root of today's Islamist terrorist theological justification. Ibn Abd al-Wahhab's fanatic quest to define Islamic orthodoxy as a violent struggle against anyone who disagreed with him belies claims by today's Islamists that theirs is a struggle to defend their religion against an aggressive Christian West.

Although Ibn Abd al-Wahhab's views are now increasingly common among Muslims around the world, they represented a severe break from nearly every practitioner of Islam up to that time — even from Ibn Taymiyyah. Ibn Abd al-Wahhab was condemned by most Muslims (including many members of his family). The Ottoman caliph issued a fatwa condemning Ibn Abd al-Wahhab's radicalism. Ibn Abd al-Wahhab and some of his followers sought refuge with an Arabian tribal leader by the name of Muhammad ibn Saud (d. 1765). In 1745, Ibn Saud and Ibn Abd al-Wahhab formed an alliance, with Ibn Abd al-Wahhab viewing Ibn Saud as the vehicle for spreading his version of Islam and Ibn Saud viewing Ibn Abd al-Wahhab as the means to legitimize his dreams of conquest. Ibn Saud and Ibn Abd al-Wahhab waged a campaign of violence across the Arabian Peninsula, imposing their puritanical version of Islam and killing those who dissented — especially Shiites. In 1801, the Wahhabis and Saudis brutally attacked the holy city of Karbala and destroyed the tomb of Huseyn, the Prophet Muhammad's grandson, whose death at the Battle of Karbala in 680 had sealed Islam's schism between Sunnism and Shiism. Through their alliance with the House of Saud, the Wahhabis gained control of the two holiest places in Islam, Medina and Mecca, and the Saudi rulers subsequently declared Wahhabism their official state religion. The unification of Wahhabism and political authority in Saudi Arabia set a precedent for Islamists the world over (including the Shiite leaders of the Iranian revolution), who insist there can be no separation of mosque and state.

From the early nineteenth century onward, the fortunes of the Wahhabi–Saudi alliance waxed and waned as it contended with rival tribes and challenges from the declining Ottoman Empire. By the early 1930s, following the collapse of the Ottoman Empire, Abdul Aziz bin Saud, a descendant of Muhammad ibn Saud, had consolidated control over most of the Arabian Peninsula, creating what is now the Kingdom of Saudi Arabia. The Wahhabis continued their campaign against other forms of Islam; to this day, they teach that Shiism is an invention of Jews and that its followers are not "real Muslims." The wealth generated by Saudi oil, coupled with the Wahhabis' status as custodians of Islam's holiest sites, helped the Wahhabis pursue what the Khawarij could never achieve: establishment of their supremacist interpretation of Islam as mainstream.

But the same event that enabled Islamism to emerge as a religious-political movement — the collapse of the Ottoman Empire at the end of World War I — also saw the emergence of its primary challenger: secular and nationalist modernizers, first in Turkey and then across the broader Middle East and North Africa. The growth of secular states with

Muslim-majority populations — the choice of some Muslims to separate politics from religion — reminds us that Islamism was by no means an inevitable development within Islam in the twentieth century.

The most significant secular modernizer was Mustafa Kemal Atatürk (1881–1938), who founded the Turkish Republic in 1923. A brilliant military strategist and tactician, Atatürk became one of the pivotal statesmen of the twentieth century. Turks credit him with saving their country by rejecting the Treaty of Sèvres imposed on the Ottoman rulers by the Allies at the end of World War I; this treaty, which ceded control of much of the Anatolian Peninsula to Greece, France, and Italy, was viewed by many Turks as an unacceptable humiliation. Atatürk led Turkish forces to victory against the Allies before establishing new governing institutions for the fledgling republic. He replaced sharia with the rule of secular law (patterned after that of Switzerland) and laid the foundation for a modern democracy in which authority derived from the votes of citizens rather than religious scholars' interpretation of God's intent. He launched a top-down "cultural revolution" to modernize and Westernize Turkey. He changed the alphabet of the Turkish language from Arabic to Latin, reformed the dress code (forbidding Islamic headgear, i.e., the headscarf for women and the fez for men), and transformed the basis of Turkish identity from membership in the Muslim *millet* (religious community) to citizenship in the Turkish Republic; henceforth, all Turkish citizens would be treated equally under the law — regardless of their religious affiliation.

Atatürk looked to France's model of a mixed presidential-parliamentary political system for inspiration, and to the country's secularist ideal of *laïcité*, which prohibits religious practices that contradict the political and cultural freedoms enshrined in its constitution. Atatürk envisioned his goal as the liberation of his fellow Turks from centuries of religious dogma imposed by the caliphate and the ulema (council of religious elders), thereby establishing the values of the Enlightenment in a modern Turkey. In a sense, Atatürk's reforms were intended to reopen the gates of *ijtihad*, and thus to restore the central role of rational thinking that had catapulted Islamic civilization to scientific and intellectual greatness in the past.

Atatürk was not the region's only secular modernizer. The first constitution of any Muslim-majority country was drafted in Tunisia in 1861. Egypt followed in 1866 with democratic reforms and the first elections in a Muslim society.[34] Meanwhile, in Muslim-populated areas outside Ottoman control, the ideas of the Enlightenment were also taking hold.

---

34 Bernard Lewis, "Why Turkey Is the Only Muslim Democracy," *Middle East Quarterly* 1(1):

In 1918, Azerbaijan became the first Muslim country to establish a secular democracy; although this experience was regrettably brought to an end by Bolshevik military intervention, it offered inspiration to Atatürk and his supporters in the following decade. Similar movements to promote secularism and democracy in Muslim societies arose in the region stretching from the Balkans to Uzbekistan.

These reformist initiatives helped generate a spirit of nationalism in the early twentieth century, which broadened into a call for secular modernization across the broader Middle East and North Africa, embodied in the late twentieth century by leaders such as President Habib Bourgiba of Tunisia and President Gamal Abdul Nasser of Egypt.

After World War II, as Western colonial powers began their exodus from the Middle East, Arab nationalism morphed into Pan-Arabism and emerged as a pervasive ideological force. The two most prevalent forms of Arab nationalism are Nasserism (named for President Nasser in Egypt) and Ba'athism (first in Syria then in Iraq). Despite periodic hostility between these two movements, they share four key similarities: they are pro-modernization, pro-Arab unity, anti-Western, and anti-Israel.[35]

The Ba'ath ("resurrection") Party was founded in 1947 by Michel Aflaq (1910–1989), an Orthodox Christian and political philosopher, and Salah al-Din al-Bitar (1912–1980), a Sunni Muslim.[36] Both were Syrian, born to Damascene merchant families and brought up in the atmosphere of intense pro-Arabism in the 1920s and 30s. The party hoped that once the Arab nationalist parties of all Arab states formed, the Arab spirit and intellect would be revived after languishing for centuries.[37] In 1954, the Ba'ath Party gained a number of seats in the Syrian parliament, and, in keeping with Aflaq's contention that the ends justify the means, abandoned democratic organizational structures in favor of Marxist–Leninist

---

41–9, available at: www.meforum.org/216/why-turkey-is-the-only-muslim-democracy (accessed January 22, 2011).

35   David Downing, *The Making of the Middle East* (Chicago, IL: Raintree, 2005), p. 26. Adeed Dawisha makes the point that for quite a while Israel was not a primary rallying cause but was considered "just another imperialist state." Adeed Dawisha, *Arab Nationalism in the Twentieth Century: From Triumph to Despair* (Princeton, NJ: Princeton University Press, 2003), p. 243.

36   This section relies upon John F. Devlin, "The Baath Party: Rise and Metamorphosis," *American Historical Review* 96(5): 1396–407.

37   To quote the party constitution of 1947: "The Arabs form one nation. This nation has the natural right to live in a single state. [As such] the Arab Fatherland constitutes an indivisible political and economic unity. No Arab country can live apart from the others." Cited in Dawisha, *Arab Nationalism*, p. 3.

"democratic centralism." Thus the groundwork was laid for the dictatorial regimes in Syria in 1966 and Iraq in 1968 (with Hafez al-Assad seizing power in Damascus in 1970 and Saddam Hussein taking over in Baghdad in 1979).

Arab nationalism lost steam as a political ideology as secular modernizers abandoned those elements of Atatürk's reforms that had stressed democracy. The heavy-handed policies of the Ba'athist dictatorships — which failed to provide basic education, jobs, or human rights — created openings for Islamist movements, which had been consolidating their strength since the 1920s while waiting for anti-regime sentiment to increase. Pan-Arabism's decline accelerated with Israel's humiliating defeat of Arab forces during the 1967 Six-Day War, in what became known among Arabs as "al-Nakbah" (the catastrophe).[38] Pan-Arabism then fused with Islamism, which subsequently assumed a position of ideological predominance among Muslims in the broader Middle East and North Africa. Islamism emerged as a mixture of Wahhabism and Arab nationalism, with the *umma* replacing Arab unity as the movement's core objective, and with Israel and the West increasingly cited as the cause of the injustices plaguing Muslims.[39]

Islamism's Emergence as a Global Movement

The seeds of the modern Islamist movement were planted by a handful of ideologues who drew inspiration from Ibn Abd al-Wahhab's totalitarian political ideology and draconian interpretation of Islam. The most significant Islamist movement to date emerged in Egypt in 1928, when Hasan al-Banna (1906–1949) founded the Muslim Brotherhood to fill the vacuum left by the abolishment of the caliphate four years earlier. Al-Banna, a schoolteacher, was concerned that the Islamic world had fallen behind the West and believed, like Ibn Abd al-Wahhab before him, that Muslims needed to return to "pure" Islam. He borrowed the term *salafi* from Egyptian jurist and liberal reformer Muhammad Abduh (1849–1905) to suggest Muslims' need to return to an "original" interpretation of Islam

---

38   Fouad Ajami pronounced the end of Arab nationalism in his famous article, "The End of Pan-Arabism," *Foreign Affairs* 57(2): 355–73, available at: www.foreignaffairs.com/articles/30269/fouad-ajami/the-end-of-pan-arabism (accessed January 22, 2011).

39   For a short summary, see Thomas L. Friedman, "1977 vs. 1979," *New York Times* (February 13, 2010), available at: www.nytimes.com/2010/02/14/opinion/14friedman.html (accessed January 22, 2011).

for guidance in modern life.[40] Al-Banna created the Muslim Brotherhood as an Islamist political movement to gradually "re-Islamize" Muslims and then once again politically unite them under a new caliphate.

Activists of the Muslim Brotherhood engaged in bottom-up Islamization, meaning they spread Islamist ideology through grassroots education, propaganda, and civic activism. The organization emerged as a political party in Egypt, where its candidates ran for public office with the aim of overthrowing the country's secular system of government. In response to government repression of the movement in the 1950s, the Muslim Brotherhood instigated public uprisings, some of them violent, against the government. As political tension increased, a Muslim Brotherhood member attempted to assassinate President Nasser in 1954; the organization was banned the same year.[41]

The Egyptian government's banning of the Muslim Brotherhood led many of its activists to flee — to other Muslim-majority countries, Europe, and the United States. This exodus helped Brotherhood activists spread Islamist ideology well beyond the group's Arab homeland. Banna's Muslim Brotherhood thus became the parent organization of a number of Islamist offshoots, which themselves would take root abroad and produce offshoot groups of their own. During this period, the Muslim Brotherhood's leading ideologue was Sayyid Qutb (1906–1966), whose ideas continue to radicalize generations of Muslims into Islamists even five decades after his death. Qutb had begun his activist career in the 1930s as a secular reformist. However, as Arab nationalism gained strength, Qutb was increasingly repulsed by the ethnic supremacist rhetoric, corrupt tendencies, and repressive techniques of the Pan-Arabists. He gravitated instead toward what he viewed as a higher goal: the elevation of the

---

40   Al-Banna's use of the term *salafi* differed significantly from that of Abduh, who is widely considered to be the founder of the modernist and rationalist Islamic movement. To make Islam compatible with contemporary norms, Abduh believed Muslims needed to go back to the Islamic understanding of the *salaf* (the first generations of Muslims, or the "righteous ancestors") and then use reason to reinterpret Islamic texts; they could not merely follow the traditions and interpretations provided by clerics of medieval times. Thus Muslims would reopen the gates of *ijtihad* and modernize Islam by leaving aside religious and social norms that had become fossilized over the course of a millennium. His ideas were gradually transformed into the political–religious ideology of Islamism, initially by his disciple Muhammad Rashid Rida (1865–1935), and then by Hassan al-Banna, both of whom wanted to make the adoption of sharia law compulsory for Muslims.
41   Muslim Brotherhood members were involved in the assassination of Egyptian prime minister Mahmud Fahmi Nokrashi in 1948; President Anwar El Sadat was assassinated by a Muslim Brotherhood offshoot, al-Gamaa al-Islamiyya, in 1981.

Islamic *umma*. During the 1950s and 60s, Qutb's writings became increasingly radical. Like Ibn Abd al-Wahhab, Qutb argued for sharia law to be established as a comprehensive system that would govern all aspects of life, and described military jihad as essential to defend Islam against the West.[42] In 1964, Qutb published his most famous work, *Ma'alim fi al-Tariq* (Milestones), which offered a blueprint for how Islamists could take over secular governments. In it, Qutb argues that Muslims have fallen into the "state of ignorance" (*jahilliyah*) that existed prior to God's revelation to Muhammad because they have failed to follow divine law. To remedy this, a vanguard of Muslims should reject everything except the Qur'an, separate themselves from society, emulate the Prophet's companions (*sahaba*), and proselytize others to become "true Muslims." Once a critical mass of these "true Muslims" was reached, this vanguard would then remove existing systems and political powers by any means necessary. The Egyptian authorities viewed *Milestones* as seditious extremism; they hanged Qutb for the crime of subversion in 1966.

After Qutb's execution, there was a second exodus of Muslim Brotherhood members from Egypt. Many went to Saudi Arabia, which had begun its global Islamization project to counter Nasser's Pan-Arab nationalism, an ideology that called for the overthrow of the Saudi monarchy. The ruling family had founded the Muslim World League (MWL) in 1962 to defend itself against Nasserism and to export Wahhabi Islam globally, and they recruited Muslim Brotherhood teachers and scholars to staff the Wahhabi institutions created under the MWL, both at home and beyond the Arabian Peninsula. As Ibn Abd al-Wahhab had done before them, the Muslim Brotherhood members formed a mutually beneficial partnership with the Saudi leaders: the Saudis provided institutions and funding, while the Brotherhood spread its version of Islamist ideology, aiming to undermine secular rule around the world (a process described in detail in Chapters 3–5).

Outside the Arab world, another key Islamist ideologue who both drew on and inspired Qutb was the Indian thinker Maulana Abdul Ala Maududi (1903–1979). Maududi shared Qutb's (and Ibn Abd al-Wahhab's) belief that secular governments in Muslim-majority countries that did not implement sharia law were apostate regimes, against which Muslims were obliged to wage political and military jihad. To advance such thinking, Maududi founded the Jamaat-e-Islami (JI) movement and political party in 1941 in British India. After the independence and

---

42   Paul Berman, *Terror and Liberalism* (New York: W. W. Norton, 2003), p. 98.

partition of India and the establishment of Pakistan as an Islamic republic in 1956, JI became the primary supporter of Islamist ideology in Pakistan and the broader South Asian region. Indeed, Maududi became a crucial agent in spreading Islamist ideology across South and Southeast Asia.

Despite its grounding in the specifically Sunni extremism of Ibn Abd al-Wahhab, Islamism spread to the Shiite world in the early 1970s, thanks in large part to the writings of Iranian sociologist Ali Shariati (1933–1977). Shariati is often called "ideologue of the Iranian Revolution."[43] While studying in Paris in the mid-1960s, he was highly influenced by Marxist ideas, especially the call for revolution to bring about a just and classless society. The Sunni Islamists Maududi and Qutb also had a significant impact on Ayatollah Khomeini and other leaders of the 1979 Iranian Revolution, with some of their works translated from Arabic into Farsi by Iran's revolutionary Islamists.

Shariati's intellectual development in Paris demonstrates that twentieth-century European thought influenced Islamist as well as secular movements. The Muslim Brotherhood, its radical offshoots like HT, JI, and Iranian revolutionaries, as well as secular Nasserists and Ba'athists, were all influenced by contemporary European political and social movements, especially Fascism, Nazism, and Communism.

In recent years, there have been a number of books written on the impact of Nazism on Arab nationalist and Islamist movements.[44] The similarities between previous totalitarian movements and Islamism are remarkable — and are not purely coincidental. The Islamists were strongly influenced by leaders and thinkers of these movements, and superimposed their ideas on the Islamic societal and theological context. Well after Nazism was defeated in Europe, its mindset and organizational principles remained relevant in the Arab world. Even now, two decades after the collapse of Communism, HT and many other Islamist organizations continue to use the cell-based organizational structures of the Bolsheviks.

Hasan al-Banna admired Adolf Hitler and Benito Mussolini,[45] and

---

43   Ervand Abrahamian, "Ali Shariati: Ideologue of the Iranian Revolution," in Edmund Burke and Ira Lapidus, eds., *Islam, Politics, and Social Movements* (Los Angeles, CA: University of California Press, 1993), pp. 289–97.

44   On the impact of Nazism on Islamism, see, for example, Jeffrey Herf, *Nazi Propaganda for the Arab World* (New Haven, CT: Yale University Press, 2009); Matthias Kuntzel, *Jihad and Jew-Hatred: Islamism, Nazism and the Roots of 9/11* (New York: Telos Press, 2007); Laurent Murawiec, *The Mind of Jihad* (New York: Cambridge University Press, 2008).

45   Efraim Karsh, *Islamic Imperialism: A History*, upd. ed. (New Haven, CT: Yale University Press, 2007), p. 214.

the Muslim Brotherhood and its various splinter groups have sponsored translations of *Mein Kampf* and of the infamous but fraudulent *The Protocols of the Elders of Zion.*[46] Heinrich Himmler, the main architect of the Holocaust, was involved in pro-Nazi indoctrination of Muslims as well.[47]

In Palestine, Haj Muhammad Amin al-Husayni (1921–1948), who, as grand mufti of Jerusalem, was the supreme spiritual leader of Palestinian Muslims, aided a pro-Nazi coup in 1941 in Iraq[48] and recruited Bosnian Muslim troops for Hitler's SS.[49] Al-Husayni also helped establish the religious and organizational foundation of the international Islamist movement, including the Islamists' embrace of anti-Semitism. In other words, Islamists' adoption of anti-Semitism *preceded* the establishment of the State of Israel.

In fact, anti-Semitism has become a fundamental element of Islamism. In his Qur'anic commentary *Fi Zilal al-Qur'an* (In the Shade of the Qur'an), Qutb declares bluntly that Jews are "the worst of all creatures" and adopts a literal interpretation of the verse, labeling them "pigs" and "apes."[50] This kind of anti-Semitism was not found within Islam until the

---

46   *The Protocols* was an anti-Semitic text that appeared in the *Znamya* newspaper in Russia in 1903. It was deliberately fabricated by Russian journalist Matvei Golovinski and "unearthed" a Jewish plot to take over first Russia, and then the rest of the world. The purpose of the monograph was to scare away anti-Semitic Russian czar Nicholas II from introducing further reforms. Yet many people, especially Islamists, believe the book to be a true account of a worldwide Jewish conspiracy — one that is still active.

47   See Herf, *Nazi Propaganda*, p. 199: "On May 14th, 1943, Himmler requested that the SS's Reich Security Main Office (RSHA) examine 'themes in the Koran that lead Muslims to the view that the Koran predicts and assigns to the Führer the mission of completing the Prophet's work.' Himmler wanted the RSHA to examine the issue because 'we can very probably use this idea in the Muslim population, above all our own Muslim troops.'"

48   United States Holocaust Memorial Museum, "Hajj Amin Al-Husayni; Arab Nationalist and Muslim Leader," *Holocaust Encyclopedia* (Washington, DC: United States Holocaust Memorial Museum, n.d.), available at: www.ushmm.org/wlc/en/article. php?ModuleId=10007666 (accessed January 22, 2011).

49   When the SS decided in February 1943 to recruit among Bosnian Muslims for a new division of the Waffen-SS, SS Main Office Chief Berger enlisted al-Husayni in a recruiting drive in Bosnia from March 30 and April 11. On April 29, Berger reported that 24,000–27,000 recruits had signed up and noted that the "visit of the Grand Mufti of Jerusalem had had an extraordinarily successful impact." (United States Holocaust Memorial Museum. "Hajj Amin Al-Husayni: Wartime Propagandist," *Holocaust Encyclopedia* [Washington, DC: United States Holocaust Memorial Museum, n.d.], available at: www. ushmm.org/wlc/en/article.php?ModuleId=10007667 [accessed January 22, 2011]).

50   Middle East Media Research Institute (MEMRI), *Contemporary Islamist Ideology Authorizing Genocidal Murder*, Special Report No. 25 (Washington, DC: MENRI, 2004), available at: www.memri.org/report/en/0/0/0/0/0/0/1049.htm#_ednref15 (accessed

1930s, just as Hitler was consolidating his Nazi rule. In fact, just prior to Islamism's spread, Jews in the Middle East and North Africa were fully integrated in public life, served in parliaments, and were respected members of the political and economic communities.[51] Though there are anti-Jewish suras in the Qur'an, traditional Islamic scholarship often interpreted them in a way that led to a greater tolerance of Jews than that displayed in much of Europe. After the creation of the State of Israel, anti-Semitism took hold in earnest within Islamist ideology.

The exodus of European colonial powers from the Middle East, North Africa, and Central and South Asia facilitated the spread of Islamism beyond Arabia. In North Africa and India, colonial powers had set up secular institutions (e.g., schools, military and other government bureaucracies) that separated religion from public life and enabled secular enterprises to flourish alongside religious faith. As a result, many Muslims in these regions came to believe that Islam was compatible with democracy and modernity. In opposition to this secular order, anti-colonial movements often took an Islamist form.

Following decades of ideological preparation, Islamism truly took off in 1979 thanks to three monumental events. First, and perhaps most importantly, the Iranian Revolution demonstrated that Islamists were able to overturn a secular regime, seize political power, and establish sharia rule. Though the Iranian revolutionaries were Shiites, Sunni Islamists were emboldened by this great Islamist success. Now, instead of drawing inspiration from only Sunni sources, Islamists in different parts of the world were also reading Iranian sources like Shariati and Khomeini and observing how the Iranians were applying Islamist theory in real life.

Second, Sunni Islamists briefly seized control of Islam's holiest shrine,

---

January 22, 2011). Islamists often call Jews and Christians "apes" and "pigs," respectively, citing the Qur'an itself, for example: "You surely know of those among you who exceeded the bounds with respect to the Sabbath, and so We said to them, 'Be you apes, miserably slinking and rejected'" (2:65). Wahhabi literature also highlights the remark of Ibn Abbas, the Prophet's cousin: "The apes are Jews, the people of the Sabbath; while the swine are Christians, the infidels of the communion of Jesus." Non-Islamists do not read such lines literally and as valid for all times, but contextualize them. Moreover, there are many different ways to translate the same ancient Arabic phrases. (Ibn Abbas, quoted in: Center for Religious Freedom of Freedom House and Institute for Gulf Affairs, *Saudi Arabia's Curriculum of Intolerance with Excerpts from Saudi Ministry of Education Textbooks for Islamic Studies* (Washington, DC: Center for Religious Freedom of Freedom House and Institute for Gulf Affairs, 2006), p. 24, available at: www.freedomhouse.org/uploads/special_report/48.pdf [accessed January 22, 2011]).

51   See Kuntzel, *Jihad and Jew-Hatred*.

the Ka'ba in Mecca. Saudi authorities were worried that Iran's Islamist revolutionaries might inspire an uprising either by Saudi Arabia's Wahhabi extremists or by its restive Shiite minority, either of which could destroy the kingdom. Saudi leaders further feared that Iran might emerge as the new leader of the world's Muslims, especially if the Ka'ba was no longer under Saudi control.

Third, the Soviet Union's invasion of Afghanistan provided Islamists around the globe with a new rallying cry. Bringing down the Soviets through armed jihad gave Wahhabi groups and the Muslim Brotherhood a shared sense of purpose, and these two groups began cooperating closely despite their differences. This cooperation continued when Wahhabi and Muslim Brotherhood members moved to Europe and the United States, where — as explained in the next several chapters — the two groups spread their Islamist ideology to Muslims in the West. The government of Saudi Arabia viewed this burgeoning cooperation among Islamist groups against the Soviet invaders as an opportunity to keep Sunni extremists outside the country and to restrain their own Shiite population. Thanks to skyrocketing oil revenues after the 1973 oil embargo, the Saudi government began spending considerable amounts of money to indoctrinate Sunni Muslims with militant jihadist ideologies, focusing on resisting the Soviet invasion of Afghanistan and blunting the spread of Iranian Shiism. Since 1979, the Saudi government has provided Wahhabi groups and Muslim Brotherhood branches tens of billions of dollars to fund lobbying and publications around the world, which have helped to create the misperception in the West that the Islamist extremism of Ibn Taymiyyah and Ibn Abd al-Wahhab constitutes moderate mainstream Islamic thinking.

And the West has aided these efforts. After Iranian revolutionaries seized the US Embassy in Tehran in 1979, the Saudi aim to spread Sunni extremism as a shield against Iranian Shiism appealed to the United States. As the war in Afghanistan continued, Washington welcomed — and then actively supported — the armed jihad by Wahhabi mujahedeen against Soviet troops. Over time, Washington's support of Wahhabi activists led to a great strengthening of the international Islamist movement, including, of course, al-Qaeda.

The Wahhabis were not the only Islamists who received Western support. For decades the West assisted the Muslim Brotherhood, even helping it to bring its radical ideology to Western lands. As Ian Johnson reported in the *Wall Street Journal*, during World War II tens of thousands of Muslims in the Soviet Red Army ... switch[ed] sides ... [to] fight for Hitler. After the war, thousands sought refuge in West Germany, building one of the largest Muslim communities in 1950s Europe ... [The] Muslim Brotherhood formed a working arrangement with U.S. intelligence organizations, outmaneuvering German agencies for control of the former Nazi soldiers and their mosque [in Munich].[52]

Among these Islamist activists working with US intelligence operatives was Said Ramadan (1926–1995), the son-in-law of Muslim Brotherhood founder Hasan al-Banna. With help from Western operatives, Ramadan made the Munich mosque a Europe-wide center. Ramadan moved to Geneva in 1958 to head the secretariat of the World Islamic Congress, as part of an effort, according to Johnson, "to unite Muslims around the world."[53] Today, Ramadan's son, Tariq Ramadan, is one of Europe's most prominent Islamists.

Yet because of their lasting alliance with Saudi Arabia, it is Wahhabi groups who have enjoyed the most success in spreading and popularizing Islamist thinking. Through massive propaganda campaigns financed by Saudi Arabia's enormous oil revenues, Wahhabi extremists have used their status as custodians of Islam's holy sites in Mecca and Medina to claim they are the sole legitimate authority on the history and interpretation of Islam. The proliferation of Wahhabi propaganda around the globe has so distorted the prevailing understanding of Islamic history and theology that hundreds of millions of Muslims are unable to recognize Wahhabism as an extreme movement distinct from Islam as a whole — even though it is at odds with hundreds of other schools of Islamic thought. Wahhabi activists further this obfuscation by referring to themselves as "moderate Muslims."

In their effort to impose their narrow interpretation of Islam on all Muslims, Wahhabis have sought to erase any hint of other forms of Islam, including Islamic tombstones, mausoleums, and shrines dedicated to non-Wahhabis. In 2002, King Fahd of Saudi Arabia ordered the destruction of the fortress of al-Ajyad overlooking the Grand Mosque in Mecca; the fortress had been built in 1780 by an Ottoman regime eager to keep the Wahhabi sect out of Islam's holiest place. Saudi authorities have demolished many Ottoman-era mosques to obliterate these symbols of cultural

---

52 Ian Johnson, "Beachhead: How a Mosque for Ex-Nazis Became Center of Radical Islam," *Wall Street Journal* (July 12, 2005).
53 Johnson, "Beachhead."

and religious diversity. This Islamist desire to enforce a single, narrow view of Islam was also reflected in the Taliban's destruction of the statues of Buddhas in Bamyan, Afghanistan, in the spring of 2001, as well as in Sunni radicals' attacks on Shiite shrines in Iraq. But the Wahhabis go even further than their fellow Islamists: they seek to eliminate physical signs of the life of the Prophet Muhammad. Such extremist behavior stands in sharp contrast to centuries of mainstream Islamic thinking that called for Muslims to emulate all aspects of the Prophet's actions and deeds. Wahhabis, on the other hand, believe it is only in the literal words of the Qur'an, not in the Prophet's own human example, that God's revelation can be found. In other words, too much attention on the Prophet detracts from the Wahhabis' strict and draconian interpretation of Islam. Wahhabis therefore advocate demolishing architectural monuments connected to Muhammad's life, including even his family members' houses in Mecca and the mausoleums of hundreds of his companions.

Over the course of the twentieth century, Islamism expanded beyond a single Arabian kingdom to become a regional movement based in Egypt and then a global phenomenon. Thanks to the Machiavellian calculation that "the enemy of my enemy is my friend," Western governments facilitated Islamism's spread into Europe in the 1950s and its global expansion later on through support for Wahhabi mujahedeen in Afghanistan and for the Pakistani Islamist extremists in the early 1980s. All the while, Western strategists remained oblivious to the ideological danger Islamism posed not only to them, but to Muslims as well.

By the start of the new millennium, Islamism was a universal movement that had identified the United States as the main enemy and primary target of global jihad. Islamists were confident that because their mujahedeen had defeated the Soviet Union in Afghanistan and catalyzed that country's dissolution, they could easily destroy the United States. For over 20 years, Iran had been calling for the destruction of both the "Great Satan" (the United States) and the "Little Satan" (Israel). Pakistan seemed on the brink of an Islamist takeover, with Pakistani prime minister Benazir Bhutto warning President George H. W. Bush in a 1989 phone call about the rising danger of the violent Islamist Osama bin Laden.[54] Meanwhile, the governments of Sudan, Yemen, and Somalia were taken

---

54   This incident was mentioned by her husband, Asif Ali Zardari, on *Meet the Press*, NBC, May 10, 2009. Hamid Karzai, Asif Ali Zardari, Steve Coll, and Andrea Mitchell, "'Meet the Press' transcript for May 10, 2009" (May 10, 2009), available at: www.msnbc.msn.com/id/30658135/ns/meet_the_press/page/2/ (accessed January 22, 2011).

over by Islamists, leading to severe political tension, insurrection, and even civil war.

The Islamist terrorist attacks of September 11, 2001, briefly awakened Western leaders to the threats their societies faced from Islamist extremism. Yet today, most Western governments seek to "engage" Muslims regardless of their political-religious ideology, so long as those Muslims forswear violence. Western leaders are overlooking the threat to secular democracy and universal human rights posed by Islamist radicals — including nonviolent ones. This failure to recognize that Islamists do not represent the religion of Islam has enabled Islamists to win elections (like the Muslim Brotherhood's militant wing Hamas in the Palestinian territories) and to pass off their extreme interpretation of Islam as mainstream thinking in Western societies.

CHAPTER 3

The Rise of Islamism in Europe

Tasked with making their countries' barren fields and bombed-out farms bloom with life once again, the postwar leaders of Western Europe did what any expert horticulturist would do: they found an external source of thriving growth to transplant. The transplanted Muslim "guest workers" who came to European countries (primarily Germany, the Netherlands, Britain, and France) in the 1940s and 50s were not intended to supplant existing workers, but to strengthen economies temporarily during their recovery. But the decision to rely on guest workers had unintended consequences.

First, the Muslim residents of Europe soon put down permanent roots of their own. With their development shaped by the distinctive conditions of European soil, the children and grandchildren of the first "transplanted" generation became different from their forebears in important ways. Second — and again, without any conscious intent — these first European Muslims would facilitate the invasion of a later and far more problematic element to Europe: the Islamists, who arrived with the second wave of Muslim immigrants to Europe in the 1960s and 70s. Like invasive weeds, the Islamists thrived in the conditions created by others, taking over established community organizations and exploiting the legitimate political and spiritual grievances of a society they had played no part in constructing. Third, the European governments of that later time were unable to distinguish between the largely nonpolitical and traditionalist Muslims of the first wave and the Islamists of the second; thus, instead of eradicating the Islamist presence, government policies mistakenly nourished it.

Although this chapter — and much of this book — focuses on the resulting rapid growth of Islamism and the subsequent public struggle to uproot it, any account of the postwar establishment of Islamic communities in Europe would be incomplete without mention of a fourth unintended consequence: the emergence of *differentiated communities.* These are ethnic groups (such as the Berbers) or distinctive religious denominations (such as the Alevis) who, in the absence of the ethnicities or sects dominant in their countries of origin, were able to establish thriving niches of their own by creating and retaining control of separate, independent community organizations. Retaining connections to non-Islamist interpretations of Islam, the differentiated communities have represented thriving if isolated flowerings of moderation within European Islam, though they are now being threatened by the encroachment of the new Islamist mainstream. These communities remain a source for potential optimism in the larger struggle against Islamism — provided that effective action can be taken to strengthen them.

Economic Transplants: The First European Muslims

The Muslim guest workers' move to Europe in the middle of the twentieth century was not the first such transcontinental migration to take place in such relative obscurity; after all, the Massachusetts Native Americans in the seventeenth century and the Ottoman governors of Palestine in the nineteenth could not have realized that the small groups of English Pilgrims and Eastern European Jews were only the vanguard of movements that would definitively alter the destiny of the host societies. It is thus unremarkable that ordinary Europeans were at most "bemused" by the Muslims' arrival.[1] What is distinctive about the European Muslims is

---

1   Colin Nickerson, "A Lesson in Immigration: Guest Worker Experiments Transformed Europe," *Boston Globe* (April 19, 2006), available at: www.boston.com/news/world/europe/articles/2006/04/19/a_lesson_in_immigration/ (accessed January 22, 2011).

that the migrants *themselves* had no sense of their historical significance. In contrast to the Pilgrims and Zionists (and in contrast to some of the later Islamists), they had no religious "mission" to fulfill. Whether South Asian, North African, or Middle Eastern in origin, this first generation of migrants instead shared a "preoccupation with work"[2] and had in common with the host governments a set of prosaic objectives: to work, earn as much money as possible, and then return home.

This is not to say that all Muslim guest workers were identical. As explained in greater detail below, they came from different ethnic groups and religious denominations. More than that, they were individuals, some of whom were pious, and some of whom were only nominal adherents to Islam. Indeed, as the Swiss author Max Frisch put it, the Europeans had "called for workers, but we got human beings."[3] But for those human beings — all of whom had chosen or been selected by their governments to go to Europe on short-term labor contracts — religious practice (or lack thereof) was not their primary source of identity. Even after they put down roots in Europe, the guest workers' religion would not become a political issue for their host societies. Yet why was this the case?

Coming from the poorest and least-developed peripheral regions of their own countries,[4] these guest workers were largely immune to politicized religion. Of course, they had their own traditions and cultures, based to varying degrees on village, tribal, or Islamic values. But none of these were formal, systematic schools of thought with clearly defined political objectives. In other words, their Islam was cultural and traditional

2   Parveen Akhtar, "Transience Participation: The Politics of First Generation Pakistani Migrants in the UK (Post-1945)," in M. Black and K. McKillop, eds., *Human Ends and the Ends of Politics*, vol. 23 (Vienna: IWM Junior Visiting Fellows' Conferences, 2009), available at: www.iwm.at/index.php?option=com_content&task=view&id=135&Itemid=125 (accessed January 22, 2011).
3   Max Frisch, "Vorwort" (Introduction), in Alexander J. Seiler, ed., *Siamo Italiani — die Italiener: Gespräche mit italienischer Gastarbeitern* [*Siamo Italiani*, the Italians: Conversations with Italian Guest Workers] (Zurich: E.V. Z. Verlag, 1965), pp. 7–11 (author's translation).
4   Even those who emigrated to Europe from cities had initially lived in rural areas:

> A majority of migrating Muslims had already experienced an internal migration in the country of origin from rural to urban regions prior to emigrating abroad. Very often, before recruitment by German firms, they had lived two or three years in large cities and waited for an arrangement through ... the German authorities.

(*Renaissance*, "Islam in Germany," *Renaissance* 9[11], available at: www.monthly-renaissance. com/issue/content.aspx?id=702 [accessed January 22, 2011].)

rather than learned or political. This is a very important distinction, given that learned Islam was corrupted by Islamism, whereas the Islam of oral tradition has even today maintained its moderate spiritual and ethical elements. Moreover, when many of the guest workers first moved to Europe, the mainstream political culture in their homelands was geared toward modernization and secularization; Islamism in its current form was only beginning to penetrate their societies. Thus, whether they were firmly devoted to ancient traditions emphasizing "honor" above all else, or they were determined to enjoy the latest economic benefits of modernity, the guest workers had no interest in the purported benefits of Islamism.

Rejecting Tradition: The Next Generation(s)

Islamism therefore would not become an issue until the coming of age of the guest workers' children and grandchildren. But how did the next generations of European Muslims become so quickly cut off from the beliefs and traditions of their forebears? The reasons differed from family to family, although generally a combination of the following factors prevailed.

The first was a seemingly simple matter of timing. Islamism took root in the guest workers' countries of origin only after the initial wave of guest workers reached Europe. As noted above, neither the guest workers themselves nor their host societies expected the workers to stay long term. It was therefore only *after* governments recognized that these human beings couldn't simply be packed up and shipped home that the guest workers began starting families at all; in Germany (the slowest-reacting host country), it was only in 1973 that the guest workers could begin making arrangements to bring their families from home.[5] By the end of the 1970s, the Islamist movements in the countries of origin had gained considerable momentum, even in peripheral areas — thus ensuring that immigrating family members had a much greater chance of being exposed to Islamist views before arriving on European soil.

---

5   This decision in Germany was (in yet another example of unintended consequences) due to the government's imposing a moratorium that year on the guest-worker program (Elisabeth Beck-Gernsheim, "Preface: Looking at Immigration through Immigrant Eyes," in Gökçe Yurdakul, *From Guest Workers into Muslims: The Transformation of Turkish Immigrant Associations in Germany* [Newcastle: Cambridge Scholars Publishing, 2009], pp. xiii–xvi [p. xii]). In Britain, the Bangladeshi and Pakistani communities had begun arranging such "familial migration" up to a decade earlier; see Akhtar, "Transience Participation."

The second factor inhibiting the passing of the first generation's non-Islamist religious traditions to subsequent generations was the oral, informal nature of those traditions. The fact that these traditions, free of the political agenda dominating Islamist scholarship of that era, were *not* written down made them harder to pass on to the second generation. Certainly, there was no artificial "clean break" between parents and children; however, as any kindergarten student who has played the game "telephone" knows, oral messages often become distorted when passed from one person to another. Such distortions tended not to occur in the rural communities of origin — where economic and social conditions remained largely stable from generation to generation, and where deference to the collective wisdom of a community's elders was often the norm. In Europe, however, with social and family life in a state of near-constant flux, untrained parents often passed on traditions like gender segregation or honor killings, while neglecting to emphasize others like tolerance of dissenting viewpoints or respect for older people.

A third factor that explains why European-born Muslim children tended to be cut off from their families' tradition has to do with competing European norms of parent–child and other family relationships. The expectations of European cultures were often dramatically different from those of the guest workers' cultures: children were expected not to obey their parents blindly, but to challenge them and establish their own independent identities. Meanwhile, parents were expected to talk about these challenges and share their experiences about how to respond to them, not to handle family matters in a closed, exclusively private fashion. Of course, the guest workers' children enthusiastically took up the burden of this "responsibility to challenge" — but the immigrants themselves did not suddenly conform to European expectations. Muslim immigrant parents often became confused and distraught by their children's rebelliousness, which generated tension within families that led children to reject their parents' teachings about the traditions of their families as being "out of touch" with European society. This socio-psychological dynamic cleared the way for Islamists' appeals to the children of guest workers.

The rebellion described above was not sparked solely by the second generation's desire to copy the adolescent experiences of non-Muslim European peers. A *fourth* factor, what might be termed the "frozen-in-time phenomenon," sparked further rebellion: parents responded to their perceived (and actual) loss of control by keeping their nuclear families under much stricter control than they would have done "back home." Guest workers were unaware that village and small-town norms were changing and adapting over time under the influence of urban political and popular cultures in countries such as Morocco and Turkey.

Dual Alienation: Social and Spiritual

This rebellious European youth culture, combined with the failure of guest workers to pass on their traditional religious practices, alienated children both from mainstream European society and from their spiritual identity as Muslims. This situation was further aggravated by Europeans' unreadiness to absorb a growing population of Muslims with traditions differing from the Judeo-Christian norm. Second-generation Muslims were not the first in the history of migration to reject or modify traditions held by their parents. The distinctiveness of their experience — especially compared to that of migrants to countries of immigration such as the United States, Canada, or Australia[6] — lies in the fact that, once they had abandoned their parents' values, European Muslims had no "local" alternative in their adopted societies with which to replace them. Lacking any real historical experience of large-scale immigration, European countries were unable to redefine their identities overnight to be more inclusive.[7] Even in the United States, Canada, and Australia, a long process of debate and reflection was necessary before immigrants from cultures of origin such as Southern Europe or later East Asia could be accepted as "American," "Canadian," or "Australian"; and before September 11, there was virtually no public discussion (let alone reevaluation) in Europe of what it meant to be "Dutch" or "British." Thus, even though many second-generation Muslims had ceased to think of *themselves* as "Moroccans" or "Pakistanis," *Europeans* would not think of them as anything else.

European Muslims' sense of separation from mainstream society

---

6   In those countries, among others, an immigrant group's rejection, modification, or abandonment of the first generation's "Old World" values was the first step in a process of establishing itself in the context of — and eventually as an integral part of — the new country.

7   Even though it would be a mistake to consider Europe as a monolithic entity, it is fair to say that *none* of the European countries was administratively, culturally, or institutionally prepared to integrate or assimilate large numbers of immigrants. This was especially true for immigrants belonging to another major religion (one with its own priorities, cultural norms, and universal claims), as Europe's own century-long trend toward secularism only accelerated after World War II. This was of course in complete contrast to developments in the Muslim-majority countries, especially among the political and social elites, where Islamism — politicized Islam — was becoming more significant than ever before.

deepened due to a combination of misguided government policies and widespread discrimination in access to jobs and education, which curtailed European Muslims' involvement in their host countries. "Out of sight and out of mind," the second-generation Muslims of Europe played only a minimal role in the European public consciousness — and, therefore, a European consciousness played only a minimal role in their own. Prohibited from active participation in their countries of birth, these second- and third-generation Muslims felt social alienation from the European society surrounding them, and cut off from the faith traditions of their ancestral countries, they also suffered spiritual alienation from Islam.

Social alienation is evident in the persistent gap between the educational attainment of European Muslims and that of the indigenous population. In the Netherlands, for example, as of 2005, 45 percent of ethnic Moroccan adults and 40 percent of ethnic Turkish adults had completed only elementary education, as compared with 6 percent of non-Muslims. Overall, "the education level of non-Western non-natives is still significantly lower than that of natives."[8] Moreover, even those Muslims who have completed their education — even through university — tend not to be accepted in society on the same terms as their classmates. This problem of "blocked upward migration" was a direct contributor to the rising sense of social alienation; it also contributed to radicalization. As German Islamist terrorism expert Guido Steinberg has argued, young European Muslim men

> reach limitations at some point in their history. For example, they go to university, but still don't get the job they want . . . [They] are forced to make their way as petty criminals. Individual failure then frequently turns into an aggressive, radical attitude toward society. Then . . . [they] are receptive to militant ideologies.[9]

---

8   Sociaal Cultureel Planbureau [Socio-Cultural Planning Bureau], Wetenschappelijk Onderzoek- en Documentatiecentrum, [Scientific Research and Documentation Center], and Centraal Bureau voor de Statistiek [Central Bureau of Statistics], *Jaarrapport integratie 2005* [Annual Report on Integration 2005] (The Hague: Sociaal Cultureel Planbureau, Wetenschappelijk Onderzoek- en Documentatiecentrum, and Centraal Bureau voor de Statistiek, 2005), p. 44 (author's translation).
9   Guido Steinberg, interview by Aladdin Sarhan, "Jihadism is a Greater Problem Today Than it Was in 2001," *Deutsche Welle*, November 30, 2006, available at: www.dw-world.de/dw/article/0,2144,2252945,00.html (accessed January 24, 2011).

The problem of discrimination in employment, even against highly qualified Muslims, has been doubly damaging. First, it has left young Muslim men in a state of unemployment or underemployment,[10] ensuring them more than enough time to listen to the entreaties of radical Islamists. Second, it has fueled such intense distrust toward state and society that the *perception* of discrimination has remained even after more than two decades of legal (and increasingly practical) equality in the Continent's labor markets.[11]

Even if we allow that discrimination against Muslims in the search for employment may be more perceived than actual, its impact is nevertheless real and consequential. Ordinary Muslims continue to suffer; the more they hear about their coreligionists facing insurmountable difficulties, the more they look for "answers" — which Islamists readily provide. Thus, they remain angry and alienated from mainstream European societies because of secular factors such as unemployment and social discrimination, and they remain beyond the power of governments to affect. This sense of social alienation is deepened by the refusal of Europeans as a whole — the inclusive rhetoric of most government, media, and academic elites notwithstanding — to extend the meanings of the terms "British," "German," or "Dutch" to encompass European Muslims. Europe's second- and third-generation Muslims are thus left in a state of confusion about their national identities. Feeling that they lack the option of becoming fully European, many have chosen "Muslim" as their identity.

The shift to a "Muslim" identity occurs fairly quickly and completely among people with no specific ties to a particular country "back home." For those Muslims born in Europe, who have never visited their ethnic "homeland" and don't even speak that country's language, it is not irrational to conclude that the only meaningful identity available is Islam. As a British-born child of Pakistani immigrants said,

> I am called a "Paki" because of my looks, but I don't feel Pakistani — I have never even visited the country. But I don't feel British either. Neither

---

10 Muslim women were also denied career opportunities due to discrimination, although in their case it was their own families, not European societies, who were responsible.

11 Many researchers disagree, arguing that discrimination remains actual and entrenched; however, careful analysis of the studies they cite (which, rather than collecting data on actual outcomes, ask respondents what they "feel" about the level of discrimination in the labor market — to take a 2003 British Cabinet Office survey as an example) suggests that perceptions are the current driving factor.

of these identities means much to me, and they will mean even less to my children. But we can definitely be Muslim.[12]

This trend of identifying Islam as an "ethnic category, rather than a religious category,"[13] existed even before Islamist recruiters began following guest workers to Europe in the 1970s. But, for years, it remained confined to a minority.

Islamism spread in Europe due mainly to the spiritual alienation arising from the failure of guest-worker parents to pass on their traditional version of Islam to their children. As the children tried to figure out what their "Islamic" identity meant in the midst of an alienating European society, they grew anxious for answers about what it was to be a "true Muslim." Unfortunately, the arrival of Islamist students and asylum seekers provided the teachers these young European Muslims sought.

Invasive Weeds: Islamists Come to Europe

As governments from Anatolia to the Levant to North Africa became increasingly repressive from the late 1960s through the 1980s, their citizens — whether ambitious students, marginalized minorities, or persecuted political opponents — looked toward Western Europe as a land of greener pastures. At first glance, the migrants of the resulting "second wave" resembled those of the first, as they mostly came from the same countries that had sent guest workers to Europe a few decades before and initially planned only temporary stays in Europe. But unlike those who had gone before, these second-wave Muslims enjoyed a general familiarity with the languages and/or political systems of their destination countries because of colonial-era ties and pre-existing networks established by guest workers from their origin countries. Generally highly educated, these second-wave immigrants mainly came from their countries' more dynamic urban centers, not from conservative rural villages. Many were secular-minded students or refugees — notably those fleeing the ayatollahs' revolution in Iran, as well as members of the minority communities

---

12   Interview with the author, London, 2006.
13   Netherlands Ministry of the Interior and Kingdom Relations, *From Dawa to Jihad: The Various Threats from Radical Islam to the Democratic Legal Order* (The Hague: Ministry of the Interior and Kingdom Relations, 2004), p. 29, available at: www.minbzk.nl/contents/ pages/42345/fromdawatojihad.pdf (accessed January 30, 2011).

such as the Alevis or Berbers — and had legitimate grounds for political asylum in Europe.

But many others were Islamists, who sought to exploit Europe's political freedom and relative ethno-religious tolerance as they prepared a global campaign to establish a new world order based on Islamist political ideology. Their long-term goal was to overthrow the very freedoms that had attracted them to Europe and replace the rule of secular law with theocratic regimes based on sharia; before this would happen, however, they planned to return to their countries of origin and overthrow the regimes that had repressed them. European officials did not attempt to discern the goals of the Islamists' political ideology, and they granted asylum to many immigrants who presented far more of a threat to democratic rule than the regimes they had fled. The fact that they were often persecuted at home *because* of their militantly political religiosity, not a commitment to democracy or liberalism, was not taken into account.

The Islamists themselves were not surprised by their success at obtaining student visas or political asylum; indeed, they had counted on it in choosing Europe as the destination and refuge for their short-term *hijra* (migration). In this, as in many other ways, the Islamists saw themselves as emulating the example of Muhammad and the first Muslims. For example, they cited the case of the *sahaba* (companions of the Prophet) who, seven years before Muhammad's own escape to Medina, had been advised by him to flee across the Red Sea to the Christian kingdoms in what is now Ethiopia. There, as a Muslim community that was "numerically insignificant in a predominantly non-Muslim kingdom," they grew in strength and numbers before eventually returning to Arabia in triumph.[14] Persecuted by nationalist (or "apostate" Muslim) governments, the Islamists who fled to Europe during the 1970s and 80s envisioned that they too would stay in Europe only until they gained enough strength and support to return and overthrow the "persecutors." With their focus on the political developments in their home countries, they had no long-term plans to gain control of the existing Muslim communities of Europe — something they would accomplish quickly once the decision was made to remain on the Continent.

Several factors combined to make it both desirable and possible for

---

14   H. A. Hellyer, "Muslims in Europe: Precedent and Present," *American Journal of Islamic Social Sciences* 25(1): 40–62 (41), available at: http://i-epistemology.net/attachments/925_ajiss-25-1-stripped%20-%20Hellyer%20-%20Muslims%20in%20Europe%20-%20Precedent%20and%20Present.pdf (accessed January 24, 2011).

Islamist groups to develop a permanent base and permanent networks in Europe. First, the strengthening of regimes "back home" made them less vulnerable to Islamists' coup attempts, and further curtailed Islamists' freedom of action there. Second, as indicated in Chapter 2, the financial bonanza of petrodollars following the 1973 oil shock generated enormous funding from sympathetic Persian Gulf states, which expanded Islamists' capabilities for agitation globally. Third, the collapse of the Soviet Union in 1991 emboldened the Islamists to adopt a universalist vision, as they attributed the collapse to their success in defeating the Soviets in Afghanistan. Fourth, the horrific war in Bosnia sensitized Muslims worldwide to the suffering of Muslim brethren in Europe, expanding the focus of outrage at the injustices they perceived the West to heap upon Islam beyond the plight of Palestinian Arabs. Fifth, Islamists in Europe recognized that the Muslim communities established there by the guest-worker generation had become permanent, and these communities provided a target for recruitment that was impossible to resist. Finally, Islamists decided to remain in Europe because they enjoyed full freedom of action, since Europeans continued to offer them the full range of civil liberties that defined their civilization — a civilization the Islamists were dedicated to defeating.

Recruitment Strategies: Off-the-Shelf and Custom Tailored

Since many of the incoming Islamists were well-trained, highly indoctrinated activists, they were able to shift focus away from their planned return home and toward the new objective of recruiting European Muslims. The Islamist movement's characteristic flexibility and adaptability was crucial to its success, as different organizations modified their strategies in different circumstances to advance the movement's common universalistic ideology. Of course, such adaptations in the Islamists' approach did not take place overnight, occurring instead as part of a sequence that exploited changes within the target communities themselves. As they entered a given community, Islamists appealed to the specific local (usually ethnic or national) concerns back home. Then, as their influence spread (and as the movement became more internationalist due to global developments), the emphasis shifted to the global *umma*.

One can see this dynamic at work in the recent history of the Masjid-e-Umer (Mosque of [the Caliph] Omar), located in the South Asian

Muslim neighborhood of Walthamstow in northeast London. Perhaps better known as the "Queens Road mosque," *The Times* reported in 2008 that the facility had "been a recruiting ground for 20 years" — in other words, beginning very soon after the permanent establishment of Islamist cells in Europe.[15] At that time, it was affiliated with the Tablighi Jamaat (roughly, "conveying group"), an organization founded and based in the Asian subcontinent. Without interrupting its role as a center for radicalization focused on the subcontinent, the mosque increasingly became a stage for more universalistic appeals to Islamism for two reasons. First, younger members were less interested in the "parochial" concerns of organizations that had retained an emphasis on events in the guest workers' origin countries;[16] second, the Islamist movement was rapidly developing an internationalist approach (and dense global network), making the Syrian extremist cleric Omar Bakri Mohammed of HT and later al-Muhajiroun an in-demand speaker at Queen's Road despite his lack of ties to Pakistan or Bangladesh.

While Queen's Road may be one of the more notorious mosques in Europe (especially after it emerged that 7/7 bomber Mohammad Sidique Khan had worshiped there), its experience is far from unique. Local variations exist, of course; the Muslim Brotherhood played the internationalist role in place of HT in countries with a larger percentage of ethnic Arabs, such as Germany (and the United States, as Chapter 4 discusses). HT proved particularly adept at making a tactical shift in the heavily secular Turkish Cypriot community in Britain — with its "mostly empty Turkish mosques."[17] Due to the informal (sometimes even alcohol-fueled) practice of religion within the community — as well as the absence of any significant extremist group among Turkish Cypriots back on the island of Cyprus itself— Islamists made little headway in their recruitment efforts. Accordingly, a new tactic was tried by HT. Rather than continuing to preach to the concerns of the community as a whole, HT focused on recruiting particular *individuals selected* for their potential to influence the community. Cosh Omar, a London actor and playwright and son of the Turkish Cypriot community's *hoca* ("teacher," or one who

15   Sean O'Neill, "Airline Bomb Plot: Coded E-mail Trail Exposed Plan," *Times Online* (September 9, 2008), available at: www.timesonline.co.uk/tol/news/uk/crime/article6818722.ece (accessed January 24, 2011).

16   Ed Husain, *The Islamist* (London: Penguin, 2007), p. 77.

17   Cosh Omar, "Rebel with a Cause: A Personal Journey from Sufism to Islamism and Beyond," in Zeyno Baran, ed., *The Other Muslims: Moderate and Secular* (New York: Palgrave Macmillan, 2010), pp. 83–106 (84).

carries out religious rituals), was one such person. Approached individually and invited to HT meetings (the first was a fiery sermon by Bakri Mohammed), Omar gradually entered the group's influence and was on the path to becoming an activist — before finally discovering the motive behind his being "chosen":

> Why had the group invested so much time and attention in me? . . . One day I was invited to the house of a high-ranking party member. I explained my conundrum, and my significance to the party was spelled out. Hizb ut-Tahrir had successfully penetrated most sections of the Muslim community in Britain, but the one group that they could not maneuver into was the Turkish Cypriots . . . I was reminded that for over two decades, my father had served his community by performing all their ritual needs. Now that the preliminary work had been done, the time had come for his son to take over from his father, and gradually disseminate the knowledge of Hizb ut-Tahrir's "authentic" Islam.[18]

Islamist groups did not generally have to devise such "custom" recruitment strategies to appeal to European Muslims. When recruiting among those without the distinctive traits of communities like the Turkish Cypriots, it was sufficient to appeal to social and spiritual alienation. The more visible and tangible aspects of social alienation were targeted first. Despite declared efforts to reduce discrimination in education and employment beginning in the 1970s, there was little or no change in the relative differences between Muslim and non-Muslim communities. Counterterrorism specialist Marc Sageman argues that such relative deprivation "is probably a necessary factor" for radicalization, since those "who are satisfied with life are unlikely to join a religious revivalist terrorist movement."[19] The first recruits were therefore the "poor, unemployed, angry people" who could not satisfy their actual or perceived material needs.[20] Islamist groups, supported by petrodollars, were able to provide immediate financial assistance as well as help with finding work, especially in the parallel society of Islamic community organizations and charities that were in the process of being established.

---

18   Omar, "Rebel with a Cause," p. 98.

19   Marc Sageman, *Understanding Terror Networks* (Philadelphia, PA: University of Pennsylvania Press, 2004), p. 95.

20   Jason Burke, *Al-Qaeda: The True Story of Radical Islam* (London: I. B. Taurus, 2004), p. 284.

Appeals to those suffering from social alienation were necessary but not sufficient to recruit new Islamists; spiritual alienation was the crucial factor in transforming a disgruntled European Muslim into an Islamist. Islamist recruiters thus provided more than just material support; they reassured their targets that they bore no responsibility for their poverty or deprivation, but were instead victims of the infidel West and of "apostate" governments back home. Perhaps most significantly, the Islamists offered prospective recruits searching for their Islamic identity clear answers to questions about what it meant to be a "true Muslim." Islamism's "brew of revolutionary ideology, a search for identity, and socio-economic aspirations"[21] contained all the ingredients these angry people needed to strike back against those they held responsible for their problems.

By the 1990s, as material conditions for European Muslims improved — and as the increasingly global Islamist movement grew in strength and influence — the deprivation that fostered social alienation was no longer a necessary condition for radicalization. In fact, many of the perpetrators of recent terrorist attacks (notably the 2007 attempted car bombing of Glasgow International Airport, carried out by an aeronautics engineer and an obstetrician with the assistance of several other medical doctors) come from middle-class or even from wealthy backgrounds. Yet even as the importance of economic factors diminished, the pace of recruitment did not decline, since Islamist groups redoubled their focus on spiritual alienation. Islamists' growing control over community institutions proved equally valuable in preying upon young Muslims' feelings of loneliness and confusion about their Islamic identity. With mosques and community centers at their disposal, radical organizations were able to turn the mosque from a place of prayer into a social nexus where the alienated could feel welcome among their "brothers" and "sisters." They organized a wide range of activities, from adult-education classes to youth summer camps, soccer matches, and communal dinners. For those within this mosque-centered social circle, the transition to participation in more political Islamist activities such as demonstrations or protests was not a large one.

Even for Muslims without a background in political Islamism, the religious rhetoric of the movement was comforting; as Bernard Lewis has noted, it provided "an emotionally familiar basis of group identity, solidar-

---

21   Loretta Napoleoni, "Modern *Jihad*: The Islamist Crusade," *SAIS Review* 23(2): 53–69 (64).

ity, and exclusion."[22] The latter factor is perhaps the most distinguishing feature of Islamist "community activism." Common identities and feelings of fellowship are shared by the members of virtually any faith community; exclusion — especially of those whose faith is deemed insufficiently "pure" — is a trait shared instead with revolutionary ideological movements such as Bolshevism. Being part of such an "exclusive" movement was a great source of pride for its new recruits; after joining, one former Islamist recalled, "Instantly, I felt important. Special. Chosen. Better than the others . . . I no longer needed to search for the earthly paradise, the one my parents never found."[23] Thus, exploitation of young European Muslims' spiritual alienation became the most important tool of Islamist recruiters.

Islamist Tactics Inside the Mosque

The Islamist movement relied on flexibility of both strategy and (especially) tactics to achieve considerable success in recruiting European Muslims within a few short years of arriving in Europe. The Islamists' flexibility and adaptability were a consequence of the decentralized nature of a movement that was made up of independent organizations sharing a common ideology and set of political objectives, and which enjoyed significant financial support from governments and individuals in the Gulf. In their takeover of European mosques and Muslim community organizations, the Islamist groups exhibited a high degree of tactical skill in areas ranging from intragroup politics to public relations and human-resources management. Moreover, when using these mechanisms to secure strategically important objectives — like the institutional resources necessary for exploiting social and spiritual alienation — Islamists showed a high level of tactical awareness that must be taken into account when developing means of resisting and reversing their advances.

Although from time to time the various Islamist groups founded their own charities, community centers, or mosques after arriving in Europe, the general pattern was to co-opt and take over existing institutions, which required less effort and offered greater recruitment possibilities.

---

22   Bernard Lewis, *The Crisis of Islam: Holy War and Unholy Terror* (New York: Modern Library, 2003), p. 22.
23   Naema Tahir, conference presentation, European Conference on Active Participation of Ethnic Minority Youth in Society, Copenhagen, Denmark, September 7, 2006.

First, Islamists would secure places on the organization's board of directors or governing committee on the basis of their credentials as "Islamic scholars"; over time, they would become "respected community leaders." The Islamist board members would then push to add like-minded individuals (whether local recruits or Islamists from elsewhere) to the committee. After this process was repeated often enough to give Islamists a majority, they could fire their opponents (imams and board members alike) and replace them without consultation. Usually, this process took place without attracting the attention of the average Muslim in the congregation.

Even when the non-Islamists realized what was happening and tried to fight back, they were hampered by several key disadvantages. To begin with, their opponents were "professional Muslims" who were able to devote their full time and attention to their task. The moderates — of whom a majority were guest workers at this point — were of course focused above all on their jobs and careers, and could not devote their working lives to board politics. Second, while the non-Islamists were dependent on voluntary contributions from like-minded individuals, their rivals enjoyed access to funding sources that were lavish by comparison. This is not to say that the Islamists spent money flashily or carelessly; on the contrary, their spending tactics were much more subtle and directed toward winning over ambivalent or undecided members of governing committees.

Why did Islamists choose to co-opt boards of directors over other alternatives, such as installing their allies as imams? The answer lies in the distribution of power within the organizational structure of the average mosque. Even on paper, the balance of power lies not with the imam, who has no guaranteed salary or other fixed source of income, but (in the words of former HT activist Ed Husain) with the "all-powerful mosque committees with their loud-mouthed chairmen," who "bully" the typically "meek" imams.[24]

Thus, it was far easier for Islamists to marginalize any hostile imams than to replace them. Even if the Machiavellian governing-committee maneuvers had not been possible, the imams were never a serious threat to the Islamist takeover for several reasons. In the first place, they were generally older than the swelling population of second- and third-generation Muslims in their mosques, and unable to relate to the needs or concerns of European-born Muslims. Moreover, the newly minted Islamists — in contrast to many imams even today — were fluent in

---

24   Husain, *The Islamist*, p. 39.

European languages and became intimately familiar with European cultures; this was especially critical to the Islamist effort to reach out to (or create) new converts among indigenous Europeans. Moreover, as the next generations became less and less interested in the homelands and cultures of their grandparents, the Islamists' superior linguistic and cultural awareness set them apart from their moderate rivals in terms of communication skills. Beginning with local television and continuing with the platforms of radio and the internet, the Islamists mastered each means of communicating with potential Muslim and non-Muslim recruits. Young enough to be comfortable with emerging technology, and capable of speaking the languages with the widest audience, the Islamists' campaigns reached far more ears than the imams' sermons delivered in the languages of the "old countries." With more visibility, of course, came support, recognition, money, and, most significantly of all, legitimacy: in short, the key attributes of mainstream religion.

One final tactic to note is the Islamist movement's careful appeal to — and exploitation of — women. Though it ran seemingly counter to their fundamentalist religious precepts, women's participation became key to the Islamist takeover of European Islam in several ways. First, of course, is the significance of numbers: even though women were allowed to participate only in carefully constrained ways, they enabled Islamist organizations to effectively double their strength as needed. Second, even limited opportunities represented an improvement over the situations in some traditional Muslim communities where women could not even enter the mosque: former HT activist Ed Husain, for instance, was "impressed" by the separate women's prayer area at the JI-controlled East London mosque, which "seemed like feminist progress" compared to the men-only prayer house on Brick Lane.[25] Third, as political activity increased, Islamist leaders saw the effectiveness of having "feminist" women on the front lines of their protests, demanding the right to make the "personal choice" to live under sharia law and to wear the burqa. Though "Islamist feminism" remains an oxymoron at best, the failure of moderate Muslims to respond by increasing women's role in their own organizations helped to push Muslim women away from Islam's mainstream in Europe.

---

25   Husain, *The Islamist*, p. 28.

Fertilizing the Wrong Crop: How Governments Facilitated the Islamist Takeover

Even as the first professional Islamist militants began preparing for their journey to European shores as part of the second wave of Muslim migration in the late 1960s and 70s, the Continent's policymakers slept blissfully unaware of the dangers these new arrivals posed to European societies; after all, the jolting tones of the 9/11, 3/11, and 7/7 wake-up calls would not ring out for decades to come. But as any sleepwalker who awakens without remembering a fall down the stairs can testify, taking steps in *any* direction while unconscious is likely to have painful consequences. It is thus not surprising that in three decades of sleepwalking, Western Europe's governments made countless policy blunders regarding Islam and Islamism. These policy mistakes broadly fit into three categories: "gentlemen's agreements," permitting Islamist groups to enjoy virtually unlimited freedom of operation on their territory; reliance on Islamist "partner" governments abroad; and dependence on partnerships with Islamist-controlled "representative" Muslim institutions at home.

1 Ungentlemanly Disagreements

Although for decades European governments remained almost pathologically unable to comprehend the Islamist threat to Europe itself, this was not due to incompetence. European intelligence services and police forces had gained considerable experience in dealing with extremist groups, ranging from leftist radicals like the Red Army Faction to violent separatists such as ETA (Euskadi Ta Askatasuna, or "Basque Homeland and Freedom"). The European security services were well informed about the Islamist "careers" of many of the new Muslim arrivals thanks to intelligence sharing with governments in their countries of origin. Unaware of the *universal* nature of Islamist ideology, however, Europeans were confident that the scope of Islamist groups' aims would remain confined to their countries of origin — and thus outside their own responsibilities for security in Europe. To ensure that this aim would not change in the future, European governments concluded so-called gentlemen's agreements with the Islamist groups. These pacts had allowed the Islamists to operate unhindered so long as they did not commit violent acts in Europe itself. In hindsight, the decision to end such agreements seems inexplicable, even absurd. We can begin to understand this decision — and, more importantly, the longtime dominance of the security mindset within European approaches to Islam — only when we recall how *unimportant* Islam and Muslims were as a priority at the time. In the absence of active interest from academia, civil society, or the media, concerns about Muslim migrants were thus easily delegated to the security community.

Within that community, the gentlemen's agreements were supported largely because of the belief — justified in regard to the guest-worker generation — that Islam's "self-enforcing" norms and customs were responsible for lower rates of violent crime among Muslim immigrant communities. Unaware of the distinctions between first- and second-wave migrants, law enforcement officials assumed that this self-enforcement mechanism would operate equally effectively on the leaders of violent organizations and other successful Islamist asylum seekers.[26] Some Islamists did keep to the literal meaning of their agreement. For example, after obtaining the status of "political refugee" in France, the leaders of the Tunisian group Hizb-al-Nahda "tended not to be very active" in politics — but only because they were instead enthusiastically promoting the so-called return to Islam among second-and third-generation Muslims.[27] In time, it became obvious that Islamists, such as Omar Bakri, were not subject to the judgment of first-generation Muslim community elders. Yet policy did not change, and law enforcement continued to uphold the gentlemen's agreements and ignore Islamist activity, even when it included the arrangement of flights to transport European-born recruits to Afghanistan for training. Even when the assumption about "self-enforcement" was directly refuted by increasing "complaints from local Muslims infuriated by the behavior of the Islamists," no move was made to alter the agreements; as the Danish researcher Michael Taarnby explains, this was because policymakers were guided by political correctness; "[t]he fear of provoking Muslim communities without reason created a climate in which the Islamists felt quite secure."[28]

As Europeans were becoming more afraid of upsetting the status quo, the Islamists began to worry less that they would lose what had become

---

26 Michael Clarke, "The Contract with Muslims Must Not Be Torn Up," *Guardian* (August 26, 2005), available at: www.guardian.co.uk/terrorism/story/0,12780,1556818,00. html (accessed January 24, 2011).

27 Samia Labidi, "Faces of Janus: The Arab-Muslim Community in France and the Battle for its Future," in Zeyno Baran, ed., *The Other Muslims: Moderate and Secular* (New York: Palgrave Macmillan, 2010), pp. 107–22 (111).

28 Michael Taarnby, *Recruitment of Islamist Terrorists in Europe: Trends and Perspectives* (Aarhus: Centre for Cultural Research, University of Aarhus, 2005), p. 8.

a secure position on the Continent. They felt freer to ignore not just the implicit gentlemen's agreements, but also explicit European law. HT, to take but one example, evaded British attempts at overseeing its university-oriented activities by registering shell organizations under false names and by setting up recruiting stalls just a few inches off university property. Now that there was no more pretense of "agreements" to maintain — and increasingly able to use their power as representing "mainstream" Islam to silence any critics — the Islamist organizations were able to concentrate entirely on working against the governments themselves (see Chapter 5).

2 Unfaithful "Partners" Abroad

With Islamism relegated to the purview of the security services, European foreign ministries took little notice of it in the conduct of their countries' international relations. Saudi Arabia was thus viewed primarily as a partner in the realm of energy and trade policy. As the Saudis gained credibility in these areas, the scope of their partnerships with Europe gradually expanded to include Middle East peace talks and finally the religious life of Muslims in the West itself. The Saudi kingdom's government could *openly* contribute funding to the spread of its extreme Wahhabist interpretation of Islam, thereby complementing its clandestine financing of Islamist organizations. It encountered no objections in the mid-1980s, when the MWL, "flush with petrodollars and substantial contributions from [the state oil and gas firm] ARAMCO, paid the salaries of Turkish imams in West German mosques."[29] Even direct intervention in European Islamic communities by officials of the Saudi government itself did not trigger any European countermove, as shown in the following example from Italy.

In the 1970s, the ambassadors of several Muslim countries had created a small charitable organization called the Centro Islamico Culturale d'Italia (CICI; Islamic Cultural Center of Italy) Emboldened by Saudi activities elsewhere, the Saudi representation in Rome transformed the scale and purpose of the CICI's activities: "due principally to the

---

29 Joel Beinin, *Political Islam and the New Global Economy: The Political Economy of Islamist Social Movements in Egypt and Turkey*, paper prepared for French and US Approaches to Understanding Islam conference, France-Stanford Center for Interdisciplinary Studies, September 12–14 (Stanford, CA: France-Stanford Center for Interdisciplinary Studies, Stanford University, 2004), available at: www.stanford.edu/dept/france-stanford/ Conferences/Islam/Beinin.pdf (accessed January 24, 2011).

intervention of Saudi Arabia, [the CICI] became involved in efforts to promote Islam in Italy," specifically through the construction of the €30 million Mosque of Rome, Europe's largest.[30] There are many other such examples. Using a combination of clandestine, indirect, and direct funding, the Saudi government has, as of the time of writing, constructed over 1,500 mosques and 2,000 religious schools, the vast majority of which are located either in Europe or in North America.[31]

Long before these numbers reached quadruple digits, the spread of such bases for religious extremism had indeed caused much worry in government circles — not in Europe but in secular regimes in Muslim-majority countries. Since they were directly affected by — and deeply familiar with — Islamism and Islamist terrorism, these secular regimes were better able to predict the end result of Europe's lax policies. An Egyptian government official once issued a prophetic warning to those European countries giving "sanctuary" to extremists, telling them that they "should now understand it will come back to haunt them where they live."[32]

3 Unfaithful "Partners" at Home

It was not just warnings coming from abroad that were ignored; Europeans also took little heed of the hard-won lessons from their own histories about the dangers of combining religious and political authority. These lessons were not only the obvious medieval examples. In cases such as the military campaign to unify Italy in the nineteenth century and the democratic forces' struggle against authoritarianism in Portugal and Spain in the twentieth century, the political and ideological power of the Catholic Church was the main source of strength for the minorities in each country that opposed these popular movements. Having forgotten this difference between the will of religious elites and the will of the majority, European governments were thus more likely to accept at

---

30   This case is drawn from Ahmad Gianpiero Vincenzo, "The History of Islam in Italy," in Zeyno Baran, ed., *The Other Muslims: Moderate and Secular* (New York: Palgrave Macmillan, 2010), pp. 55–70 (63).

31   Hedieh Mirahmadi, "Navigating Islam in America," in Zeyno Baran, ed., *The Other Muslims: Moderate and Secular* (New York: Palgrave Macmillan, 2010), pp. 17–32 (22).

32   Evan F. Kohlmann, *Al-Qaida's Jihad in Europe: The Afghan-Bosnian Network* (New York: Berg, 2004), p. 151.

face value the Saudi claim that their mosque-construction projects were intended to meet the "religious needs" of all European Muslims.

Later, when they sought to address some of the difficulties faced by European Muslims by consulting with "Islamic organizations," they similarly failed to question *who* was really represented by their new institutional partners. They did not grasp that they were dealing with Islamists. The funding — and more importantly, the legitimacy and publicity[33] — that the Islamists obtained enabled them to cement their takeover of European Islam. Though this general pattern holds for Europe as a whole, European Muslims — to say nothing of European governments — do not form a monolithic entity. The particular ways Islamist groups were able to work so closely with governments in such different environments as those of the multiculturalist UK and assimilationist France are accordingly worth considering in greater detail.

Even compared with those living in other European countries, Britain's Muslims were quick to adopt religion as the primary basis of their identity. In addition to the common factors discussed earlier, in Britain this shift toward a Muslim identity was driven by the publication of a single book, Salman Rushdie's *The Satanic Verses*, in 1989.[34] Immediately, there was an outpouring of public rage from British Muslims (including prominent "community leaders" not yet publicly identified as Islamists), expressed in forms such as public book-burnings. The Saudi government and Islamist groups such as HT and the Muslim Brotherhood took full advantage of this public sentiment, channeling it to expand their support base and expose more people to their ideologies.[35]

The British government took no steps to prevent the usurpation of so many of its citizens' loyalties by global political Islam; in fact, it actually facilitated the process. The established policy of multiculturalism made

---

33   Soon after an official organization was designated, it became the "go-to" source for media representatives seeking "the Muslim view" on a given issue. See Lorenzo Vidino, "The Muslim Brotherhood's Conquest of Europe," *Middle East Quarterly* 12(1): 25–34, available at: www.meforum.org/687/the-muslim-brotherhoods-conquest-of-europe (accessed January 24, 2011).

34   Humayun Ansari, *"The Infidel Within": Muslims in Britain since 1800* (London: Hurst, 2004), p. 1.

35   On the rapid mobilization of the Muslim response and the assistance of extremist groups, see Salaam.co.uk, "The Rushdie Affair," (London: n.d.), available at: http://www.salaam.co.uk/themeofthemonth/september03_index.php?l=1 (accessed February 13, 2011). For Saudi involvement, see Kenan Malik, "Take Me to Your Leader," kenanmalik.com (April 23, 2009), available at: www.kenanmalik.com/essays/hp_fatwa_extract.html (accessed January 24, 2011).

it easy for Islamic lobby groups — often funded by Saudi or Pakistani extremists — to win government concessions that reinforced the concept of an Islamic identity. By courting the "Muslim vote," political leaders further strengthened this still-forming identity. At national and local levels, the British government "encouraged" (that is to say, ordered) the formation of Islamic umbrella organizations (such as the Bradford Council of Mosques, set up in 1981) to "speak for" Muslims, thereby marginalizing more secular existing groups such as the Asian Youth Movement. It was at the encouragement of the Conservative government then in power that the Muslim Council of Britain (MCB) was formed in 1997.[36]

As an umbrella group, the MCB is comprised of local communities representing a variety of Islamic perspectives, not simply those of radical Islamism. Nevertheless, it has been justly criticized for permitting groups like the Muslim Brotherhood and JI to have much influence in its operations. This influence is visible in its calls for the granting of a UK visa to Sheik Yusuf al-Qaradawi, a major Brotherhood leader notorious for his defense of suicide bombings. Indeed, many MCB imams endorse fundamentalist interpretations of Islam that conflict sharply with Britain's liberal political and cultural traditions. Criticism of the group has been largely in vain, however, since MCB officials have so successfully cultivated their relationships with government ministries and with political figures in opposition that, regardless of which party is in power, the MCB's position remains unchanged. The MCB was thus until recently perceived as the primary voice of "mainstream" Islam in the UK, as will be discussed in Chapter 5.

Due to its traditional support for strict separation of religion and the state, the French government did not begin working with Muslim organizations as partners until 2003. That year, the formation of an extremist Muslim political party, the Parti des Musulmans de France (PMF; Party of the Muslims of France) triggered a change in government policy. The French response was twofold, coupling support for certain existing organizations with the creation of a new umbrella organization, to be called the Conseil Français du Culte Musulman (CFCM; French Council of the Muslim Faith). Then-interior minister Nicolas Sarkozy and other officials expected that these measures would foster the development of a more moderate Muslim population and combat the rise of Wahhabism

---

36 Conservative Party Group on National and International Security, *Uniting the Country: Interim Report on National Cohesion* (London: Conservative Party, 2007), available at: www. conservatives.com/pdf/unitingthecountry.pdf (accessed January 24, 2011).

and Salafism. Their optimism might not have been misplaced — that is, if the partners they were supporting were not already under the control of the Islamists.

The first bodies selected to receive government support were the Mosque of Paris, the Fédération Nationale des Musulmans de France (FNMF; National Federation of the Muslims of France), and the Union des Organisations Islamiques de France (UOIF; Union of Islamic Organizations of France). Of the latter two organizations, the FNMF is the smaller and targets the Moroccan community; it was founded and financed by the Kingdom of Morocco to retain its influence over Moroccans in France, although it later received Saudi funding as well.[37] The UOIF, established in 1983 by two Muslim Brotherhood members studying in France (the Tunisian Abdallah Ben Mansour and the Iraqi Mahmoud Zuheir), is itself an umbrella organization encompassing over 200 associations throughout France. With its Brotherhood connections and relative size and strength, the UOIF soon became "the dominant voice" within the new CMCF.[38]

While maintaining a moderate public image (because it wishes to continue its government partnership), the UOIF's actions suggest that it is far more extreme than it purports to be. It enjoys close ties to the Muslim Brotherhood's Sheikh Yusuf al-Qaradawi, who has addressed the UOIF annual conference and who holds an academic position at the UOIF-affiliated European Institute of Human Sciences (EIHS), an imam training center in France.[39] Moreover, the organization raised funds for Hamas through a French-registered charity known as the Comité de Bienfaisance et de Secours aux Palestiniens (CBSP; Committee for Charity and Aid to Palestinians), which the US government designated a terrorist entity in 2007.[40] When these examples are added to the many

---

37   Michael Laskier, "Islamic Radicalism and Terrorism in the European Union: The Magrehbi Factor," in Hillel Frisch and Efraim Inbar, eds., *Radical Islam and International Security: Challenges and Responses* (London: Routledge, 2008), pp. 93–120 (96).

38   Daniel Strieff, "Forging a Voice in 'France's High-Rise Hell,'" Islam in Europe, *MSNBC.com* (May 9, 2007), available at: www.msnbc.msn.com/id/12812186/ (accessed January 25, 2011).

39   Centre Simon Wiesenthal Europe, *The True Face of the UOIF: Antisemitism, Advocacy and Financing of Terrorism, and the Call to Jihad* (Paris: Centre Simon Wiesenthal Europe, 2007), available at: www.wiesenthal.com/atf/cf/%7BDFD2AAC1–2ADE–428A–9263–35234229D8D8%7D/trueUOIF.pdf (accessed January 25, 2011).

40   US Department of the Treasury, "U.S. Designates Five Charities Funding Hamas and Six Senior Hamas Leaders as Terrorist Entities," press release JS-672 (August 22, 2003), available at: www.treasury.gov/press-center/press-releases/Pages/js672.aspx (accessed January 25,

extremist and anti-Semitic statements and sermons by UOIF leaders and imams, it becomes difficult to disagree with the conclusion of the Franco-Lebanese scholar Antoine Sfeir that the UOIF poses "a real threat to secularism."[41]

Hidden Blooms: The Differentiated Communities

As Islamism has gathered strength in Europe, some ethnic and sectarian minority groups within European Islam have been unjustly neglected. Ignored by the mainstream media, by academic researchers, and above all by governments, these non-Islamist groups, which have been referred to as "differentiated communities," remain poorly understood to this day. For the first few decades after Muslim immigrants arrived in Europe, obscurity was actually advantageous to these communities, as it helped them escape the Islamists' notice. Now that the focal point of the struggle against Islamism has shifted away from the mosques and community organizations toward the political arena, this lack of public attention is undermining these minority communities' efforts to serve as partners in government "engagement" efforts.

Two distinctive Muslim communities in Europe have, in particular, retained a strong, independent identity in the face of increasing Islamist dominance: the Alevis and the Berbers. In addition to their relative obscurity, both communities have something more important in common: their moderate nature. This moderate tendency has been encouraged by two factors. First, the generally rural origins of these communities — including those that came to Europe in the second wave — had shielded them in their own countries from Islamism's rise; their villages and small towns were the last to come under the influence of the Islamists at home. Second, once these communities were rooted in Europe, their separate organizational structures served to protect them against the Islamist ideology spread primarily through mosques and community networks. With their tightly defined cultural/linguistic/denominational identities, their "re-created villages" in European urban neighborhoods were more cohesive,

---

2011); Olivier Guitta, "Giving in to Hamas?" *FrontPageMagazine.com* (February 7, 2006), available at: http://archive.frontpagemag.com/readArticle.aspx?ARTID=5651 (accessed January 25, 2011).

41   Hugh Schofield, "France's Islamic Heartland," *BBC News* (April 18, 2003), available at: http://news.bbc.co.uk/2/hi/europe/2959389.stm (accessed January 25, 2011).

ensuring against a loss of identity in the second and third generations. As a result, these communities' religious organizations were vibrant and energetic enough to retain independence from the Islamist-dominated "mainstream" and its government-sponsored umbrella groups. In fact, they set up their *own* umbrella organizations, for example, the Avusturya Alevi Birlikleri Federasyonu (AABF; Federation of Unions of Alevites in Austria).[42]

1 The Alevis

One of the least studied differentiated communities of Muslims in Europe is the Alevis of Turkey, who have been resisting Islamization — both in Turkey and in Europe. They have never resorted to political violence; in fact, to a very large degree, they have maintained their unique spiritual and cultural traditions that happen to reject violence, which further underlines their distinctiveness from their Sunni Muslim oppressors.

The Alevis themselves are split about how to define their community in relation to Islam. Most believe that they are nonorthodox Shiites following the line of the Prophet Muhammad's son-in-law, the murdered caliph Ali. Other than this veneration for Ali, however, the Turkish Alevis have little in common with the Syrian Alawites (the denomination to which Syria's ruling Bashir family belongs). Unlike the Alawites, whose doctrines are generally not revealed outside the faith, Alevis discuss their beliefs and practices openly.

Alevis emphasize core values such as love and respect for all people, pacifism, tolerance toward other religions and ethnic groups, and equality of men and women. In traditional Alevi worship — which takes place not in mosques, but in *cemevi* (Alevi assembly houses), women and men dance, sing, and worship together. Alevism also differs from Sunni and most of Shiite Islam in many other respects; for example, it forbids polygamy while permitting alcohol. Arguing that "God does not reside in a stone, but in the heart of people," Alevis do not participate in the Sunnis' Hajj pilgrimage to Mecca (which is centered around the Black Stone of the Kaaba, Islam's most sacred site).[43]

Although their religious practices involve elements of mysticism,

---

42   Shireen T. Hunter, ed., *Islam, Europe's Second Religion: The New Social, Cultural, and Political Landscape* (Westport, CT: Praeger, 2002), p. 143.
43   Teresa Küchler, "Turkey's Alevi Muslims Look to EU for Protection from Intolerance,"

Alevis are also politically engaged, and are above all interested in obtaining protection for their cultural practices and respect from their governments — whether in Europe or in their countries of origin. In the Turkish political context, "Alevism is seen as a counterforce to Sunni fundamentalism," which makes Alevis valued political allies of secularist political leaders.[44] Alevis view this alliance as key to obtaining their ultimate goal: having the Turkish state recognize Alevism as an official Islamic community equal to — but different from — Sunni Islam.

In Europe, where there is less pressure on the Alevi community to define itself in opposition to Sunni Islam, the Alevi political agenda is broader and more reflective of Alevi core values. Free to focus on issues besides state recognition, European Alevis have, as one German journalist noted, adopted "an unflinchingly progressive stance on a number of controversial issues: Alevis favor abortion rights and equal opportunities for women and gays."[45] Finally, demonstrating that their support for secular values in Turkey is authentic (and not an Islamist-style tactical concession), prominent Alevi representatives have spoken out in favor of the right to criticize religion in European societies. After the Berlin Opera canceled a production of Mozart's *Idomeneo* (featuring, among other elements, the severed heads of Jesus and Muhammad) due to fear of Islamist response, an Alevi community leader in Cologne declared, "it is absolutely unacceptable that art should be repressed on the pretext of religion. Freedom of the imagination must not be surrendered after so many centuries of struggle and development."[46]

2 The Berbers

The issue of Berber identity has suffered almost as much obscurity and neglect in the Berbers' homelands as it has in Europe. Thanks to the long-standing efforts by Arab rulers to suppress the indigenous Berber language and culture, the differences between Arabs and Berbers have

EU Observer.com (December 19, 2008), available at: http://euobserver.com/879/27323 (accessed January 25, 2011).

44   David Zeidan, "The Alevi of Anatolia," unpublished manuscript (1995), available at: www.angelfire.com/az/rescon/ALEVI.html (accessed January 25, 2011).

45   Küchler, "Turkey's Alevi Muslims."

46   Stephen Schwartz, "Moderate Islam in Germany," *Family Security Matters* (October 10, 2006), available at: www.fsmarchives.org/article.php?id=327281 (accessed January 25, 2011).

blurred significantly. It is thus important when speaking of the Berbers to distinguish between Berber *ethnicity* and Berber *identity*. Scholars estimate that 80 percent of Moroccans, and 60 percent of Tunisians and Algerians are of Berber ancestry; however, this ethnic majority is in practice a cultural minority, as only half of these people self-identify as Berbers.[47]

To this day, the division between those who do and do not consider themselves Berbers has closely reflected patterns of urbanization. City dwellers assumed the cosmopolitan Arab identity, language, and culture, while the more isolated populations in the countryside — where some areas resisted conversion to Islam until the sixteenth century — rejected any such change.[48] This essential conservatism of the rural Berber population helped to shape the development of an atypical "Berber Islam" that retains many elements of pre-Islamic religious practice. A further aspect of this Berber Islam was a markedly tolerant and peaceful approach to Maghrebi Jews and other minority populations. Inevitably, this lack of conformity with Arab norms drew the attention of Sunni fundamentalists, who viewed the Berbers as "bad Muslims" living in a state of ignorance.

In spite of increasing assimilation and the decline in use of their traditional languages, Berbers have maintained their tradition of resistance not only against religious dictates, but also against the terminology by which they are known; rejecting the pejorative Arabic *al-Barbar*, many refer to themselves instead as "Amazigh," meaning "one who is free." In response to the pro-assimilation campaigns that accompanied the rise of Pan-Arabism in the 1960s, the Berbers — under the slogan "Freedom, Dignity, Justice" — began for the first time to organize politically.

Thanks to the escape valve offered by Western Europe, the region's governments had no need to try to satisfy the Berbers' grievances; they simply shipped the "troublesome" Berbers abroad as guest workers. Accordingly, there are significant Berber populations in France and the Netherlands, descended from first-wave Moroccan, Algerian, and Tunisian guest workers. Although the lack of clarity surrounding the question of who Berbers are makes counting difficult, estimates of the European population range from 1.5 to 2 million, of whom 1 million live in France and over 300,000 in the Netherlands.

---

47   Moheb Zaki, *Civil Society and Democratization in the Arab World: Annual Report 2007* (Cairo: Ibn Khaldun Center for Development Studies, 2007), p. 206, available at: www.eicds. org/english/publications/reports/Annual-Report-EN07.pdf (accessed January 25, 2011).
48   Marrakesh, the only urban community in North Africa with a predominantly Berber identity, is an exception; see Zaki, *Civil Society and Democratization*, p. 207.

The Berber communities in the Netherlands and France are particularly interesting, since it is in these two countries that a distinctly *urban* form of Amazigh identity has emerged for the first time. This is especially so in the Netherlands, where second- and third-generation Berbers struggled to find an identity that fitted.[49] Although for reasons outlined above they could not identify with the Islamist-promoted "Muslim" identity, they resented being known simply as "Moroccans," as this label became associated with extremism and criminal activity in the Netherlands. Even the name "Berber" was unavailable, as it was associated in Dutch minds with the Islamists — like the assassin Mohammed Bouyeri — who had hijacked it as a cover for their own "resistance" efforts both in the countries of origin and in Europe.

In this context, the Amazigh identity emerged as an alternative for these particular Dutch Muslims, among whom it fostered a sense of pride and confidence without fanning the flames of anger and alienation. Moreover, it enabled them to make a clear public distinction between themselves and the "Arabized" Berbers such as Bouyeri who had chosen Islamist ideology and sharia law over Berber Islam and traditional beliefs.

The community leaders have had some success in promoting the Amazigh identity in recent years, but there are no guarantees that this success will continue. As previously argued, the Islamist movement has a near-infinite capacity to reinvent its tactics and message to win over a target population. Having already successfully redefined mainstream Islam, the Islamists will doubtlessly find redefining what it means to be "Berber" a less daunting challenge. Already, Islamists are successfully downplaying the degree of conflict between Berbers and Arabs, arguing that the two groups have always been on the "same side," as exemplified by Tariq ibn Ziyad, the legendary Berber military commander who conquered Spain for Islam in 711 — shortly after the initial Arab incursion into the Amazigh homelands.

Since Islamists enjoy a massive financial, logistical, and political advantage, it is unlikely that *any* single group will be able to resist them on its own. A better strategy for the Berbers of Europe would be to appeal to non-Islamists outside their own community. With non-Arabs comprising

---

49 This example is based on the author's interviews with Berber and Amazigh activists opposing Islamism in the Netherlands. Similar dynamics exist in France, where Amazigh leaders, primarily from Algeria, try to combat the hold of Islamism with a revival of Amazigh identity.

over 80 percent of the world's Muslims,[50] there is a wide audience for arguments explaining how deeply the Islamist movement is rooted in Arab supremacist ideology and in its attendant cultural, economic, linguistic, and political imperialism. From Indonesia to Senegal, Arab imperialists have used religious rhetoric to encourage many peoples to ignore their own pre-Islamic pasts and to abandon remaining non-Islamist practices that still exist (such as Nawruz, the traditional celebration of the Persian New Year). By focusing on common elements among the disparate opponents of Islamism, moderates will be more likely to stay united — and to eventually emerge victorious.

As the examples of the Alevis and Berbers show, some European Muslims rely on the strength of their unique traditions to maintain the integrity of their communities in Europe and to resist inroads by Islamist recruiters. Their experiences underscore the critical importance of helping second- and third-generation European Muslims overcome their spiritual alienation by connecting with their families' traditional and vibrant forms of Islam.

---

50   RAND Project Airforce, *U.S. Strategy in the Muslim World after 9/11*, RAND Corporation research brief series, RB-151-AF (RAND Corporation, 2004), available at: www.rand.org/content/dam/rand/pubs/research_briefs/2005/RAND_RB151.pdf (accessed January 25, 2011).

CHAPTER 4

The Rise of Islamism in the United States

As an American high school student fond of partying, punk rock, and pancakes, Omar Hammami seemed an unlikely candidate for recruitment by militant Islamist networks. Born in Alabama to a Syrian immigrant father and Southern Baptist mother, Hammami became a star Bible camp student. But Hammami followed a career path never before taken by a graduate of southern Alabama's Daphne High, rising to field commander in the violent Somali Islamist group Harakat al-Shabaab al-Mujahedeen("Mujahedeen Youth Movement," more commonly known just as "al-Shabaab"). After he appeared in his first propaganda video in 2007, the unusual details of his story attracted significant media attention. Hammami was unique even compared to the other young Americans who entered al-Qaeda's ranks; both John Walker Lindh and Adam Gadahn were troubled, isolated teenagers before they fell into extremism, while Hammami enjoyed good relations with his family. Moreover, he was fully integrated into mainstream US society and living the life of a typical American teenager; he was even elected class president by his peers. Hammami nevertheless was radicalized and became one of al-Shabaab's most influential field commanders, leading its brutal rebellion against Somalia's secular society.

Though Hammami's radicalization in the United States may seem difficult to understand, it follows the same pattern seen among spiritually alienated European Muslims who are exploited by Islamist recruiters. Raised as a Christian, Hammami never developed a connection with the tolerant Islam practiced by his father. In adolescence, he grew curious about what it meant to be a Muslim, and Islamist ideologues were ready to offer simple answers to his complex questions. In 2010, in a surreptitious Facebook exchange with his sister, Hammami made clear that his militant jihadism was motivated by just one thing — Islamist ideology. Recognizing his growing notoriety at home, Hammami argued that those wondering how he became a violent Islamist could not

> blame it on poverty or any of that stuff . . . They will have to realize that it's an ideology and it's a way of life that makes people change. They will also have to realize that their political agendas need to be fixed.[1]

The United States as a Religious Nation of Immigrants

Islamist ideologues like the ones who radicalized Hammami began coming to the United States over four decades ago. Just as in Europe, the main Islamist wave of immigration reached America's shores in the 1960s. Once in the United States, Islamist groups used the same tactics and benefited from the same kind of government mistakes as their counterparts in Europe. By the time the September 11 attacks forced the United States to respond to the challenge of radical Islam abroad, it already faced an Islamist-dominated Muslim community at home.

But few US officials or analysts recognized the potential threat of Islamism to the security and democratic institutions of the United States. Conventional wisdom was that American Muslims were integrated into mainstream society. There were no "Muslim ghettos" in the United States like those in Paris, Amsterdam, and London. Muslims seemed to attend the same schools, hold the same jobs, and achieve the same levels of wealth as members of any other faith community in the United States.

---

1   Quoted in Andrea Elliott, "The Jihadist Next Door," *New York Times Magazine* (January 27, 2010), p. 26, available at: www.nytimes.com/2010/01/31/magazine/31Jihadist-t. html (accessed January 25, 2011).

Moreover, the successful integration of Muslims fit America's own self-understanding and bolstered the national belief in the United States as a country of immigrants bound together by common values, including freedom of religion. From the outset, religious freedom has been one of the most important values shaping the American identity. Many of America's original colonists traveled to the New World in search of religious freedom, and the US Constitution mandates freedom of religion in the Bill of Rights and separation of church and state in the establishment clause. As noted by perhaps the most famous European observer of early America, Alexis de Tocqueville, "Americans have succeeded ... in combining admirably ... the spirit of religion and the spirit of liberty."[2]

In reality, America's conception of itself as a melting pot and a land where religious freedom is valued has led the United States to make two mistakes relating to the Islamists. Not only were Americans initially blind to Islamism's destructive intentions in this country, but they have also been slow to grasp that where America's promise of equality has failed, the Islamists have been poised to take advantage of alienated minorities.

American Hispanics

Consider the case of American Hispanics, a culturally and linguistically distinct group whose rapidly increasing numbers, socioeconomic disadvantages, and origin from a neighboring region provide a close parallel to Europe's Muslim immigrant guest workers, such as German Turks or French North Africans. Recent studies have shown that the Latino community in the United States has not followed the usual pattern of other immigrant groups, in which each generation becomes more prosperous and more "American" in terms of their language, culture, and outlook, than the previous. A group of scholars at Brown University demonstrated that third-generation Hispanic immigrants to the United States are more likely to commit crimes and less likely to perform well in school than first- and second-generation Hispanic immigrants.[3] Furthermore, a recent Pew Hispanic Center study concludes that third-generation

---

2   Alexis de Tocqueville, *Democracy in America*, vol. 1 (New York: Westvaco, 1999), p. 60.
3   Sara Slama, Amy Kerivan Marks, Flannery Patton, and Cynthia Garcia Coll, *The Effects of Immigrant Generation on Class Preparedness in Hispanic/Latino and Asian Adolescents in the United States* (Providence, RI: Brown University, n.d.), available at: www.brown.edu/Administration/Dean_of_the_College/utra/documents/Slama.pdf (accessed January 25, 2011).

Hispanic immigrants enjoy "no difference in poverty rates" compared to second-generation immigrants.[4] As poverty and cultural isolation alienate American Hispanics from the mainstream, the pool of potential rejectionists grows. Islamists exploited feelings of alienation in Jose Padilla, a second-generation Hispanic immigrant arrested in 2002 for his involvement with al-Qaeda. He was convicted in 2005 of conspiracy to "murder, kidnap, and maim" and of providing material support to terrorists. Padilla's life reveals a familiar pattern of Islamist radicalization: alienated in childhood, he joined a gang while in middle school, found answers in religion (first Christianity, then Islam), and soon became radicalized. He then went to Yemen, ostensibly to teach English, and began traveling to sites in the Islamist network throughout the Middle East and South Asia.[5]

African Americans

Like Hispanics, African Americans have also experienced alienation from American society as they struggle to overcome the legacy of slavery. It is only during the last half century that African Americans have made significant progress toward economic and social equality with whites. Yet disparities remain between blacks and whites across a broad range of key social indicators, including income, education, and health. Nearly two centuries of government-enforced segregation and enduring racial discrimination helped to foster in many African Americans a sense of social alienation that mirrors that of Muslims in Europe. Indeed, many European Muslims interpret the plight of African Americans as analogous to their own social marginalization. During extensive meetings with the author in the Netherlands in 2005 and 2006, young Moroccans repeatedly referred to themselves as the "Blacks of Europe." "Our families were treated like slaves when they were brought here," one noted. "They did not know about their rights, [were] intentionally left uneducated, living in terrible conditions . . . And now we are blamed for not having integrated or not performing at the same level as the whites." This statement reflects the

---

4 The Pew Hispanic Center's survey results are summarized in N. C. Aizenman, "Most U.S. Hispanic Kids Have Immigrant Parents," *Washington Post* (May 29, 2009), available at: www.washingtonpost.com/wp-dyn/content/article/2009/05/28/AR2009052801506. html (accessed January 25, 2011).

5 Debra J. Saunders, "Padilla's Life and Times," *San Francisco Chronicle* (April 27, 2004), available at: www.sfgate.com/cgi-bin/article.cgi?f=/c/a/2004/04/27/EDG7H6ABSQ1. DTL (accessed January 25, 2011).

anger of many children of guest workers in Europe, who withdrew from the mainstream European societies that mistreated their parents. Perhaps unsurprisingly, many of them emulate African American youth in dress and demeanor.

Nor should it be surprising that in the United States, increasing numbers of African Americans are reacting to their own alienation from mainstream American society by converting to Islam. According to the Pew Research Center, as of 2007, 59 percent of all converts to Islam in the United States were African Americans; African Americans constituted 20 percent of all US Muslims, making them the largest group of native-born Muslims in the United States, and, after Arab Americans (24 percent of the total), the second-largest ethnic group within American Islam.[6] Many African Americans convert to Islam as a means to political empowerment, embracing the messages of Islamist recruiters who blur religion and politics to spread their vision of politicized Islam. Drawing on claims that many enslaved Africans were forcibly converted from Islam to Christianity and that true liberation can come by "reverting" to Islam, such recruiters have established Islamism as an ideology of resistance to the American establishment. Islamism is spreading fastest in US prisons, where African Americans endure perhaps the most dramatic form of social alienation: physical separation from mainstream society. Jane Smith, associate dean for faculty and academic affairs at Harvard Divinity School, estimates that more than 300,000 prisoners, many of them African Americans, are converts to Islam, and that the rate of conversion may be more than 30,000 a year.[7] Books by Maududi and Qutb are commonly found in prison libraries, along with Wahhabi translations of the Qur'an.[8]

It should be noted that millions of Muslims from countries around the world have come to the United States in search of the religious freedom

---

6   Pew Research Center, *Muslim Americans: Middle Class and Mostly Mainstream* (Washington, D.C.: Pew Research Center, May 2007), p. 22, available at: http://pewresearch.org/assets/pdf/muslim-americans.pdf (accessed January 25, 2011).
7   Jane Smith, *Islam in America* (New York: Columbia University Press, 1999), p. 165.
8   Steven Emerson, "Radicals in Our Prisons: How to Stop the Muslim Extremists Recruiting Inmates to Terrorism," *New York Post* (May 24, 2009), available at: www.nypost.com/p/news/opinion/opedcolumnists/item_mm7BW6pcTbzbjhri6DmuHM#ixzz1COxgBCGa (accessed January 25, 2011); Daveed Gartenstein-Ross, "Prison Jihad? How Radical Islamic Charities Exploit Their Access to the Prison System," *Weekly Standard* (October 12, 2006), available at: www.weeklystandard.com/Content/Public/Articles/000/000/012/777kjlzx.asp (accessed January 25, 2011).

and respect for diversity that are outlined in the country's founding documents. They are not Islamists. Nor are they uneducated, as the European guest workers generally have been. Many of the Muslim immigrants to the United States have been university students and professionals who arrived already speaking English. They have therefore been better prepared than Europe's Muslims to benefit from the educational and employment opportunities available in the United States. Easier upward social mobility in the United States relative to Europe brought success to the vast majority of Muslim immigrants who sought the American Dream; there was no comparable "Dutch dream" or "German dream" to which the unassimilated guest workers could aspire.

US Muslims and Islamism

Concerned above all with achieving educational and professional success, most Muslim immigrants to the United States focused on their families' social integration into mainstream society. While they successfully passed on to their children their families' secular traditions (food, music, holidays), they often ignored religion. The United States, rather than Islam, was supposed to be the primary source of the next generation's identity. As these children grew older, they often demanded answers to the question of what it meant to be "Muslim." When they did not receive satisfactory answers at home, they became spiritually alienated. As in Europe, young Muslims in the United States thus became susceptible to Islamist recruiters, who offered Islamist answers to questions concerning how Muslims should balance their faith with American cultural norms. Many Muslim immigrant parents inadvertently facilitated Islamist recruitment by sending their children to local Islamic schools and community centers to learn about their religion. As will be shown, such institutions were typically controlled and operated by Islamists, who had spent over three decades establishing themselves and their institutions as the social and religious anchors of "mainstream Muslim" communities in the United States.

American Youth and Islamism

Islamist groups like the Muslim Brotherhood, Wahhabis, and Salafis have extensively recruited among Muslim youth in the United States, targeting both those experiencing spiritual alienation and those educated at

Islamist institutions. These groups have achieved success by exploiting young Muslim Americans' quest for self-expression and their questioning of authority, and by reassuring them that it is natural for "real Muslims" to reject the political and legal authority of the US government. They portray their interpretation of Islam as the only one that is "truthful" and "pure," and denigrate non-Islamist traditions as "not properly Islamic" because they are "polluted" by Western culture and politics. Appealing to the norms of a secularly integrated generation of Muslims, some Islamist recruiters even downplay religious piety, emphasizing instead the need to combat the supposed injustices perpetrated against Muslims by other Americans. This approach, which taps into young American Muslims' spiritual alienation and then uses it to foster social alienation, is the reverse of the Islamists' approach in Europe (where social alienation is exploited to foster spiritual alienation). But the Islamists' final objective in both the United States and Europe is the same — to blur the boundary between religion and politics, consolidate Muslims into subcommunities that coexist with mainstream society, introduce sharia norms, and lay the foundation for the eventual establishment of the *umma*.

"Mainstream" Islamism

Islamists have spent over three decades placing their institutions and philosophy in the mainstream of American Islam. As in Europe, Islamists came to the United States in the 1960s in search of political and cultural space in which to operate. After threatening the regimes in their home countries (primarily Egypt, Syria, Jordan, Iraq, and Pakistan) by calling for their replacement with Islamic governments based on sharia, they faced political repression and fled abroad. The initial goal of Islamists arriving in the United States was to consolidate their strength to prepare for an eventual return to their home countries, where they would challenge the region's existing regimes. Over time, as Islamist immigrants became familiar with America's secular mainstream society, they shifted their primary target to the United States. Establishing schools, community centers, and places of worship, these movement elites laid the foundation for the subsequent emergence of a larger Islamist movement that is now threatening the democratic order of the United States.

The Muslim Brotherhood

With the broad geographic and social range of its organizational network, the Muslim Brotherhood has taken the lead in planting the seeds of Islamism in the United States. In this effort, the Brotherhood has enjoyed strong support from Saudi Arabia, despite its ideological differences with the kingdom's official Wahhabism. Members of the Muslim Brotherhood, who are referred to by the Arabic term "Ikhwanis," cloaked themselves in secrecy from the start, publicly and euphemistically referring to the Brotherhood as the "Cultural Society."[9] Avoiding any public mention of their quest to replace democracy with sharia rule, they instead went about establishing a spate of American and international Islamist organizations.

The first major organization formed by the Brotherhood in the US was the Muslim Student Union (MSU). According to an internal Brotherhood document, "In 1962, the Muslim Students Union was founded by a group of the first Ikhwans in North America and the meetings of the Ikhwan became conferences and Students Union Camps."[10] The next year, Brotherhood members Ahmed Totonji and Jamal Barzinji created a more formal structure under the name Muslim Students Association (MSA) at the University of Illinois at Urbana-Champaign. Over the next several decades, the Brotherhood expanded, establishing nearly 600 MSA chapters at universities throughout the United States and Canada. Although the MSA claims to represent mainstream moderate Islamic thought, it actually nurtures Islamist ideology among young North American Muslims.[11] (Evidence for this can be found in the example of Howard University dental student Ramy Zamzam, who was arrested in 2009 in Pakistan on charges of planning to commit terrorism; he was a president of the MSA Council of Washington, DC.)

The organizations established by the Brotherhood have shared not only tactics and ideology but personnel as well, further strengthening the

---

9   Noreen Ahmed-Ullah, Sam Roe, and Laurie Cohen, "A Rare Look at Secretive Muslim Brotherhood in America," *Chicago Tribune* (September 19, 2004), available at: www.chicagotribune.com/news/watchdog/chi-0409190261sep19,0,3008717.story (accessed January 25, 2011).

10   Muslim Brotherhood, "A Brief History of the Muslim Brotherhood in the US," internal document of the Muslim Brotherhood (Muslim Brotherhood, 1991). Available at: www.nefafoundation.org/miscellaneous/HLF/MBUS_History.pdf (accessed January 25, 2011).

11   Investigative Project on Terrorism (IPT), *Muslim Students Association: The Investigative Project on Terrorism Dossier* (IPT, n.d.), available at: www.investigativeproject.org/documents/misc/31.pdf (accessed January 25, 2011).

Brotherhood's emerging global network. Barzinji and Totonji worked with a third Brotherhood associate, Hisham Altalib, to broaden the Brotherhood's network beyond the MSA, both in the United States and abroad. Totonji was the first (and Altalib the second) leader of the International Islamic Federation of Student Organizations (IIFSO), founded in 1969. In its own words, the IIFSO was established to facilitate "the organized promotion of concepts such as the unity of Islamic thought, the universality of the Islamic movement, and the consolidation of a mature Muslim leadership."[12] In 1973, Barzinji and Altalib played a key role in creating the North American Islamic Trust (NAIT), a nonprofit — hence tax-exempt — organization tasked with building schools, Islamic centers, and publishing networks. NAIT received considerable sums of money from the Saudi government, which sought to forge global cooperation between Wahhabis and the Muslim Brotherhood.[13] In 2003, one national security expert claimed that NAIT owned or controlled the physical assets of 75 percent of US mosques and that the Islamic Society of North America (ISNA), an Islamist umbrella group described below, controlled the ideology of their preaching, publications, and education.[14]

Internationally, Barzinji and Totonji worked together with other Islamists to found the World Association of Muslim Youth (WAMY) in Riyadh, Saudi Arabia, in 1972. Their objective was to increase cooperation between Wahhabis and the Muslim Brotherhood and advance their Islamist ideology around the world. Totonji served as the deputy of WAMY's first secretary general, and Barzinji was listed as a WAMY senior member in the 1980s.[15] Then in 1981, Barzinji and Totonji collaborated

---

12   International Islamic Federation of Student Organizations (IIFSO), "History of the IIFSO," International Islamic Federation of Student Organizations (n.d.), available at: http://web.archive.org/web/19990202092801/www.iifso.org/hist.htm (accessed January 25, 2011).

13   Stephen Schwartz, *Wahabism and Islam in the U.S.*, 108th Congress Hearings, US Senate Subcommittee on Terrorism, Technology and Homeland Security, June 26, 2003, available at: http://kyl.senate.gov/legis_center/subdocs/sc062603_schwartz.pdf (accessed January 25, 2011).

14   J. Michael Waller, *Statement of J. Michael Waller, Annenberg Professor of International Communication, Institute of World Politics before the Senate Subcommittee on Terrorism, Technology, and Homeland Security*, 108th Congress Hearings, US Senate Subcommittee on Terrorism, Technology and Homeland Security, October 14, 2003, available at: http://kyl.senate.gov/legis_center/subdocs/101403_wallerl.pdf (accessed January 26, 2011).

15   Anwar Ibrahim, *Speech Delivered by His Excellency, The Minister of Finance of Malaysia, Bro. Anwar Ibrahim, at the Formal Opening of the 7th International Conference of WAMY*, Kuala Lumpur, Malaysia, January 28, 1993, available at: http://web.archive.org/web/20030314125221/

on the establishment of another organization, the International Institute of Islamic Thought (IIIT), which is now headquartered in Virginia and (according to its website) promotes the "Islamization of knowledge." The IIIT's other cofounders included additional senior Muslim Brotherhood activists, including Yaqub Mirza, chief executive of the now-defunct SAAR Foundation (a fundraising operation linked to the Brotherhood's militant wing, Hamas), and Sayyid Syeed, then-president of the MSA.[16]

Also in 1981, Ikhwani activists from the IIIT, WAMY, and other international Islamist groups founded a large umbrella organization called the Islamic Society of North America (ISNA). ISNA's aim is to organize the efforts of US groups like the MSA and NAIT, link them with the international Islamist organizations, and channel all these groups' efforts "to advance the cause of Islam and service Muslims in North America so as to *enable them to adopt Islam as a complete way of life.*"[17] The Brotherhood's internal documents assert that "the Muslim Students Union was developed into the Islamic Society in North America (ISNA) to include all the Muslim congregations from immigrants and citizens, and to be a nucleus for the Islamic Movement in North America."[18] According to US Senate testimony by a former FBI analyst, Saudi Arabia was the largest single source of ISNA's financing in 1991.[19]

ISNA's role in unifying the efforts of disparate Muslim Brotherhood activists and affiliated organizations — and hence in establishing Islamism as the dominant institutional representative of Islam in the United States — is evident in the biographies of its key leaders. Sayyid Syeed, one of

---

www.wamy.org/english/conferences/speech6.htm (accessed January 26, 2011); Matthew Levitt, "Combating Terrorist Financing, Despite the Saudis," Washington Institute for Near East Policy, Policy Watch #673, November 1, 2002, available at: www.ciaonet.org/pbei/winep/policy_2002/2002_673.html (subscription required; accessed February 13, 2011).

16 For Mirza, see FBI, FOIA Documents, Case ID: 1111944–000, release date: April 29, 2008, available at: www.investigativeproject.org/documents/misc/159.pdf (accessed January 26, 2011). For Syeed, see M. M. Ali, "Personality: Dr. Sayyid Muhammad Syeed," *Washington Report on Middle East Affairs* (April 1998), p. 35, available at: www.wrmea.com/backissues/0498/9804035.html (accessed January 26, 2011).

17 Islamic Society of North America, "Documents of Incorporation" (Indianapolis, Indiana: Office of the Secretary of State), July 14, 1981; italics added.

18 Muslim Brotherhood, "Brief History of the Muslim Brotherhood in the US."

19 Matthew Levitt, "Subversion from Within: Saudi Funding of Islamic Extremist Groups Undermining U.S. Interests and the War on Terror within the United States," *Washington Institute for Near East Policy*, 108th Congress Hearings, Senate Subcommittee on Terrorism, Technology, and Homeland Security, September 10, 2003, available at: www.washington institute.org/templateC07.php?CID=13 (accessed January 26, 2011).

IIIT's cofounders, has served in a range of leadership positions within ISNA throughout his professional life, including secretary general. He is currently national director of ISNA's Office of Interfaith and Community Alliances, while concurrently serving on the board of advisors of the Washington-based lobbying group, the Council on American Islamic Relations (CAIR), discussed below. Syeed's interconnection with other Brotherhood affiliates is further evident in his service as secretary general of the IIFSO and director of academic outreach at the IIIT from 1984 to 1994, while at the same time helping to lead ISNA.[20] Another important ISNA leader, Jamal Badawi, has been a member of ISNA's board of advisors since 1988. He also served on NAIT's board during 1991–1993. Additionally, Badawi is on the executive committee of the Fiqh Council of America, an organization under ISNA's umbrella that issues legal edicts according to Islamist interpretations of sharia.[21] Another key ISNA figure, Taha al-Alwani, was until recently chairman of the Fiqh Council of America. Al-Alwani was also a founding member of the Wahhabis' MWL in Mecca and a founding member and later president of the IIIT; he is currently the president of the Graduate School of Islamic and Social Sciences, a Virginia-based institution run by the IIIT.

Such overlapping relationships among Brotherhood activists and affiliates are also evident in the operations of the now defunct Islamic Association for Palestine (IAP), founded in 1981 in Chicago by senior Ikhwani leader Mousa Abu Marzook. He was joined by other high-ranking Muslim Brotherhood activists, such as Khalid Mishal (now secretary general of Hamas) and Sami al-Arian (a Florida college professor who was convicted of providing material support to Hamas terrorists in 2003). The IAP's stated purpose was to communicate the Ikhwani "point of view" and "to serve the cause of Palestine on the political and the media fronts."[22] After Hamas was created in 1987 in Gaza, the IAP became its leading representative in North America.[23]

---

20   IPT, *Islamic Society of North America: An IPT Investigative Report* (IPT, n.d.), available at: www.investigativeproject.org/documents/misc/275.pdf (accessed January 26, 2011).

21   See Fiqh Council of North America, "History of the Fiqh Council," Fiqh Council of North America (Plainfield, IN: Fiqh Council of North America, 2010), available at: www.fiqhcouncil.org/node/6 (accessed January 26, 2011).

22   Muslim Brotherhood, "Brief History of the Muslim Brotherhood in the US."

23   US Government, "*United States of America vs. Holy Land Foundation for Relief and Development: Government's Trial Brief*" (NEFA Foundation, May 29, 2007). Available at: http://nefafoundation.org/miscellaneous/HLF/U.S._v_HLF_TrialBrief.pdf (accessed January 26, 2011).

Mishal and Marzook are also tightly connected to another Brotherhood affiliate in the United States, the Holy Land Foundation (HLF), based in Texas. While the HLF did collect donations to Islamic *zakat* committees (religious charities tasked with providing food and medical care) in the Middle East,[24] the US government argued in court that these committees "were controlled by Hamas and contributed to terrorism by helping Hamas spread its ideology and recruit supporters."[25] The evidence in the HFL trials showed that Ghassan Elashi, who incorporated the HLF and served as its treasurer and board chairman, also incorporated the IAP, and is the cousin of Marzook's wife. Mufid Abdulqader, a top fundraiser for the HLF, is Mishal's half-brother. Meanwhile, Marzook's own cousin is Mohamed El-Mezain, the original chairman of the HLF board, and identified by Mishal as "the Hamas leader for the U.S."[26]

Having established these organizations for Islamist activism among American Muslims, Muslim Brotherhood leaders launched an effort to influence US politics by founding the Council on American-Islamic Relations (CAIR) in 1994. CAIR's stated mission is to "enhance understanding of Islam, encourage dialogue, protect civil liberties, empower American Muslims, and build coalitions that promote justice and mutual understanding."[27] Although these objectives sound innocuous, private statements by CAIR leaders indicate a more sinister objective: one of CAIR's founders, the Ikhwani Omar Ahmad, identified the need for "infiltrating the American media outlets, universities and research centers" to replace secular democracy with sharia rule in the United States

---

24   David Cole, "Anti-Terrorism on Trial: Why the Government Loses Funding Cases," *Washington Post* (October 24, 2007), available at: www.washingtonpost.com/wp-dyn/content/article/2007/10/23/AR2007102301805.html (accessed January 26, 2011).

25   The jury was deadlocked after the conclusion of the 2007 trial; see Leslie Eaton, "No Convictions in Trial against Muslim Charity," *New York Times* (October 22, 2007), available at: www.nytimes.com/2007/10/22/us/22cnd-holyland.html (accessed January 26, 2011). Upon retrial in 2008, however, the government did secure criminal convictions against HLF's founders. See Gretel C. Kovach, "Five Convicted in Terrorism Financing Trial," *New York Times* (November 24, 2008), available at: www.nytimes.com/2008/11/25/us/25charity.html?scp=1&sq=Kovach%2C+%93Five+Convicted+in+Terrorism+Financing+Trial&st=nyt (accessed January 26, 2011).

26   Josh Lefkowitz, *The 1993 Philadelphia Meeting: A Roadmap for Future Muslim Brotherhood Actions in the U.S.* (NEFA Foundation, November 15, 2007), available at: http://nefafoundation.org//file/93Phillyfinal.pdf (accessed January 26, 2011).

27   CAIR, "Our Vision, Mission, and Core Principles," CAIR (Washington, DC: CAIR, 2010), available at: www.cair.com/AboutUs/VisionMissionCorePrinciples.aspx (accessed January 26, 2011).

(albeit in the distant future).[28] The membership of CAIR's top leaders in the Muslim Brotherhood belies the organization's self-presentation as a typical civil rights organization. CAIR's true mission, like that of other Brotherhood organizations, is to spread Islamism among American Muslims. CAIR, along with ISNA and many other American Brotherhood organizations, was named an unindicted coconspirator in the 2007 federal trial against the HLF, which was convicted of channeling millions of dollars to Hamas terrorists.

Islamists' Bottom-Up Tactics in the United States

The HLF trial brought to public attention a Brotherhood strategy paper from 1991, which calls for a "civilizational *jihad*" in America to be conducted in six stages:

1. Establishing an effective and stable Islamic Movement led by the Muslim Brotherhood.
2. Adopting Muslims' causes domestically and globally.
3. Expanding the observant Muslim base.
4. Unifying and directing Muslims' efforts.
5. Presenting Islam as a civilization[al] alternative [to secular government].
6. Supporting the establishment of the global Islamic state wherever it is.[29]

The Brotherhood memo goes on to outline the bottom-up Islamization strategy followed by CAIR, ISNA, and other Islamist organizations in the United States. This strategy begins with the individual, then spreads to the individual's family, to his community, and to the entire country, with the final goal being to unite the now-Islamized countries into a global caliphate. Accordingly, the Brotherhood seeks as an organization to become "rooted in the spirits and minds of [the] people" and then to establish "organizations on which the Islamic structure is built." The memo states

---

28   US Palestine Committee, transcript of meeting of US Palestine Committee leaders in Philadelphia, October 1993, available at: http://nefafoundation.org/miscellaneous/HLF/93Philly_12.pdf (accessed January 26, 2011).

29   Mohammed Akram, "An Explanatory Memorandum on the General Strategic Goal for the Group in North America," internal memorandum (Muslim Brotherhood, May 22, 1991), available at: www.nefafoundation.org/miscellaneous/HLF/Akram_GeneralStrategicGoal.pdf (accessed January 26, 2011).

that Muslims should look upon this mission as a "Civilization *Jihadist* responsibility," one that "lies on the shoulders of Muslims [but especially on those of] the Muslim Brotherhood in this country."The memo clarifies that "jihad" aims to spread the Brotherhood's politicized version of Islam as an alternative to the West's existing political system. It lists various tactical and strategic methods to merge the various organizations (educational, women's, political, professional, business, youth, scientific, and media groups) established in conjunction with the Brotherhood across the United States to reach the following goal:

> The Ikhwan must understand that their work in America is a kind of grand *jihad* in eliminating and destroying the Western civilization from within and "sabotaging" its miserable house by their hands and the hands of the believers so that it is eliminated and God's religion is made victorious over all other religions.[30]

Other internal documents of the Brotherhood and its US affiliates shed light on the Islamist network's tactical use of American values and conceptions of political correctness to subvert the country's democratic institutions in pursuit of sharia rule. According to evidence from the HLF case, at a secret 1993 meeting of Hamas members and sympathizers in Philadelphia, the HLF's chief executive Shukri Abu Baker suggested that US Islamist groups speak about "democracy and freedom of expression" to deflect scrutiny from their politically subversive agenda. Arguing "war is deception," he urged that "caution should be practiced not to reveal our true identity." Future CAIR chairman Omar Ahmad, also present at the meeting, compared the HLF's Islamists' modus operandi to that of a person "who plays basketball; he makes a player believe that he is doing this while he does something else," and asserted that "politics is a completion of war." Another participant agreed on the strategy of deceiving Americans by seeming to embrace their values, of "playing a very important tune to the average American which is the issue of democracy, the issue of representation."[31]

Despite CAIR's vociferous public demands that Muslims be accorded tolerance and "Muslim cultural values" be respected, CAIR's private messages reflect the intolerance of religious diversity and pluralism at the core of Islamist ideology. In 1998, during a speech entitled "How Should

---

30   Mohammed Akram, "An Explanatory Memorandum."
31   US Palestine Committee, transcript of meeting.

We Live as Muslims in America?" Ahmad urged Muslims not to assimilate into American society, but instead "to deliver the message of Islam." Islam should not seek to be equal to any other faith in the United States, Ahmad argued; Islam must become the country's dominant religion, and the Qur'an the highest authority, in preparation for Islam's eventual emergence as the only accepted religion on earth.[32] Ibrahim Hooper, CAIR's communications director, also expressed his wish to overturn the US system of government in favor of an Islamic state. "I wouldn't want to create the impression that I wouldn't like the government of the United States to be Islamic sometime in the future," Hooper said in a 1993 interview with the *Minneapolis StarTribune*. "But I'm not going to do anything violent to promote that. I'm going to do it through education."[33] By "education," Hooper most likely meant Muslim Brotherhood indoctrination.

Islamists have blended an appeal to democratic values with this totalitarian mindset to gain control of mosques and Islamic centers established by non-Islamist Muslims in the United States. In keeping with the Brotherhood's bottom-up approach, Islamists initiated this takeover by first joining the boards of these institutions. As the numbers of Islamists increased on these bodies, they gradually pushed out remaining non-Islamist board members, which allowed them to purge non-Islamist imams from mosques, schools, and centers. Since the 1980s, Islamists have used this methodology to gain control of dozens of mosques and Islamic organizations across the United States,[34] allowing them to establish their

---

32   Lisa Gardiner, "American Muslim Leader Urges Faithful to Spread Islam's Message," *San Fernando Valley Herald* (July 4, 1998), available at: http://anti-cair-net.org/AhmadStateScanned.pdf (accessed January 26, 2011).

33   Lou Gelfand, "Reader Says Use of 'Fundamentalist' Hurting Muslims," *Minneapolis Star Tribune* (April 4, 1993), available at: www.anti-cair-net.org/HooperStarTrib (accessed January 26, 2011).

34   There are countless examples of these takeovers throughout the United States, dating back to the arrival of Islamists on American soil. To give just three: the 1982 radical seizure of the Bridgeview Mosque — originally founded by just 30 families from the West Bank village of Zeitunia — on Chicago's South Side (see Noreen Ahmed-Ullah, Sam Roe, and Laurie Cohen, "A Rare Look at Secretive Muslim Brotherhood in America," *Chicago Tribune* [September 19, 2004], available at: www.chicagotribune.com/news/watchdog/chi-0409190261sep19,0,3008717.story [accessed January 25, 2011]); the 2005 overthrow of the moderate directors of the Islamic Center of New England in the Boston suburb of Quincy, Massachusetts (see Yvonne Abraham and Stephen Kurkjia, "Praised as Beacon, Mosque Project Stalls Amid Rancor," *Boston Globe* [December 18, 2005], available at: www.boston.com/news/local/massachusetts/articles/2005/12/18/praised_as_beacon_mosque_project_stalls_amid_rancor/ [accessed January 26, 2011]); and the 2010 transformation of

extreme and politicized interpretation of Islam as mainstream Islamic thinking for American Muslims.[35]

Saudi Arabia's Critical Support for Islamists in the United States

Islamist activists received significant support in their takeover of Islamic organizations in the United States from the government of Saudi Arabia, especially from its embassy in Washington, DC. Beginning in the 1960s, the Saudi government and embassy financed the Brotherhood-affiliated organizations previously described. They paid millions of dollars to disseminate Islamist literature in US prisons, Islamic schools, and Wahhabi-run mosques.[36] Such materials have included textbooks, Wahhabi translations of the Qur'an, and theological works presenting the Wahhabis' calling for "true Muslims" to promote the seventh-century legal and social norms entailed in sharia to modern American society. A former US Treasury official estimated that, during the 1980s and 90s, Saudi Arabia's government contributed $75 billion to support Islamist causes worldwide.[37] In 1998, Saudi Arabia's Islamic Development Bank contributed $250,000 to the purchase of land for CAIR's headquarters in Washington, DC.[38] Many

---

the formerly inclusive and diverse Muslim Unity Center congregation in Bloomfield Hills, Michigan (outside Detroit), into a nexus of radical activity.

35   According to an undercover study by the Washington-based Center for Security Policy, a significant majority of American mosques have ties to the Muslim Brotherhood and Saudi supporters, and contain materials that teach hatred of the West and the need to establish sharia law in the United States. David Yerushalmi, *Mapping Sharia in America* (Washington, DC: Center for Security Policy, 2008); WorldNetDaily, "Study: 3 in 4 U.S. Mosques Preach Anti-West Extremism: Secret Survey Exposes Widespread Radicalism," *WorldNetDaily* (February 23, 2008), available at: www.wnd.com/index.php?pageId=57141 (accessed January 26, 2011).

36   Center for Religious Freedom, *Saudi Publications on Hate Ideology Invade American Mosques* (Washington, DC: Center for Religious Freedom, 2005), available at: http://crf.hudson.org/files/publications/2005%20Saudi%20Report.pdf (accessed January 26, 2011).

37   David B. Ottaway, "U.S. Eyes Money Trails of Saudi-Backed Charities," *Washington Post* (August 19, 2004), available at: www.washingtonpost.com/ac2/wp-dyn/A13266–2004Aug18?language=printer (accessed January 26, 2011); David Aufhauser, testimony before the United States Senate Committee on Homeland Security and Governmental Affairs, June 15, 2004.

38   Royal Embassy of Saudi Arabia Washington, DC, "IDB Approves New Projects Worldwide," Royal Embassy of Saudi Arabia Washington, DC (August 15, 1998), available at: www.saudiembassy.net/archive/1998/news/page199.aspx (accessed January 27,

similar efforts to promote Wahhabism in the United States were led by the Islamic Affairs Department of the Saudi Embassy in Washington. At its height in the late 1990s, the department had 35–40 diplomats and an annual budget of $8 million, according to a Saudi official.[39] The embassy also made significant contributions in that period to the local branch of a Saudi-based charity called the International Islamic Relief Organization (IIRO), which shut its US offices (located in Falls Church, Virginia) in 2002. The US government has publicly revealed the IIRO's connection to terrorist financing since then; for example, the US Department of the Treasury designated IIRO's Indonesian and Philippine offices as terrorist funders in 2006.[40] The IIRO was also implicated in funding the 1993 World Trade Center bombing, as well as the 1998 bombing of the US embassies in Kenya and Tanzania.[41] The group has recently reestablished a presence in the United States, incorporating in Florida in 2009.

Official Saudi support for Islamist education and activism continued well after the terrorist attacks of September 11, 2001. The Islamic Saudi Academy (ISA), an Islamic high school in Fairfax County, Virginia, founded by royal decree of King Fahd in 1984, continues to be financed by the Saudi Arabian government; the school's board is chaired by Saudi Arabia's ambassador to the United States. For over two decades, ISA's Islamic studies textbooks taught "the same Wahhabi interpretation of Islam that is taught in Saudi Arabia and in Saudi-funded madrassas around the world."[42] As late as 2006, the school was using textbooks prepared by the Saudi Ministry of Education, which contained passages that were anti-Semitic, anti-Christian, and intolerant of non-Islamist Muslim groups, and

---

2011); Marina Jimenez and Omar El Akkad, "Values at Heart of Islamic Tensions," *Toronto Globe and Mail* (November 8, 2005), p. A12, available at: http://muslim-chronicle.blogspot.com/2006/08/globe-and-mail-exposes-how-isna-hides-5.html (accessed January 27, 2011).

39   Ottaway, "U.S. Eyes Money Trails of Saudi-Backed Charities."

40   US Department of the Treasury, "Treasury Designates Director, Branches of Charity Bankrolling Al Qaida Network," press release (August 3, 2006), available at: http://web.archive.org/web/20080709122147re_/www.treas.gov/press/releases/hp45.htm (accessed February 13, 2011).

41   Immigration and Refugee Board of Canada, *Egypt: The International Islamic Relief Organization (IIRO) and Whether It is Involved in Funding Terrorist Activities*, EGY41087.E (January 28, 2003), available at: www.unhcr.org/refworld/docid/3f7d4d901c.html (accessed January 27, 2011).

42   Nina Shea and Ali Al-Ahmed, "Hide and Seek," *National Review Online* (August 3, 2009), available at: http://article.nationalreview.com/401913/hide-and-seek/nina-shea-and-ali-al-ahmed (accessed January 27, 2011).

that advocated violence against converts from Islam to other religions.[43] In a groundbreaking 2006 study for Freedom House, Nina Shea (a member of the United States Commission on International Religious Freedom and now a senior fellow at the Hudson Institute) exposed the hate-filled, extremist teachings of the ISA's curriculum: in Islamic studies classes, for instance, students learned that there will be no day of judgment "until Jesus Christ returns to earth, breaks the cross and converts everyone to Islam, and until Muslims start attacking Jews."[44] Shea's updated study in 2008 found that while many of the most egregious examples had been deleted from the ISA's textbooks, they remain part of the curriculum in schools in Saudi Arabia despite promises by the Saudi authorities to the US government in 2006 that they would be removed.[45]

The ISA, one of 20 Islamist schools around the world funded by Saudi Arabia's government, plays an important role in indoctrinating young Muslims with Islamism's politicized and hate-filled interpretation of Islam. One graduate of the school, Ahmed Omar Abu Ali, was convicted in late 2005 of plotting to kill President George W. Bush. Abu Ali, who was the valedictorian of his class, had also participated in paintball sessions organized by the "Virginia Jihad" group of Ali al-Tamimi, an Islamist who was sentenced to life in prison without parole in April 2005 after being convicted of conspiracy, attempting to aid the Taliban, soliciting treason, soliciting others to wage war against the United States, and aiding and abetting the use of firearms and explosives.[46] While a student at the ISA,

---

43   For example, the Saudi Ministry of Education's textbooks stated "the Jews and Christians are enemies of the believers" and that "the apes are Jews, the people of the Sabbath; while the swine are Christians, the infidels of the communion of Jesus" (quoted in Center for Religious Freedom of Freedom House and Institute for Gulf Affairs, *Saudi Arabia's Curriculum of Intolerance: With Excerpts from Saudi Ministry of Education Textbooks for Islamic Studies* [Washington, DC: Center for Religious Freedom, 2006], pp. 24–5, available at: http://crf.hudson.org/files/publications/CRF_SaudiReport_2006.pdf [accessed January 27, 2011]).

44   Center for Religious Freedom of Freedom House and Institute for Gulf Affairs, *Saudi Arabia's Curriculum of Intolerance*, pp. 17–25.

45   Center for Religious Freedom of the Hudson Institute with the Institute for Gulf Affairs, *2008 Update: Saudi Arabia's Curriculum of Intolerance; With Excerpts from Saudi Ministry of Education Textbooks for Islamic Studies* (Washington, DC: Center for Religious Freedom, 2008), available at: www.hudson.org/files/pdf_upload/saudi_textbooks_final.pdf (accessed January 27, 2011).

46   Jerry Markon, "Muslim Lecturer Sentenced to Life: Followers Trained for Armed Jihad," *Washington Post* (July 14, 2005), available at: www.washingtonpost.com/wp-dyn/content/article/2005/07/13/AR2005071302169_pf.html (accessed January 27, 2011).

Abu Ali taught Islamic classes at the Dar al-Hijrah Mosque (also located in Fairfax County), a hotbed of Islamist activism. Run by Shaker Elsayed, the former secretary general of the Muslim American Society, it included among its worshippers two of the September 11 hijackers.[47] A prominent imam at the mosque was Islamist radical Anwar al-Awlaki, who served as a "spiritual advisor" to September 11 hijackers Nawaf al-Hazmi and Khalid al-Midhar, and who communicated with the perpetrator of the November 2009 massacre at Fort Hood, Major Nidal Hasan.

Until the terror attacks of September 11, 2001, the US government neither investigated nor discouraged Saudi Arabia's active support for Islamists and Islamist institutions like the ISA. In fact, following the Iranian Revolution in 1979, Washington often encouraged Saudi Arabia's Sunnis to proselytize on behalf of Wahhabism as a counterweight to Iran's Shiite radicalism. The government believed this approach could contain the strategic threat of Iran without causing the US to appear anti-Islamic. With Saudi Arabia's support, Wahhabis gained US trust, portraying themselves as fundamentalists equivalent to Protestants and Evangelicals, who sought to cleanse their religion by returning to its purest form.

Washington's failure to recognize the strategic threat to democracy and democratic values that Saudi-supported Wahhabism posed in the United States reflected a broader failure to perceive the dangerous spread of Islamism globally. The United States actively supported Islamist mujahedeen against the Soviet Army during the Soviet-Afghan War of 1979–1989. This US support laid the foundation for the rise of the Taliban, Islamist extremists who imposed a brutal regime on their fellow Afghani Muslims and later came back to haunt the United States by offering a safe haven to al-Qaeda. Late in the Cold War, Islamists used the US government as their proxy, viewing the Soviet Union as their "harder enemy," whose defeat they welcomed by their "softer enemy," the United States. By the time the Americans had come to believe that the end of the Cold War marked, in the words of Francis Fukuyama, the "end of history," the Islamists had grown into a potent force.[48] During the next decade, they would launch dramatic terrorist attacks against New York's World Trade Center (1993), the US embassies in Kenya and Tanzania (1998), and the USS *Cole* in Yemen (2000), before attacking the World

---

47   James Dao and Eric Lichtblau, "Case Adds to Outrage for Muslims in Northern Virginia," *New York Times* (February 27, 2005), available at: www.nytimes.com/2005/02/27/national/nationalspecial3/27terror.html?pagewanted=all (accessed January 27, 2011).

48   Francis Fukuyama, "The End of History," *National Interest* 16 (Summer 1989), pp. 3–16.

Trade Center and Pentagon in 2001. Meanwhile, Washington remained oblivious to the rise of Islamist ideology within US society, reassured by its ally Saudi Arabia that Wahhabis and their Islamist partners remained loyal allies of the United States.

The United States awakened from this complacency after September 11, 2001, when 19 hijackers (15 of them Saudi Arabian citizens) flew commercial airliners into the World Trade Center and Pentagon. Despite Washington's geopolitical and geoeconomic alliance with Riyadh, President George W. Bush began to scrutinize Wahhabi and other Islamist activities in the United States and around the globe, and the US government began to investigate and prosecute Islamist activists for violating US law. One prominent case was that of Abdurahman Alamoudi, known to Washington insiders as a "moderate Muslim," who was chosen by the US Department of Defense in 1991 to select Muslim chaplains for the US military. Alamoudi even met with President Clinton and then–presidential candidate George W. Bush in the late 1990s. In 2004, Alamoudi was convicted on terrorism charges for planning to kill Saudi King Fahd and sentenced to 23 years in prison.[49] Alamoudi was later identified by the US Department of the Treasury as having funneled more than $1 million to a UK-based affiliate of al-Qaeda.[50] Another prominent case was that of Sami al-Arian, the professor at the University of South Florida and self-proclaimed civil rights activist cited above for his role in establishing ISNA in the 1980s. Like Alamoudi, al-Arian met often with top US officials, including Presidents Clinton and Bush, despite being the subject of an FBI investigation (begun in 1996) into his ties to the Palestinian Islamic Jihad (PIJ), a terrorist organization. After videotapes appeared in 2001 of al-Arian speaking at rallies calling for terrorist jihad in Palestine, he was suspended from his professorship. Al-Arian was finally indicted in 2003. The judge who presided over his trial called him a "master manipulator," saying to him, "You looked your neighbors in the eyes and said you had nothing to do with the Palestinian Islamic Jihad. This trial exposed that as a lie."[51] In 2006, al-Arian pleaded guilty to conspiracy

49   US Department of Justice, "Abdurahman Alamoudi Sentenced to Jail in Terrorism Financing Case," press release (October 15, 2004), available at: www.usdoj.gov/opa/pr/2004/October/04_crm_698.htm (accessed January 27, 2011).

50   US Department of the Treasury, "Treasury Designates MIRA for Support to Al Qaida," press release JS-2632 (July 14, 2005), available at: www.treasury.gov/press-center/press-releases/Pages/js2632.aspx (accessed January 27, 2011).

51   *St. Petersburg Times*, "Judge Moody: You Are a Master Manipulator," *St. Petersburg*

to aid the PIJ and was sentenced to 57 months in prison; at the time of writing, he remains imprisoned on contempt-of-court charges in Virginia.

The Saudi Arabian government has responded to such increased scrutiny of Islamist activities by stepping up its fight against terrorism. Under King Abdullah, the Saudi government seems less supportive of Wahhabi activism as well. Indeed, King Abdullah appears worried about the Wahhabis' potential threat to the stability of his own kingdom and to the global economy. But his efforts to stem the negative impact of Wahhabi ideology may be a case of "too little, too late," as Wahhabis continue to radicalize Muslims around the world. In 2007, even after the Saudi Arabian government had ceased its official support for Wahhabism in US schools and other Islamic organizations, Wahhabi elements remained in the curriculum. The author was told by one parent of a child enrolled at a New Jersey Islamic school that he had decided to home-school his daughter so she would not be exposed to Wahhabi views and would be raised without the corruptive influence of Islamist radicalism.[52]

This New Jersey father's fears — and the similar worries of many other Muslim parents — are stoked by the efforts of Islamist organizations in the United States, such as CAIR and ISNA, who continue to portray themselves as champions of religious freedom and civil rights while intimidating their non-Islamist opponents into silence. Drawing on their extensive networks of Islamist institutions, CAIR and ISNA have grown into the two most powerful political lobbying groups among American Muslims. Members of the US Congress and officials of the Departments of State, Defense, and Justice still embrace CAIR and ISNA as mainstream — and worse, as moderate — organizations that are representative of all American Muslims. Such political clout allows CAIR and ISNA to dismiss their non-Islamist Muslim detractors as shrill, ignorant, and even anti-Muslim. Not wishing to "rock the boat," US officials tend to play along. At an open forum held by the US Department of State in 1999, moderate non-Islamist Sufi leader Shaykh Hisham Kabbani explained that most American mosques were controlled operationally and ideologically by Wahhabi extremists. He went further, declaring (correctly) that the "organizations that claim to speak on behalf of the Muslim community . . . in reality are not moderate, but extremist" and that they were spreading their ideology among American Muslim communities across the United

---

Times (May 1, 2006), available at: www.sptimes.com/2006/05/01/news_pf/State/Judge_Moody__You_are_.shtml (accessed January 27, 2011).

52   Interview with the author, Newark, New Jersey, June 21, 2007.

States.[53] In response, Kabbani, a world-renowned scholar of classical Islam, was assailed by CAIR and ISNA for his alleged Islamophobia and subsequently shunned by US Department of State officials for several years.

The fate of Kabbani underscores how the extreme has become mainstream with respect to Islamic thought in the United States. The good news is that September 11 awakened US officials (and, slightly later, their European counterparts) to the need to counter ideologies that promote terrorist violence. The bad news is that US and European officials have been slow to broaden their focus from blunting "violent extremism" to mounting a comprehensive campaign against the corrosive and subversive ideology of Islamism. Chapter 5 explores the adjustments and mistakes Western policymakers have made since the wake-up call of September 11.

---

53   Shaykh Hisham Kabbani, remarks presented at "Islamic Extremism: A Viable Threat to US National Security," open forum, US Department of State, Washington, DC, January 7, 1999. (Transcript in possession of author.)

CHAPTER 5

September 11 Awakens the West, But Islamists Advance

Al-Qaeda's brutal attacks on September 11, 2001, forced a rapid evolution in the strategic thinking of the West. For weeks, American society was frozen in a state of shock. Major television networks ceased normal programming, replacing it with continuous discussions of the attacks and their aftermath; sporting events were canceled and comedy performances were deemed inappropriate in the context of a prolonged period of national mourning. The US government's national security apparatus suddenly developed a primary focus: military response to al-Qaeda. This would consist mainly of a campaign against the terrorist group's Taliban allies in Afghanistan, which was subsequently declared a state sponsor of terrorism. Even in the immediate aftermath of the attacks, there was an understanding — in US government circles as well as in European — that the challenge facing the West was not solely military in nature. Responding to a strategic threat would require a much more comprehensive response than firing cruise missiles and sending troops. What the United States and the West needed to do was to eradicate the root causes of terror.

111

The nature of these root causes was only vaguely understood. A consensus emerged on both sides of the Atlantic that, although the terrorists who committed the September 11 attacks declared they were acting in the name of Islam, Western governments should not blame religion as the catalyst for terrorism. Many in the West believed Islam was a religion of peace. Others thought that aspects of Islam were problematic, but worried that criticizing elements of a major religion was politically incorrect. Still others remained less concerned about political correctness than about the prospect of provoking the most radical Muslims into committing further terrorist attacks. Given these uncertainties about the role of religion (and the wisdom of focusing on it), the West did not explore whether the September 11 terrorists were motivated by a common ideology, but instead focused on secular factors such as poverty, unemployment, and anti-Muslim discrimination as terrorism's root causes. The West had a responsibility, the reasoning went, to eliminate the sense of injustice that radicalized some Muslim men to fly airliners into buildings. To prevent further attacks, the West would focus its efforts on deterring violence by integrating Muslims in the West into mainstream society and reaching out to Muslims around the globe.

Though this focus was indeed important, it did not properly address the strategic threat confronting the West. Certainly, the West's failures in integrating or engaging with Muslims were tactical challenges; but the strategic challenge was the harsh utopian ideology that bound the 9/11 terrorists into a global network of millions of individuals dedicated to overthrowing existing secular legal systems along with their broad guarantees of human rights, and replacing them with a harsh interpretation of Islamic law. The West had awakened after September 11, but diagnosed only part of the problem.

Outreach Not Ideology

Less than four weeks after the World Trade Center's towers collapsed, American military forces began striking al-Qaeda terrorists and their Taliban hosts in Afghanistan under the framework of Operation Enduring Freedom (OEF). Following the rapid success of OEF's early stages, the United States and its allies launched a counterterrorism effort that was global in reach and massive in scale.

Meanwhile, many Washington policymakers and analysts focused on eradicating the root causes of terrorism. These can be grouped into two broad categories: first, social inequities such as poverty, unemployment, insufficient educational opportunities, ethnic and religious discrimination, and lack of political freedom in the broader Middle East, which caused social alienation among Muslims; second, the poor image of the United States among the world's Muslims. According to this train of thought, the two types of problems — and hence the solutions — were intimately related: as Muslims around the world realized the United States was working to alleviate the injustices that caused them to feel alienated from the West, their impressions of the United States would improve; viewed more positively by Muslims, the United States would be able to alleviate further the factors causing alienation (which drove some radical Muslims to commit acts of terrorism).

A major flaw in this view was its optimistic expectation that mere familiarity with the United States would diminish anti-American sentiment. While this optimism would eventually be discarded even at the highest levels, it endured for several years, fueled by recollection of the Cold War era. After all, the United States had won the hearts and minds of tens of millions trapped behind the Iron Curtain merely by offering them a glimpse of what American life was truly like. Likewise, it was reasoned, Muslims around the world would also become less hostile toward the United States once they saw it outside the distorting filter of Islamist propaganda. Once they discovered that American Muslims were fully integrated into US society and enjoyed the same freedoms as all other Americans, they would realize that American government and society were not fundamentally "anti-Islamic." US policymakers thus determined that "Muslim outreach" should improve the US image in the "Muslim world," which in turn would mitigate hostility toward the United States and reduce the likelihood of terrorism.

There was a fundamental problem with this effort to replicate Cold War–era public diplomacy: it was only half complete. Not only did the United States construct a positive image of itself during that period, but it also labored to *deconstruct* the propaganda of the other side. Public diplomacy was a key element of a broad counter-ideology strategy, which not only promoted the West's achievements, but highlighted the Communists' shortcomings. One key element of this effort was engagement with the citizens of Communist states to familiarize them with "the real America" and its political, economic, and cultural freedoms; another was to tell the truth about Soviet repression. Outreach was an important tactic for achieving a broader strategic goal, but not an end in itself. After September 11, on the other hand, the promotion of America abroad was not accompanied by any discussion of the flaws of Islamist ideology. For most US policymakers, the goal was operational and devoid of ideological content. US public diplomacy veterans revived familiar Cold War programs (e.g., cultural festivals, dissemination of American literature, academic exchanges), but did not tailor them to meet an ideological objective. Without any link to a broader aim of defeating Islamist ideology, however, these efforts only represented engagement for engagement's sake.

In 2002, the US Department of State launched the Shared Values Initiative to highlight what it hoped were common values shared by Muslims and Americans, and to underscore that the United States was not at war with Islam. This $15 million initiative was centered on a television campaign, developed by a private advertising firm, which illustrated the daily lives of Muslim Americans. It also featured a booklet on Muslim life in America, speaker tours, and an interactive website to promote dialogue among Muslims in the United States and abroad. The initiative was a tactical failure, as media outlets in many countries viewed the television ads as propagandist; the flagship television campaign aired only for the holy month of Ramadan in the winter of 2002–2003 and was subsequently discontinued. Following the demise of the Shared Values Initiative, the US Department of State launched the Arabic-language *Hi* magazine in July 2003 with an annual budget of $4.5 million. Designed to highlight American culture, values, and lifestyles, *Hi* was directed at Arab youth in the Middle East and North Africa and was expected to generate a more positive perception of American culture among Muslim youth. This effort failed to attract a following.[1] The US government also had high hopes for its Al-Hurra ("the free") television network, launched in February 2004 with broadcasts to many Arabic-speaking countries. Facing stiff competition from commercial television stations in the region, Al-Hurra has yet to attract a significant audience. But these programs would never succeed in achieving strategic impact, even if they had attracted large audiences, because they were designed to pursue a tactical goal. An improved US image might slow the spread of Islamism, but without exposing Islamism's weaknesses — like its rejection of democracy and basic human rights — this positive view could

---

1   The Shared Values Initiative and *Hi* magazine are discussed in United States Government Accountability Office (GAO), *Report to the Chairman, Subcommittee on Science, the Departments of State, Justice, and Commerce, and Related Agencies, Committee on Appropriations, House of Representatives: U.S. Public Diplomacy; State Department Efforts to Engage Muslim Audiences Lack Certain Communication Elements and Face Significant Challenges* (Washington, DC: GAO, 2006), available at: www.gao.gov/new.items/d06535.pdf (accessed January 27, 2011).

never replace it. In the absence of strong leadership at the political level, US public diplomacy specialists were unlikely to confront Islamism or any religious issue. For decades, they had been taught that the establishment clause of the US Constitution mandated full respect for freedom of religion in all US government programs; they were warned that any criticism of religion could lead to lawsuits. Furthermore, as Cold War veterans, they were psychologically predisposed to avoiding discussions of religion. The Cold War had been a struggle about politics, not religion; moreover, the West's respect for freedom of religion was itself a major point of contrast with the brutally atheist policies of Communist states. As a result, public diplomacy bureaucrats in the United States were unprepared to recognize that the core ideological threat to the United States in the post-9/11 world had a deep religious component — namely, Islamists' plan to impose their narrow view of Islam and draconian interpretation of sharia on the world.

By 2003, President Bush and his White House team recognized that improving the US image among Muslims was necessary but not sufficient for winning the so-called war of ideas. President Bush signaled a shift in US public diplomacy in the autumn of 2003, which aimed to adapt the tactic of Muslim outreach to the strategic challenge of Islamist ideology:

> Just as our diplomatic institutions must adapt so that we can reach out to others, we also need a different and more comprehensive approach to public information efforts that can help people around the world learn about and understand America. The war on terrorism is not a clash of civilizations. It does, however, reveal the clash inside a civilization, a battle for the future of the Muslim world. This is a struggle of ideas and this is an area where America must excel.[2]

President Bush was asserting that simply "getting to know" Americans and their society would not dissuade Islamists from hating or attacking the United States. After all, many Islamists, including Sayyid Qutb and 9/11 mastermind Khalid Sheikh Muhammad, had lived in the United States — and yet grew to despise the country.[3] The most important ideological

---

2   White House, *National Security Strategy of the United States of America* (Washington, DC: White House, 2002), p. 31, available at: www.au.af.mil/au/awc/awcgate/nss/nss_sep2002. pdf (accessed January 27, 2011).

3   Qutb became even more anti-American after his time in the United States. He wrote negatively about women dancing with men in the United States; this was a stark contrast to the positive impact jazz had on the citizens of Communist states. Khalid Sheikh

struggle in the post-9/11 world was among Muslims for the heart and soul of Islam, as Islamists strove to impose their Wahhabi-rooted interpretation of Islam everywhere. The United States would have to find a way to influence an ideological struggle in which it was a target rather than a participant.

In 2004, *The 9/11 Commission Report*, the definitive official account of the attacks, moved the Bush administration further toward recognizing Islamist ideology as the key factor contributing to radicalization and terrorism. The report warned that victory in the war against terrorism is not possible unless the United States and its allies "prevail in the longer term over the ideology that gives rise to Islamist terrorism."[4] The report cautioned that a generic description of the threat as simply "terrorism" was far too vague: "The catastrophic threat at this moment in history is more specific. It is the threat posed by *Islamist* terrorism — especially the al Qaeda network, its affiliates, and its ideology."[5] The report added:

> Usama Bin Ladin and other Islamist terrorist leaders draw on a long tradition of extreme intolerance within one stream of Islam (a minority tradition), from at least Ibn Taymiyyah, through the founders of Wahhabism, through the Muslim Brotherhood, to Sayyid Qutb. That stream is motivated by religion and does not distinguish politics from religion, thus distorting both.[6]

The report noted that the United States can help defeat the Islamists'

Muhammad was a mechanical engineering student in North Carolina in the early 1980s, and left the country convinced that the United States was morally corrupt and racist, and more convinced Islam should and would rule the world. An intelligence summary of his interrogation concluded that Khalid Shaikh Muhammad's "negative experience in the United States . . . almost certainly helped propel him on his path to becoming a terrorist . . . [It] confirmed his view that the United States was a debauched and racist country." See Peter Finn, Joby Warrick, and Julie Tate, "How a Detainee Became an Asset: Sept. 11 Plotter Cooperated after Waterboarding," *Washington Post* (August 29, 2009), p. A1, available at: www.washingtonpost.com/wp-dyn/content/article/2009/08/28/AR2009082803874. html (accessed January 27, 2011).

4   National Commission on Terrorist Attacks Upon the United States, *The 9/11 Commission Report* (New York: W. W. Norton, 2004), p. 363, available at: http://govinfo. library.unt.edu/911/report/911Report.pdf (accessed January 27, 2011).

5   National Commission on Terrorist Attacks Upon the United States, *The 9/11 Commission Report*, p. 380.

6   National Commission on Terrorist Attacks Upon the United States, *The 9/11 Commission Report*, p. 379.

political-religious ideology by offering an alternative vision of its "moral leadership in the world," and by ensuring that "America and Muslim friends can agree on respect for human dignity and opportunity." But the United States is limited in its ability to wage this ideological battle, the report stated: America's "own promotion of these messages is limited in its effectiveness simply because we are its carriers." Thus, the report concluded, non-Islamist Muslims must be the primary actors against Islamist ideologues in the battle for Islam.[7]

The White House's National Security Council, in collaboration with the US Department of State, began in early 2004 to implement these findings and thereby counter Islamism's extremist ideology.[8] Initially labeled "Muslim World Outreach," their strategy was aimed at empowering those described as "moderate Muslims" to resist and discredit Wahhabis and other extremist ideologues who manipulated the popular understanding of Islam in ways that ignored local traditions in favor of the norms of seventh-century Arabia. The White House assumed that hundreds of millions of Muslims around the world, even those who disliked the United States, nevertheless shared Washington's strategic goal of preventing Islamist ideologues from hijacking Islam with a political agenda. After all, it was Muslims who suffered most from Islamists' draconian interpretation of sharia. In October 2005, President Bush identified the differentiation between Islam and Islamism as the fundamental challenge facing the West:

> Islamic terrorist attacks serve a clear and focused ideology, a set of beliefs and goals that are evil, but not insane. Some call this evil Islamic radicalism; others, militant Jihadism; still others, Islamo-fascism. Whatever it's called, this ideology is very different from the religion of Islam. This form of radicalism exploits Islam to serve a violent, political vision: the establishment, by terrorism and subversion and insurgency, of a totalitarian empire that denies all political and religious freedom.[9]

---

7   National Commission on Terrorist Attacks Upon the United States, *The 9/11 Commission Report*, p. 393.

8   For details on The White House's Muslim World Outreach strategy, see David Kaplan, "Hearts, Minds, and Dollars: In an Unseen Front in the War on Terrorism, America is Spending Millions . . . To Change the Very Face of Islam," *US News and World Report* (April 17, 2005), available at: www.usnews.com/usnews/news/articles/050425/25roots_print.htm (accessed January 27, 2011).

9   George W. Bush, speech at the National Endowment for Democracy, Washington, DC, October 6, 2005, available at: www.presidentialrhetoric.com/speeches/10.06.05.html (accessed January 27, 2011).

Though accurate, such pointed rhetoric was difficult for many Muslims to accept, especially coming from a US president who had launched the war in Afghanistan and who spoke of an American "crusade" against terrorists. To its credit, the Bush administration recognized that the United States' lack of credibility among Muslims would require a less visible US approach. Rather than leading the ideological charge against Islamism, the US government would quietly support "moderate Muslims" already involved in the ideological fight against Islamism. Such support had to be granted indirectly; it was clear by this point that any overt US government support would discredit these moderates as American puppets. Thus, according to this strategy, Washington would discreetly provide funding to civic activists around the globe who sought to rekindle their own societies' traditional Islamic values as a shield against Islamist extremists' proselytizing. Specific programs would include developing secular schools as alternatives to Islamist madrassas; preserving, digitizing, and disseminating moderate hadiths ignored by extremists; and publishing and distributing school textbooks highlighting the indigenous religious and cultural traditions that extremists successfully sought to suppress. In addition, the United States would work with governments and business leaders in Muslim-majority countries to fund such programs directly.

Meanwhile, Washington would launch a complementary high-profile effort to advance freedom and democracy in Muslim-majority countries. The underlying goals of this effort, called the Broader Middle East and North Africa Initiative (BMENA), were to offer Muslims around the world a more hopeful (and peaceful) vision than that of Osama bin Laden and other Islamist extremists, while simultaneously portraying the United States as a partner in helping Muslims attain the same political and economic freedoms enjoyed by Americans and their Western allies. Under BMENA, Washington would use direct US government funding and multilateral diplomacy to support democratic reform across the broad region stretching from Morocco through the Middle East to Afghanistan and Pakistan. Senior US officials hoped BMENA and Muslim World Outreach would complement each other: as BMENA generated impulses for democratic reform, moderate Muslims would gain traction in their quest to protect their Islamic beliefs from Islamist ideologues.

In the end, this relatively sophisticated US approach failed, primarily due to bureaucratic inertia at home and mistrust abroad. In Washington, US public diplomacy veterans were reluctant to shift their focus from improving the US image abroad to waging ideological warfare against Islamist extremists; senior US officials balked at upsetting Islamist lobbying groups such as CAIR and ISNA. Abroad, elements in the governments of Saudi Arabia and Pakistan were uncomfortable with a US effort to weaken their own Islamist allies, while potential partners in other Muslim-majority countries resisted cooperation with an unpopular president.

Beyond these difficulties, the Bush administration faced deeper conceptual problems. Washington had not yet conducted a thorough analysis of Islamism. Except for a select few, US policymakers were largely unaware that Islamism and its intellectual founders (e.g., Ibn Abd al-Wahhab, Ibn Taymiyyah, and Ibn Hanbal) represented only one strain among dozens of traditions of Islamic thought. As a result, American officials as a group were unable to identify the crucial differences between Islamism (the ideology) and Islam (the religion). Had Washington policymakers been able to do so, they would then have been able to establish clear criteria to identify who they would engage as "moderate" Muslims — namely, those who believe Islam is compatible with democracy and universal human rights. Instead, without such ideological guidance, US officials were left to embrace any Muslim who denounced violence. This crucial mistake cleared the way for Islamists to use peaceful rhetoric to mask their political agenda of undermining the West's security and its core societal values.

Europe's Flawed Tactics

Europeans reacted to the September 11 terror attacks with an outpouring of sympathy for the United States. Though their governments initially counseled Washington to avoid the rash use of military force, they also invoked Article 5 of the North Atlantic Treaty for the first time in NATO's history, meaning that the attack on one member country (the United States) was considered an attack against all. European governments also made significant contributions to coalition military operations in Afghanistan. They did this even while considering themselves to be largely immune from the threat of similar terror attacks in their own countries, as the conventional wisdom held that the 9/11 attacks were motivated largely by Muslims' opposition to American foreign policy (especially Washington's support for Israel).

European attitudes began to shift when Islamist terrorists bombed a rush-hour commuter train in Madrid in March 2004 and London public transportation in July 2005. Suddenly, Europeans awakened to the reality that they too were threatened by terrorism in the name of Islam. Like their American counterparts, Europeans now strove to eradicate the root causes of terrorism. As in the United States, most policymakers in Europe focused on social alienation and its underlying factors (poverty, unemployment, lack of educational opportunities, ethnic/religious discrimination), which they viewed as generating a sense of injustice that fuels terrorism. Also, like their American counterparts, European government officials and civil society leaders were reluctant to explore the political-religious ideology of Islamism that was much more influential than social alienation in inciting pious Muslims to violent action. By ignoring Islamist ideology, European leaders were unable to recognize how Islamist recruiters played on European Muslims' spiritual alienation to radicalize them.

In Spain, Prime Minister José María Aznar initially blamed the bombing of March 11, 2004, on terrorists of the Basque separatist organization ETA. Aznar's attempt to place the attack in a familiar political context was understandable, given that the Madrid bombing took place just days before Spain's general election. Aznar's mistake nevertheless cost him the election. His successor, Jose Luis Rodríguez Zapatero, correctly identified the perpetrators as Islamist terrorists, but misjudged the solution to the burgeoning problem of homegrown terrorism in Europe — rather than developing a campaign to counter Islamist ideology, Zapatero sought to placate Islamists through dialogue in the form of the Alliance of Civilizations, a forum he launched with Turkish prime minister Recep Tayyip Erdogan.

After the 7/7 bombings, British prime minister Tony Blair's initial diagnosis was an accurate one: he explained that the problem was "not just the terrorists' methods, but their views . . . not only what they do, but what they think, and the thinking they would impose on others."[10] Blair's statement generated scathing criticism from Islamists, leftist intellectuals, and frightened bureaucrats in the UK, prompting the prime minister to shy away from confronting Islamist ideology. As time passed, the orthodox view — that terrorism committed by Muslims stems from their social alienation — hardened among British political and intellectual leaders. By 2009, British foreign secretary David Miliband would completely discount Islamist ideology as a driver of terrorism, and equate Islamist terrorist groups with other European terror organizations:

The idea of a "war on terror" gave the impression of a unified, transnational

---

10 Tony Blair, speech at the Labour Party national conference, Brighton, England, July 16, 2005, available at: http://news.bbc.co.uk/2/hi/uk_news/4689363.stm (accessed January 27, 2011).

enemy, embodied in the figure of Osama bin Laden and al-Qaeda. The reality is that the motivations and identities of terrorist groups are disparate. Lashkar-e-Taiba has roots in Pakistan and says its cause is Kashmir. Hezbollah says it stands for resistance to occupation of the Golan Heights. The Shia and Sunni insurgent groups in Iraq have myriad demands. They are as diverse as the 1970s European movements of the IRA, Baader-Meinhof, and ETA. All used terrorism and sometimes they supported each other, but their causes were not unified and their cooperation was opportunistic. So it is today.[11]

Miliband's response was typical of those of most Europeans, who in spite of the evidence found it hard to believe that a unified and transnational enemy existed, especially an enemy touted by President Bush and Vice President Cheney, whom many Europeans viewed as anti-Muslim ideologues.

In France, then–minister of internal affairs Nicholas Sarkozy saw the situation more clearly than Miliband. Recognizing that Islam was related to violence in France's troubled immigrant neighborhoods, he complemented a traditional law-and-order response with an invigorated campaign to reach out to France's Muslims and to assimilate them into mainstream French society. As mentioned in Chapter 3, the centerpiece of the outreach component was the establishment of an official representative body of all French Muslims, the CFCM. The council would provide a forum through which to build mutual understanding and accelerate Muslims' integration into French society. But when launching the council, Sarkozy failed to differentiate between Islamists and mainstream Muslims. This oversight cleared the way for the UOIF, a close affiliate of the Muslim Brotherhood, to dominate the council and turn it into a de facto Islamist organization. This embrace of the UOIF demoralized many non-Islamist Muslims in France, and complicated the French government's own effort to train a cadre of homegrown imams who could develop "French Islam" — that is, an interpretation of Islam that was compatible with France's democratic values of liberty, equality, and fraternity.[12]

---

11   David Miliband, "'War on Terror' was Wrong: The Phrase Gives a False Idea of a Unified Global Enemy, and Encourages a Primarily Military Reply," *Guardian* (January 15, 2009), available at: www.guardian.co.uk/commentisfree/2009/jan/15/david-miliband-war-terror/print (accessed January 27, 2011).
12   Reuters, "Uncertain Future for France's Muslim Council," Reuters (May 5, 2008), available at: http://blogs.reuters.com/faithworld/2008/05/05/uncertain-future-for-frances-muslim-council/ (accessed January 27, 2011).

The Balkenende government in the Netherlands heeded warnings from the General Intelligence and Security Service (known by its Dutch-language acronym AIVD) that Islamist recruiters were promoting both antidemocratic ideas and violent jihad among the country's Muslims. Like France, the Netherlands has also concentrated on preventing terrorist attacks and on fostering the integration of its Muslim populations. However — as described below — the political influence of Islamist groups in the country has hampered the effectiveness of these integration policies. A similar pattern was evident in Germany under the government of Chancellor Schröder.[13]

Like the Americans, European policymakers responded to Islamists' violence by adopting tactics (e.g., counterterrorism and social integration/welfare programs) but have ignored the strategic threat to Europe's security and political-legal order posed by Islamist ideology. Europeans in general shared Americans' discomfort with religious debates, especially those that would appear to be critical of Islam. In much of Western Europe — though not in the United States — secularism in the twenty-first century had come to mean freedom *from* religion more than freedom *of* religion. European leaders ignored the politically sensitive issue of spiritual alienation, and instead pressed for social integration of European Muslims through policies of multiculturalism or assimilation. Integration was a path of least resistance, which embraced all Muslims without messy debates about Islamism versus Islam; all Muslims could be "engaged" as partners, provided they renounced violence.

Thus, like their American counterparts, European officials chose not to confront the specific problem of Islamist terrorism and ignored Blair's call to focus on what their enemies thought, as well as what they did. Instead, they chose to focus on the less-precise threat of "violent extremism." This politically correct formulation avoided any suggestion that Islam might be connected to the murderous acts committed in its name, thereby obviating the distinction between Islamists and moderate Muslims. "Muslim engagement" would now be simpler to achieve, though it would consist of dialogue that ignored a crucial strategic fact: nonviolent Islamists and violent extremists have the same ideological goal: to replace

---

13   Under Chancellor Angela Merkel, however, Germany has taken a firmer line against political Islamism. As this book went to press, a serious debate was taking place in the country about radicalism and about integration issues more generally: see for example Matthew Weaver, "Angela Merkel: German Multiculturalism Has 'Utterly Failed,'" *The Guardian*, October 17, 2010, available at: http://www.guardian.co.uk/world/2010/oct/17/angela-merkel-german-multiculturalism-failed (accessed February 13, 2011).

secular democracy and respect for universal human rights with Islamic governments ruled by sharia.

European and American policy circles became flooded with proposed forums to facilitate dialogue for dialogue's sake. A key example was the forum organized by the US Embassy in Belgium in March 2006. This gathering in Brussels sought to reduce European Muslims' hostility toward the US by bringing them together with American Muslims. Embassy officials shared the hope of the US Department of State's public diplomacy specialists that once European Muslims became aware that their American coreligionists were integrated into mainstream society and enjoyed the same rights as all other Americans, anti-American hostility would begin to soften. The conference won rave reviews within the US government as the first official trans-Atlantic forum connecting American and European Muslims. Lost on many US officials was the discussion's failure to address how Islamist ideologues exploit European Muslims' spiritual alienation to gain new recruits for their campaign to undermine the West's fundamental legal and social structures. The American organizers of the conference included in the discussion representatives of the Islamist organizations CAIR, ISNA, the Muslim Public Affairs Council (MPAC), and the MSA, and even referred participants to them for follow-up discussions. This well-intended initiative thus facilitated Islamist networking efforts and helped to legitimize the very ideology that threatened the United States and its allies.

A rare example of a government conference that did in fact focus on the strategic threat of Islamism was held in The Hague in November 2006 by the US Embassy in the Netherlands.[14] This conference, entitled Diversity Dialogues, not only aimed to foster dialogue and counteract social alienation, but also to counter spiritual alienation and the spread of Islamism by focusing on the pluralism within Islam. To avoid embracing Islamist umbrella groups, participants were invited only in their individual capacity, not as representatives of any organization. Moreover, when compared especially to the Brussels conference, these participants reflected a wide range of ethnicities, professions, and religious traditions within Islam. These discussions laid the foundation for a grassroots network of non-Islamist Muslims seeking to accelerate their integration into mainstream societies while reaffirming their families' various moderate traditions of

---

14   The author was involved in the planning of this conference at the request of the late Roland Arnall, then–US ambassador to the Netherlands.

Islam, thereby countering the spiritual alienation that Islamist recruiters seek to exploit.

The Costs of Ignoring Ideology

The conference in The Hague was an exception to the more general pattern of the United States and Europe ignoring the strategic threat posed by Islamist ideology while readily engaging any Muslim who denounced violence. Islamists quickly recognized that they could divert Western leaders from scrutinizing their political ideology if they condemned terrorism and kept silent on the utopian goals they shared with violent extremists.

Islamist organizations were forced by the changes to the Western political context after September 11 to begin denouncing terrorism. As a prominent Muslim Brotherhood figure in the United States explained to the author in 2006, "9/11 hurt us; now we are under scrutiny and can't work as effectively." Only those groups involved solely in lobbying or public relations had to change their rhetoric entirely; the rest — which interacted with Muslims living in the West as well as with Western governments — simply adopted two different style guides for use in each context. One such organization is HT; though HT officially proclaims itself a nonviolent organization, just three months before September 11, an HT website declared that the methods that were used in those attacks are justified by Islamic doctrine:

> All ways and means which a Muslim uses to kill unbelievers is permitted as long as the enemy unbeliever is killed — whether they are killed by weapons from afar or if their ranks are penetrated; whether their stronghold is captured and penetrated before their eyes, or whether you blow up their planes or shoot them down; or whether you blow yourself up amongst their military encampments or blow yourself and them up with a belt of explosives. All of these are permissible means of fighting unbelievers.[15]

Omar Bakri, the founder of HT's offshoot organization, al-Muhajiroun, a group that also deems itself nonviolent, has consistently encouraged Muslims to join the global jihad by fighting in Kashmir, Afghanistan,

---

15   *Al Waie*, "Martyrdom Operations," *Al Waie*, 15(170), available at: www.al-waie.org/home/issue/170/doc/170w02doc.zip (accessed January 27, 2011). The English translation quoted here is that of Michael Whine.

and Chechnya. At least one al-Muhajiroun member traveled to Israel to engage in suicide terrorism; furthermore, 9/11-hijacker Hani Hanjour appears to have been connected to the organization. In January 2004, al-Muhajiroun's website featured this call to militant jihad:

> Those Muslims living abroad, they are not under any covenant with the *kufir* [unbeliever] in the West, so it is acceptable for them to attack the non-Muslims in the West whether in retaliation for constant bombing and murder taking place all over the Muslim world at the hands of the non-Muslims, or if it is an offensive attack in order to release the Muslims from the captivity of the *kufir*. For them, attacks such as the September 11 hijackings [are] a viable option in jihad.[16]

Due to their inflammatory nature, these types of statements tend to be disseminated privately, through narrowly targeted websites or via networks of extremist recruiters. In this way, Islamist organizations can reach Muslims in the West who are feeling both spiritual and social alienation while avoiding any negative attention from their "counterterrorism partners" in Western governments. The religious content of the messages helps the spiritually alienated find answers to their questions about their Muslim identity, while the political content spurs them to action. Thus, even nonviolent Islamist groups serve as a conveyor belt to terrorism for a growing number of radicalized Muslims. Without such radical propaganda, it is inconceivable that a British citizen like Mohammad Sidique Khan, born and raised in the UK, would have become a terrorist. Shortly before Khan killed scores of his fellow citizens (and himself) on July 7, 2005, he made a videotape in which he explained his imminent actions:

> Until we [Muslims] feel security, you [the rest of the British society] will be our targets. And until you stop the bombing, gassing, imprisonment and torture of my people, we will not stop this fight. We are at war and I am a soldier.[17]

---

16   www.muhajiroun.com, "Al-Jihad," editorial (2004), originally published at www.muhajiroun.com (accessed January 29, 2004; the site is no longer functioning. For evidence that al-Mujahiroun provided recruits for training in camps run by Osama bin Laden in Pakistan and Afghanistan, see Mateen Siddiqui, "The Doctrine of Hizb ut-Tahrir" and Michael Whine, "Hizb ut-Tahrir in Open Society," in Zeyno Baran, ed., *The Challenge of Hizb ut-Tahrir: Deciphering and Combating Radical Islamist Ideology* (Washington, DC: Nixon Center, 2004), pp. 1–32, 99–109.

17   Anton La Guardia and Neil Tweedle, "We Are at War: I am a Soldier," *Telegraph*

Khan's farewell statement, delivered in English with a distinctive Yorkshire accent, provides a window into how Islamist ideology transforms the mindset of Muslims in the West. Over time, Khan had come to identify with Muslims as a separate global community. As his fellow citizens became an "enemy" whose killing was justifiable, he stopped viewing himself as British. This dramatic change in worldview was justified by a narrowly limited interpretation of Islam — and could not have occurred in the absence of the political ideology that is Islamism.

The majority of Islamists in the West reject violence. But they share the legal, political, and social goals of their fellow Islamists who do espouse violence. All Islamist leaders follow the same strategic plan, as outlined by Muslim Brotherhood theorist Qutb in his seminal work *Milestones*. Their goal is to Islamize secular societies in a step-by-step, grassroots process. According to this plan, Muslims should set themselves apart from mainstream society rather than become loyal citizens of the countries in which they live. Muslims should adjust their social norms to consolidate themselves into a single and separate community; they should ignore their ethnic differences and consider "Muslim" as their primary identity. In Muslim-majority countries, Islamist leaders encourage this separation by suppressing not only apparently Western customs, but also distinctive local customs — anything not derived from the seventh-century Arabian practices that Islamists view as the only legitimate example for Muslims. For example, Wahhabi Islamists reject music, dancing, singing, theater, and virtually all other secular traditions. In Afghanistan and northwest Pakistan, local Islamist leaders have banned kite flying and associated festivals because they supposedly foster un-Islamic behavior.[18] In Western countries, Islamists urge the Muslim community to strengthen itself by seeking equal rights and benefits with non-Muslims, while cautioning them that such equality is not an end in itself; their primary allegiance is to the Muslim community rather than to the country in which they reside.

Integration of Muslims into mainstream society thus runs contrary to Islamist ideology, but remains a primary focus of Western policy. Since urging Western governments to abandon this goal would fail, Islamist organizations like the Muslim Brotherhood have instead focused on reshaping the Western understanding of the term "integration." They

---

(September 2, 2005), available at: www.telegraph.co.uk/news/worldnews/middle east/1497473/We-are-at-war-I-am-a-soldier.html (accessed January 27, 2011).
18   Nicolas Brulliard, "The Kite Stunner: Authorities Ground a Popular Festival Tradition," *Washington Post* (March 22, 2010), p. A9.

call for Europeans and Americans to "accept" the Muslims in their midst — but as "Muslims first" and not as fellow citizens. HT has made public statements warning that integration can be "dangerous," and has urged British Muslims to "fight assimilation into British society."[19] Islamists thus press various Muslim groups to become a unified community, and they use the political institutions and rhetoric of mainstream society to undermine the countries where they reside, with the aim of eventually demanding sharia rule. Over time, as similar Islamization processes occur in other countries, Islamized societies would eventually consolidate into the *umma* ruled by a caliphate according to a restrictive interpretation of sharia. Typical of this Islamist mindset are the views of Hamza Andreas Tzortzis, an outwardly nonviolent Islamist academic and supporter of Hamas:

> We as Muslims reject the idea of freedom of speech, and even the idea of freedom. We see under the Khilafa [caliphate], when people used to engage in a positive way, this idea of freedom was redundant, it was unnecessary, because the society understood [that] under the education system of [the] Khilafa state, and under the political framework of Islam, . . . people must engage with each other in a positive and productive way to produce results, as the Qur'an says, to get to know [one] another.[20]

Rejecting the very notion of freedom as superfluous, Tzortzis argues that Muslims should prepare for a return to the "political framework of Islam" as it existed under the caliphate. His statement sharply underscores the political nature of Islamist ideology, as it aspires to reshape modern social and political institutions to reflect the norms of Arabia in the first millennium.

Similarly blunt are the internal pronouncements of the Islamic Forum of Europe (IFE), a British group that has placed its members in staff positions in government agencies and political parties. A Channel 4 television documentary featured an IFE leaflet claiming that the organization is

---

19   Andrew Gilligan, "Islamists Who Want to Destroy the State Get £100,000 Funding, *Telegraph* (October 25, 2009), available at: www.telegraph.co.uk/news/uknews/6427369/Islamists-who-want-to-destroy-the-state-get-100000-funding.html (accessed January 27, 2011).

20   Hamza Andreas Tzortzis, "Stand for Islam," lecture, London, April 23, 2008, available at: www.hizb.org.uk/hizb/in-the-community/community-events/event-hamza-tzortzis-speaks-on-refutation-of-secular-beliefs-and-proof-of-quran-in-central-london.html (accessed June 28, 2010).

dedicated to changing "the very infrastructure of society, its institutions, its culture, its political order, and its creed from ignorance to Islam." One speaker at an IFE event explained that "our goal is to create the True Believer; to then mobilize these believers into an organized force for change who will carry out *da'wa* [preaching], *hisbah* [enforcement of Islamic law], and jihad. This will lead to social change." Another IFE pamphlet reads, "The Islamic Forum of Europe strives for the establishment of a global society, the Khilafah [caliphate], based on truth and justice." An IFE radio talk-show host said that if democracy can be maintained only "at the expense of not implementing the sharia, no one's going to agree with that."[21]

In their public pronouncements to wider audiences, European Islamists are more circumspect. When appealing to Western officials and other non-Muslims, Islamists couch their demands for a separate, parallel Muslim community in the Western rhetoric of diversity and cultural rights. The Arab European League, a Muslim advocacy group operating in Belgium and the Netherlands, states as its vision: "We believe in a multicultural society as a social and political model where different cultures coexist with equal rights under the law." In other words, the League demands specific rights for Muslims that would allow them to "coexist" separately but equally with their non-Muslim fellow citizens; integration into mainstream society on the basis of a shared national citizenship is contrary to this goal. Its founder, Dyab Abou Jahjah, has vociferously attacked this notion, calling assimilation "cultural rape," because "it means renouncing your identity, becoming like the others."[22]

In the United States in the 1990s, as mentioned in Chapter 4, the Muslim Brotherhood's local organizations outlined their ideological strategy in an internal memorandum. Brotherhood members

> must understand their work in America is a kind of grand *jihad* in eliminating and destroying the Western civilization from within and "sabotaging" its miserable house by their hands and the hands of the believers so that it is eliminated and God's religion is made victorious over all other religions.[23]

---

21   Channel 4, "Britain's Islamic Republic," *Dispatches* (Channel 4 [UK], 2010). Information about this episode is available at: www.channel4.com/programmes/dispatches/episode-guide/series-54/episode-1 (accessed January 27, 2011).

22   Marlise Simons, "An Outspoken Arab in Europe: Demon or Hero?" *New York Times* (March 1, 2003), available at: www.nytimes.com/2003/03/01/world/the-saturday-profile-an-outspoken-arab-in-europe-demon-or-hero.html (accessed January 27, 2011).

23   Mohammed Akram, "An Explanatory Memorandum on the General Strategic Goal for

Of course, neither the Muslim Brotherhood nor its key US affiliates like CAIR repeat such statements in public. Like their European counterparts, Islamist organizations in the United States disingenuously use American political rhetoric to advance their agenda, denouncing violence in order to deter US government scrutiny of their ideology. Their calls for equal rights for Muslim Americans may sound like a push for integration; but their underlying goal is to separate Muslim from non-Muslim Americans. Consider the statement of CAIR's executive director, Nihad Awad, in August 2008:

> We have about 600 lawyers today in the United States who are Muslim. And that's very important. In fact we encourage Islamic centers, in addition to raising funds for their own centers, to ... give scholarship[s to] five students every year to encourage them to pursue the field of journalism, law, humanities, political science, and whatever, American history or something like that. If 2,000 mosques nationwide do this, persistently with a positive and hopeful vision, then it can be done. Imagine if we do it nationwide; five years from now you will have an army of lawyers, you will have an army of politicians, and an army of journalists, an army of teachers who go to schools, universities and can educate people about the history of Islam and the true Islam.[24]

As in Europe, few US officials recognize the true meaning that cloaks itself in the Islamists' democratic-sounding rhetoric. They assume that all Muslim Americans are loyal to the United States and believe that CAIR, ISNA, and other Islamist organizations are concerned with ensuring that Muslim Americans enjoy equal rights with all other Americans. How do Islamists maintain this deception? One way is by claiming that Islamism is the same thing as Islam. Representative Keith Ellison of Minnesota, a convert to Islam and the very first Muslim member of Congress, openly embraces Islamism. In April 2007, the author asked Congressman Ellison if he would be using his elected position to counter Islamist ideology. He replied, "You must be an immigrant if you ask me this question. In the US, we don't differentiate Islam from Islamism. We are all Islamists here."[25]

---

the Group in North America," internal memorandum (Muslim Brotherhood, May 22, 1991), available at: www.nefafoundation.org/miscellaneous/HLF/Akram_GeneralStrategicGoal. pdf (accessed January 26, 2011).

24   Nihad Awad, speech at CAIR banquet, Houston, TX, August 23, 2008.

25   This exchange occurred after a meeting at the Rayburn House Office Building entitled

Similarly, in 2005, a staffer of the US Department of State who worked for Under Secretary for Public Diplomacy Karen Hughes, in charge of the government's "Muslim engagement" efforts, told the author, "You are not a real Muslim," presumably because the author's secular clothing and views were different from what the Islamists had described to him as appropriate for "real" Muslim women.[26]

Convinced by CAIR and ISNA that Islamism is the same thing as moderate Islam, American officials have thus worked to spread it. US Department of State exchange programs routinely bring foreign Muslims to the United States and put them in contact with Islamists recommended by these organizations. A US Embassy official working on such exchange programs in Jakarta told the author of the surprising report of an Indonesian imam who had traveled to the United States as part of a government-funded program: with horror, the imam related that he had met more Wahhabi Muslims in America over the course of a week than he had in his entire life in Indonesia. He also warned that these programs make it much harder for people like him to prevent the spread of Wahhabi ideology in Indonesia.

Another tactic Islamists use in the West to deflect scrutiny and advance their ideological agenda is to secure employment in political and government organizations. Once inside, Islamists can gain the trust of officials and try to skew policies to advance their political, legal, and social agenda. In February 2010, the British member of parliament James Fitzpatrick (then environment minister) revealed that IFE members had infiltrated British political parties:

> They are . . . placing people within the political parties, recruiting members to those political parties, trying to get those individuals selected and elected so they can exercise political influence and power, whether it's at local government level or at national level.[27]

August Hanning, the state secretary for the interior ministry and former director of the secret intelligence service (*Bundesnachrichtendienst*)

"Islam and Democracy: Promoting Dialogue and Political Participation among Muslims in Western Societies," April 25, 2007.

26 The remark was made after a presentation the author gave at the Nixon Center, Washington, DC, December 22, 2005.

27 Andrew Gilligan, "Islamic Radicals 'Infiltrate' the Labour Party," *Telegraph* (February 27, 2010), available at: www.telegraph.co.uk/news/newstopics/politics/labour/7333420/Islamic-radicals-infiltrate-the-Labour-Party.html (accessed January 27, 2011).

in Germany, had warned over a year before that Islamist activists who collaborate with terrorists appeared to have insinuated themselves into Germany's mainstream political life. Hanning cited the case of Bekkay Harrach, a German citizen and Islamist radical, who appeared in an al-Qaeda video entitled "A Bailout Plan for Germany" in October 2008. In this film, he displays a detailed understanding of the domestic political issues surrounding Germany's military engagement in Afghanistan and calls for German voters to support parties that favor withdrawal. Confronted with an extremist who "knows our home affairs, and who knows the internal conditions here," Hanning concluded that Germany faces "a new quality of threat."[28]

Hanning's concern that Islamists with knowledge of domestic affairs pose serious security risks has been the exception. Many of his official counterparts have instead embraced Islamists as partners in implementing counterterrorism and social integration policies that contradict Islamists' strategic goals. The most egregious examples occurred in the UK. In 2002, Scotland Yard established the Muslim Contact Unit (MCU) to manage outreach to Muslims; this unit promptly formed partnerships with some of the most radical individuals within London's large Salafi community. The first head of the MCU, Robert Lambert, publicly advocated "police negotiation leading to partnership with Muslim groups conventionally deemed to be subversive to democracy."[29] According to Lambert, only these groups have the credibility to challenge al-Qaeda's violent narrative and influence young Muslims.[30] Lambert argued that although nonviolent or political Salafis might have views that contradict the feelings of most British citizens, this factor is outweighed by their ability to prevent young men from becoming terrorists.[31] Under Lambert's leadership, Scotland Yard worked with Mohamed Ali Harrath, an Islamist extremist wanted by Interpol since 1992 for his links to the Tunisian Islamic Front (FIT), a radical Islamist organization that seeks to replace Tunisia's secular government with an Islamist state — by force if necessary. Scotland Yard

---

28 Antje Kraschinski, *Al-Qaida's "A Bailout Plan for Germany": A NEFA Analysis; February 10, 2009* (New York: NEFA Foundation, 2009), available at: www.nefafoundation. org/newsite/file/FeaturedDocs/nefa_harrach0209.pdf (accessed January 27, 2011).

29 Robert Lambert, "Empowering Salafis and Islamists Against Al-Qaeda: A London Counterterrorism Case Study," *Political Science and Politics* 41(1): 31–5 (31).

30 See Lorenzo Vidino, "Europe's New Security Dilemma," *Washington Quarterly* 32(4): 61–75 (68), available at: www.twq.com/09october/docs/09oct_Vidino.pdf (accessed January 27, 2011).

31 Lambert, "Empowering Salafis and Islamists Against Al-Qaeda," 31–4.

appointed Harrath to the MCU as an advisor on preventing extremism and terrorism. In a letter of support, Lambert wrote that Harrath had made a "key contribution to our efforts to defeat the adverse influence of al-Qaeda in the UK."[32]

Beyond Scotland Yard, other British leaders have repeatedly partnered with prominent Islamists whose harsh public statements undermine British values and Western values generally. For example, while serving as mayor of London, Ken Livingstone hosted Muslim Brotherhood spiritual leader Yusuf al-Qaradawi, who has praised suicide bombing as a legitimate means of defending Islam, and British (as well as other European and American) officials have hailed Tariq Ramadan as a "moderate," even though he refused during a television interview to unconditionally condemn the stoning of women, because sharia — as Ramadan interprets it — condones this brutal form of public execution.[33] The British Foreign and Commonwealth Office works closely with the MCB to help design and implement "Muslim outreach" programs.[34] This is despite the fact that MCB head Sir Iqbal Sacranie has done much to increase tensions between Muslims and non-Muslims in the UK. One of Sacranie's preferred rhetorical tactics is to invoke Muslims' status as victims. In January 2005, the British government held an official ceremony at Westminster Hall to mark the sixtieth anniversary of the liberation of Auschwitz and other Nazi death camps, with the Queen, the Duke of Edinburgh, and then–Prime Minister Tony Blair in attendance. Though invited, Sacranie boycotted the ceremony because it "excludes ongoing genocide and human rights abuses around the world and in the occupied territories of Palestine," including what Sacranie termed "the holocaust of the Palestinian *intifada*."[35]

Although others echoed Sacranie's tone in the MCB, the group still

32   Richard Kerbaj and Dominic Kennedy, "Terrorism Adviser to Met is on Wanted List: Interpol Notice Urges Arrest of Islam TV Chief," *Times* (December 15, 2008), available at: www.timesonline.co.uk/tol/news/uk/crime/article5342730.ece (accessed January 27, 2011).

33   For Ramadan's Islamism and double-talk, see Caroline Fourest, *Brother Tariq: The Doublespeak of Tariq Ramadan* (New York: Encounter, 2008) and Paul Berman, "Who's Afraid of Tariq Ramadan? The Islamist, The Journalist, and the Defense of Liberalism," *New Republic* (June 4, 2007), available at: www.tnr.com/article/who%E2%80%99s-afraid-tariq-ramadan (accessed January 27, 2011).

34   Martin Bright, "Radical Links of UK's 'Moderate' Muslim Group," *Observer* (August 14, 2005), available at: www.guardian.co.uk/uk/2005/aug/14/religion.immigrationpolicy (accessed January 27, 2011).

35   David Leppard, "Muslims Boycott Holocaust Remembrance," *Sunday Times*

did not arouse concern among top UK officials. MCB deputy head Inayat Bunglawala spoke out in favor of suicide bombing in Israel in 2005 — yet was chosen by Downing Street as one of the heads of a Home Office task force called "Tackling Extremism Together."[36] In 2002, Bunglawala acknowledged that he had distributed literature written by Osama bin Laden, whom he regarded as a "freedom fighter";[37] Bunglawala also noted his deep respect for Maududi, who played a crucial role in spreading Islamism to South Asia: "The book that brought me to practice Islam was 'Now Let Us Be Muslims' by Maududi. As for Jamaat-i-Islami [the core Islamist group in South Asia], it is a perfectly legal body in Pakistan."[38] Bunglawala's staunch Islamist agenda was also evident in his reaction to the organization called British Muslims for Secular Democracy, which he attacked because the group's leaders declined to force women to wear the *hijab* and believed the drinking of alcohol was permitted in Islam.[39]

Meanwhile, Kamal Helbawy, a prominent Islamist who helped create the MCB, became the chairman of the Centre for the Study of Terrorism. In their anxious hunt for Muslim partners, British officials accepted Helbawy's renunciation of violence at face value. Had they investigated even briefly, however, they would have discovered Helbawy's long history of public anti-Semitism, reflected in a stunning speech he delivered at a conference of the Muslim Arab Youth Association in 1992:

> Do not take Jews and Christians as allies, for they are allies to each other ... Oh, brothers, the Palestinian cause is not a conflict of borders and land only. It is not even a conflict over human ideology and not over peace. Rather, it is an absolute clash of civilizations, between truth and falsehood. Between two conducts — one [is] satanic, headed by Jews and their co-conspirators — and the other is religious, carried by Hamas, and

(January 23, 2005), available at: www.timesonline.co.uk/tol/news/uk/article505388.ece (accessed January 27, 2011).

36 Alasdair Palmer, "Top Job Fighting Extremism for Muslim Who Praised Bomber," *Telegraph* (August 21, 2005), available at: www.telegraph.co.uk/news/uknews/1496621/Top-job-fighting-extremism-for-Muslim-who-praised-bomber.html (accessed January 27, 2011).

37 Charlotte Edwardes and Chris Hastings, "Blair-link Muslims Backed Bin Laden," *Telegraph* (March 10, 2002), available at: www.telegraph.co.uk/news/uknews/1387288/Blair-link-Muslims-backed-bin-Laden.html (accessed January 27, 2011).

38 Bright, "Radical Links of UK's 'Moderate' Muslim Group."

39 Martin Bright, "Muslim Chief Blasts Islamic Group for its 'Zionist Support,'" *Jewish Chronicle Online* (December 3, 2009), available at: www.thejc.com/news/uk-news/24557/muslim-chief-blasts-islamic-group-its-zionist-support (accessed January 27, 2011).

the Islamic movement in particular and the Islamic people in general who are behind it.[40]

This statement is not anomalous; it is typical of the rhetoric Helbawy and other Islamists use when speaking among themselves, as experienced by this Muslim author firsthand at similar Islamist gatherings.

European officials nevertheless continue to partner with Islamists on sensitive initiatives, which Islamists seek to hijack to advance their political-religious objectives. A key example is imam training. Following the September 11 attacks, European governments realized that some foreign-born imams were delivering hate-filled sermons and encouraging Muslims in Europe to segregate their communities from mainstream society. In response, several European governments decided to train a cadre of imams to develop a "European Islam" — that is, a version of Islam compatible with European culture and values, and preached in European languages. Because they failed to screen out Islamist ideologues, imam training became dominated by Islamist activists who squeezed out Muslim moderates. The training programs thus backfired, producing European-born imams who understood how to relate to fellow European Muslims — and successfully used this understanding to promote Wahhabi extremism. In the UK, the Muslim Brotherhood and its South Asian counterpart, the Deobandis (whose members committed the November 2008 terror attacks in Mumbai), have played a major role in determining which imams become accredited to preach in British mosques. Moreover, in London, following the dismissal and arrest of the notorious Egyptian cleric Abu Hamza al-Masri, who had delivered hate-filled sermons at the Finsbury Park Mosque, the UK government actually *invited* the Islamist Muslim Association of Britain (MAB) to take over the mosque in 2005.[41]

Islamists have been less successful in the United States than in Europe in gaining jobs in political parties and government organizations. Still, in several high-profile cases, Islamist activists have obtained sensitive positions by taking advantage of US officials' impulse to engage Muslims regardless of ideology. As mentioned in Chapter 4, Abdurahman Alamoudi ostentatiously denounced violence and voiced support for democracy to ingratiate himself with top US officials, who in turn conferred credibility

---

40   Kamal Helbawy, speech at the Muslim Arab Youth Association and Islamic Association for Palestine conference, Oklahoma City, OK, December 1992, transcript available at: www. investigativeproject.org/238/kamal-helbawy-maya-iap-1992 (accessed January 27, 2011).
41   For details of the example, see Vidino, "Europe's New Security Dilemma," 65–7.

on him as a prominent and respected Muslim American and cleared the way for him to found the US military's Muslim chaplaincy program. US officials apparently did not know or care that Alamoudi maintained close ties to Muslim Brotherhood and Hamas leaders, nor that he had predicted during a large Islamist gathering in Chicago that Muslims would transform the United States into an Islamic country.[42] In 2004, Alamoudi was convicted and sentenced to 23 years in prison for violating financial laws pertaining to sanctions against Libya and for participating in an al-Qaeda-linked conspiracy to assassinate King Abdullah of Saudi Arabia (who was crown prince at that time). The Muslim chaplaincy program begun by Alamoudi has nevertheless continued under the Islamist auspices of ISNA.

Leaders from Islamist organizations like ISNA and CAIR have also succeeded in insinuating themselves into powerful US government entities. In one particularly important example, ISNA obtained direct access to the highest levels of the US Department of Defense in 2005, when Hesham Islam was appointed as special assistant for international affairs to Deputy Secretary of Defense Gordon England.[43] As the point person for outreach to Islamic groups, Islam was responsible for England's decision to speak at ISNA's September 2006 convention and also facilitated the visit of an ISNA delegation to the Pentagon in April 2007.

ISNA and CAIR have shaped US policy by convincing law enforcement officials they are committed to fighting terrorism. In particular, CAIR has been able to present itself as an effective partner in fighting terrorism. Hence this statement in November 2006 by the deputy head of the FBI's Los Angeles Field Office:

> Since the tragic events of September 11, 2001, the Los Angeles FBI has worked closely with CAIR, and a multitude of other community based organizations, to develop and foster relationships that encourage an open exchange of ideas and concerns relative to the FBI's mission. In order

---

42   At the Islamic Association of Palestine's 1996 conference in Illinois, Alamoudi assured his audience that "either we do it now or we do it after a hundred years, but this country will become a Muslim country" (quoted in "Affidavit in Support of Criminal Complaint," *United States of America v. Abdurahman Muhammad Alamoudi*, US District Court for the Eastern District of Virginia, Alexandria Division, no. 03–1009M, September 30, 2003, available at: http://fl1.findlaw.com/news.findlaw.com/hdocs/docs/terrorism/us alamoudi93003cmp.pdf (accessed January 27, 2011).

43   Claudia Rosett, "Questions for the Pentagon: Who is Hesham Islam?" *National Review Online* (January 25, 2008), available at: www.nationalreview.com/articles/223495/ questions-pentagon/claudia-rosett (accessed January 27, 2011).

to prevent another act of terrorism from occurring on American soil, government agencies and communities must work together, and the FBI is extremely pleased to be partners with CAIR, and the other members of the Multi-Cultural Advisory Committee, in pursuing this mission.[44]

CAIR and ISNA, like the IFE and the MCB in the UK, as well as many other Islamist groups across Europe, have succeeded in gaining access to and jobs with key government organizations in the West by exploiting officials' desperate search for Muslims apparently willing to help in the fight against terrorism. They gain trust and spark enthusiasm among Western officials through political slogans espousing Western values and renouncing violence, and they portray themselves as uniquely equipped to understand and fight "violent extremism." This deceptive use of reassuring rhetoric to conceal their underlying intentions and ideology is an example of the Islamic principle of *taqiyya* (discussed in Chapter 2).

This Islamist approach has succeeded in the West not only with government officials, but also with academics and activists on the political left, with whom Islamists' anti-American and anti-Israeli rhetoric resonates. Like government officials, those on the left don't grasp that Islamists seek to segregate Muslims from mainstream society and to impose their interpretation of Islam on all Muslims. Instead, they see Islamists as sharing their call for "social justice," which is thought to be fully compatible with the integration of Muslims into mainstream society. In embracing the Islamist perspective, the Western left ignores the great diversity that characterizes Islamic thought and Muslim life, which is ironic in light of its own emphasis on diversity.

Many left-of-center politicians, activists, and academics accept Islamist demands to establish sharia as a parallel legal system in Europe's Muslim communities on the grounds that the principle of freedom of religion requires equal treatment for religious minorities. The archbishop of Canterbury, Dr. Rowan Williams, has argued that mainstream society should accept Islamic legal norms if it accepts Jewish legal norms (halacha): "The whole idea is that there are perfectly proper ways the law of the land pays respect to custom and community." He has further pointed

---

44 The remark is from J. Stephen Tidwell, Assistant Director, Los Angeles, California Field Office of the FBI; see J. Stephen Tidwell, quoted in CAIR, "What They Say About CAIR," CAIR (2008), available at: http://web.archive.org/web/20080708205919/http://www. cair.com/AboutUs/WhatTheySayAboutCAIR.aspx#Tidwell (accessed January 27, 2011). As indicated on p. 149, the FBI severed its connection with CAIR after it was named an unindicted coconspirator in the Holy Land Fund case (concerning the HLF's ties to Hamas).

out that Orthodox Jewish courts were already operating in the UK, and that British law accommodated the anti-abortion views of some Christians. The suggestion is that logically and ethically, Muslims should enjoy analogous rights on issues such as family law, and should not have to choose between "the stark alternatives of cultural loyalty or state loyalty."[45]

But Archbishop Williams' perhaps well-intentioned argument misses three key points. First, Islamists have no problem with the "stark alternatives" of religion versus state because they have no wish to accommodate both; they value cultural loyalty to a single Muslim community and denigrate state loyalty. Second, whereas halacha governs only Orthodox Jewish communities, Islamists want *all* people (even non-Muslims) in *all* places (even those with a non-Muslim-majority) to live according to sharia. Third, the Islamists' vision of sharia is draconian; it undercuts universal human rights, above all the rights of women. Indeed, where sharia has been applied in European communities, female Muslims have faced serious restrictions of their fundamental rights, including forced marriage, polygamy, and denial of the right to divorce.[46] A December 2009 report by the Center for Islamic Pluralism concluded that the application of sharia in Muslim communities in the UK, Germany, the Netherlands, France, and Spain was undermining basic rights of Muslims, especially women.[47]

By accommodating Islamist demands for sharia in some communities, European authorities have emboldened Islamists to insist on further changes to the fabric of mainstream society. German schools are increasingly grappling with cases of Muslim girls pushing for exemption from coeducational swimming and sports on religious grounds.[48] After one school caves in to these demands, it becomes increasingly difficult for others to oppose them. In the UK, the London Borough of Croydon

---

45   *BBC News*, "Sharia Law in UK is 'Unavoidable,'" *BBC News* (February 7, 2008), available at: http://news.bbc.co.uk/2/hi/7232661.stm (accessed January 27, 2011).

46   See John Bingham, "At Least 85 Sharia 'Courts' Operating in Britain, Says Civitas Report," *Telegraph* (June 29, 2009), available at: www.telegraph.co.uk/news/newstopics/religion/5675166/At-least-85-sharia-courts-operating-in-Britain-says-Civitas-report.html (accessed January 27, 2011).

47   Irfan Al-Alawi, Stephen Suleyman Schwartz, Kamal Hasani, Veli Sirin, Daut Dauti, and Qanta Ahmed, *A Guide to* Shariah *Law and Islamist Ideology in Western Europe 2007–2009* (Washington, DC: Center for Islamic Pluralism, 2009), available at: www.islamicpluralism.org/documents/shariah-law-islamist-ideology-western-europe.pdf (accessed January 27, 2011).

48   Sonia Phalnikar, "When Faith is More Important than School," *Deutsche Welle* (April 23, 2004), available at: www.dw-world.de/dw/article/0,,1152539,00.html (accessed January 27, 2011).

launched separate swimming sessions for Muslim men and women two days a week. Increasing numbers of municipal swimming pools across the UK (and other European countries) are following suit. In some cases, local authorities have now begun to impose strict dress codes that accord with Islamist doctrine but contradict Western norms: all swimmers — including non-Muslims — are barred from entering the pool in normal swimming attire and must comply with the "modest" dress code required by Islamic custom, with women covered from neck to ankles and men, who swim separately, covered from navel to knees.[49]

Even in advertising, a reflexive adherence to political correctness has allowed Islamist norms to supplant Western ones. Banks such as Halifax and NatWest have banned piggy banks, the time-honored Western symbol of private saving, from their promotional material. Why? Because of Islamist complaints that any depiction of pigs offends all Muslims. Novelty pig calendars and toys have also been banned from one local council's social welfare office in Britain.[50] Many British nursery schools in Muslim neighborhoods have even banned stories that feature swine, including the classic children's tale "The Three Little Pigs."[51]

The more serious problem involves left-leaning academics, journalists, and human rights organizations. Especially in the UK, these have continued to provide platforms for radical Islamists. In 2005, Professor Anthony Glees (then of Brunel University, now of the University of Birmingham) warned that British campuses had become a safe haven for Islamist extremists.[52] Douglas Murray, director of the Centre for Social Cohesion, in early 2010 noted that "the U.K.'s universities offer the most conducive environment an Islamic extremist could inhabit outside Waziristan."[53] Human rights organizations have done more than provide platforms to Islamists; their support has lent them legitimacy. A particularly prominent case involved Amnesty International and its treatment

---

49   Patrick Sawer, "Swimmers Are Told to Wear Burkinis," *Telegraph* (August 15, 2009), available at: www.telegraph.co.uk/news/newstopics/politics/6034706/Swimmers-are-told-to-wear-burkinis.html (accessed January 27, 2011).

50   *Sun*, "Muslims Win Toy Pigs Ban," *Sun* (October 1, 2005), available at: www.thesun.co.uk/sol/homepage/news/article102182.ece (accessed January 27, 2011).

51   *BBC News*, "School Bans Pig Stories," *BBC News* (March 4, 2003), available at: http://news.bbc.co.uk/2/hi/uk_news/england/2818809.stm (accessed January 27, 2011).

52   Anthony Glees and Chris Pope, *When Students Turn to Terror: Terrorist and Extremist Activity on British Campuses* (London: Social Affairs Unit, 2005).

53   Douglas Murray, "British Radicalization Studies," *Wall Street Journal* (January 8, 2010), available at: http://online.wsj.com/article/SB10001424052748704130904574643912730752216.html (accessed January 27, 2011).

of Gita Sahgal, head of the gender unit at Amnesty's secretariat. Sahgal publicly opposed Amnesty International's collaboration with former Guantanamo Bay detainee Moazzam Begg, declaring,

> I believe the campaign fundamentally damages Amnesty International's integrity and, more importantly, constitutes a threat to human rights . . . To be appearing on platforms with Britain's most famous supporter of the Taliban, whom we treat as a human rights defender, is a gross error of judgment.

In response, Amnesty International fired Sahgal.[54]

This desire to accommodate Islamists in Western society has not been limited to the political left. Conservative academics have also been anxious to partner with nonviolent Islamists in the effort to deter violent extremists from committing terror. Despite the Muslim Brotherhood's quest to replace the international order of secular states with a global *umma* governed by sharia, two researchers at the Nixon Center in Washington, DC, took a very lenient line toward the organization in a 2007 article in *Foreign Affairs*:

> The Brotherhood claims success at sifting radicalism out of its ranks through organizational discipline and a painstaking educational program . . . It appears that the [Brotherhood] works to dissuade Muslims from violence, instead channeling them into politics and charitable activities. As a senior member of the Egyptian Brotherhood's Guidance Council told us in Cairo, "If it wasn't for the Brotherhood, most of the youths of this era would have chosen the path of violence. The Ikhwan has become a safety valve for moderate Islam." The leader of the Jordanian Islamic Action Front, the Muslim Brotherhood's political party in Jordan, said that this group outdoes the government in discouraging *jihad*: "We're better able to conduct an intellectual confrontation, and not a security confrontation, with the forces of extremism and fanaticism."[55]

---

54 IPT News, "Amnesty Official Slams Rights Group's Ties with 'Taliban Supporter,'" *Investigative Project on Terrorism* (February 8, 2010), available at: www.investigativeproject.org/blog/2010/02/amnesty-official-slams-rights-groups-ties-with (accessed January 27, 2011).
55 Robert S. Leiken and Steven Brooke, "The Moderate Muslim Brotherhood," *Foreign Affairs*, March/April 2007, p. 112, available at: www.foreignaffairs.com/articles/62453/robert-s-leiken-and-steven-brooke/the-moderate-muslim-brotherhood (accessed January 27, 2011).

Right-of-center political leaders in Europe and the United States have also played into Islamist hands through certain integration policies and statements that aggravate the social alienation of their Muslim compatriots. While they have insisted that second- and third-generation Muslims have to adopt European norms if they want to be treated as full-fledged citizens, they are unable to define what these norms are. Dutch parliamentarian Geert Wilders (who, as of this writing in spring 2011, is the most popular politician in the Netherlands) has gone so far as to compare the Qur'an to Hitler's *Mein Kampf*, calling for the Qur'an to be banned and proclaiming, "I don't hate Muslims. I hate Islam."[56] Wilders has simultaneously inflamed anti-Muslim sentiment and incensed Muslims in the Netherlands with his incendiary film *Fitna* (Arabic for "sowing discord"), a 17-minute documentary highlighting hate-filled preaching by Islamist extremists, selective citations from the Qur'an, and footage of 9/11 and other terrorist attacks. Such provocations increase the polarization between Muslims and non-Muslims that Islamists seek to foster.

Not surprisingly, anti-immigrant and anti-Muslim sentiments have in general aggravated Muslims' sense of alienation from Western society. In the UK, second- and third-generation British citizens chafe at being called "Pakis" or "Muslims" when they (and sometimes their parents) were born in the UK. Similarly, many Turks in Germany complain, even after they become naturalized, that they are not socially accepted as fully German. As one prominent German sociologist noted, "Quite a number of second- and third-generation Turks now have German citizenship, while they are still perceived as being Turkish and live in the Turkish communities."[57] In France, some government officials told Muslims they faced a stark choice: either assimilate into French culture or leave the country.[58] In Italy, journalist and author Oriana Fallaci made the same point in 2006 that Wilders would make later: "The Qur'an is the *Mein Kampf* of this [Islamist] movement. The Qur'an demands the annihilation or subjugation of the other, and wants to substitute totalitarianism

---

56   Ian Traynor, "'I Don't Hate Muslims. I Hate Islam,' says Holland's Rising Political Star," *Observer* (February 17, 2008), available at: www.guardian.co.uk/world/2008/feb/17/netherlands.islam (accessed January 27, 2011).

57   H. Julia Eksner, *Ghetto Ideologies, Youth Identities and Stylized Turkish German: Turkish Youths in Berlin-Kreuzberg* (Berlin: Lit Verlag, 2006), pp. 25–6.

58   James Graff, "Love it or Leave it: Xenophobia Goes Mainstream," *Time* (May 1, 2006), available at: www.time.com/time/world/article/0,8599,1189794,00.html (accessed January 27, 2011).

for democracy ... All the evil that the sons of Allah commit against themselves and against others is in it."[59]

In the United States, several prominent public figures on the political right made similar inflammatory statements, which proved similarly helpful to Islamist efforts. In 2001, just a few weeks after September 11, President George W. Bush referred to a "crusade" against terrorism; though he retracted his use of the word, Islamist activists exploited the remark, claiming it indicated the president's true feelings and his desire to fight a "war against Islam." Also shortly after 9/11, one of the world's most influential Christian evangelists, the Reverend Franklin Graham, claimed Islam was "an evil and a wicked religion."[60] Similar sentiment was expressed by a high-ranking US military officer and counterterrorism official, Lieutenant General William G. Boykin, who noted of a Somali warlord, "I knew that my God was bigger than his. I knew that my God was a real God and his was an idol."[61] Members of the US Congress periodically fed Islamists' claims that the US government was Islamophobic; Then-Congressman Tom Tancredo of Colorado (who, three years later, would campaign for the Republican presidential nomination on a heavily anti-immigration platform) blurted out while on a radio call-in show in 2005 that if Muslim fundamentalist extremists attacked the United States with nuclear weapons the United States "could take out their holy sites," and bomb Mecca.[62]

Prominent ex-Muslims in Europe and the United States have attacked Islam as incompatible with peace and democracy, and have thus reinforced Muslim sentiment that the West is at war with Islam. Ayaan Hirsi Ali, a Somali ex-Muslim and former member of the Dutch parliament, claimed in 2007 that "violence is inherent in Islam. It's a destructive, nihilistic cult of death. It legitimizes murder."[63] She co-produced with

---

59   Oriana Fallaci, *The Force of Reason* (New York: Rizzoli International, 2006), p. 306.
60   Jarrett Murphy, "Pentagon's Preacher Irks Muslims" *CBS News* (April 16, 2003), available at: www.cbsnews.com/stories/2003/04/16/national/main549684.shtml (accessed January 27, 2011).
61   William M. Arkin, "The Pentagon Unleashes a Holy Warrior," *Los Angeles Times* (October 16, 2003), available at: http://articles.latimes.com/2003/oct/16/opinion/oe-arkin16 (accessed January 27, 2011).
62   Associated Press, "Tancredo: If They Nuke Us, Bomb Mecca," *Fox News* (July 18, 2005), available at: www.foxnews.com/story/0,2933,162795,00.html (accessed January 27, 2011).
63   David Cohen, "Violence is Inherent in Islam: It is a Cult of Death," *London Evening Standard*, (February 2, 2007), available at: www.islamophobia-watch.com/islamophobia-watch/2007/2/7/violence-is-inherent-in-islam-it-is-a-cult-of-death.html (accessed February 13, 2011).

Dutch filmmaker Theo van Gogh the movie *Submission*, which portrayed Islam as systematically oppressing women. Many Muslims, especially Islamists, took great offense. One of them, Mohammed Bouyeri — a second-generation Moroccan Muslim radicalized by Islamist preachers, and who was previously mentioned in Chapter 3 — murdered van Gogh in Amsterdam for "insulting Islam."[64] Islamists issued death threats against Hirsi Ali for committing apostasy, deepening anger on both sides of the divide, which, in turn, further aggravated the separation of European Muslims from mainstream European societies. Meanwhile, in the United States, Syrian American psychiatrist Wafa Sultan has argued that one cannot be a Muslim and a loyal American, warning that regardless of how well integrated into Western societies Muslims may seem to be, they "will always be loyal first to Islam."[65] Arguments such as these stoked anger within many Muslim communities and left Muslims in the West feeling like outcasts, thereby helping Islamists consolidate them into discrete communities segregated from secular society.

Islamists have exploited criticism of Islam or Islamism as part of another key tactic: accusing their Western critics of Islamophobia. The goal of this tactic is twofold: to catalyze Muslims' self-identification as a single community with allegiance to their religion rather than their country of citizenship, and to deflect scrutiny of Islamist objectives by putting Western critics on the defensive. Islamists cite polling data indicating that 53 percent of Americans viewed Islam unfavorably in 2009 to support their claim that American society is Islamophobic. Islamists also condemn as Islamophobic anyone who uses the phrase "Islamist terrorism" or who recognizes a possible connection between Islam and terrorist acts committed in the name of Islam.[66] Even top US military officials appear to have been intimidated by outlandish Islamist claims. According to an

64   *New York Times*, "Dutch Court Sentences Van Gogh Killer to Life," *New York Times* (July 26, 2005), available at: www.nytimes.com/2005/07/26/world/europe/26iht-web.0726theo.html (accessed February 1, 2011).

65   Quoted in TBird, "Bush Empowering Terrorists, Charges Vocal Muslim Critic," Goofigure.com (November 11, 2006), available at: www.goofigure.com/UserGoofigureDetail.asp?gooID=6156 (accessed January 28, 2011).

66   Of the faiths Gallup asked Americans about, Islam elicits the most negative views. A slight majority of Americans (53 percent) say their opinion of the faith is either "not too favorable" (22 percent) or "not favorable at all" (31 percent). When asked about their level of knowledge about Islam, many Americans tell Gallup they have either "very little knowledge" (40 percent) or "none at all" (23 percent). The study also reveals that Americans view Islam more negatively than they view Muslims. (Gallup and the Coexist Foundation, *Religious Perceptions in America: With an In-Depth Analysis of U.S. Attitudes Toward Muslims*

August 2008 report prepared for the US military's Central Command (CENTCOM) entitled *Freedom of Speech in Jihad Analysis: Debunking the Myth of Offensive Words*, the US Department of Defense has hampered its own ability to develop counterterrorism options by censoring the use of vocabulary connecting Islam to terrorism.[67]

Playing on Muslims' sense of victimization, Islamist propaganda portrays wars led by the United States and its coalition partners in Afghanistan and Iraq, as well as Israel's military operations in Lebanon and Gaza, as intended to "kill Muslims." Such propaganda highlights civilian victims without mentioning the terrorist brutality of violent Islamists like al-Qaeda, the Taliban, and Hamas. Though deeply inaccurate, such reports are effective in radicalizing some Muslims into believing they have a religious duty to defend Islam against its Western enemies. According to a 2006 report by the Canadian Security Intelligence Service, "[t]he most important factor for radicalization is the perception that Islam is under attack from the West."[68]

Islamists are carrying out these aggressive propaganda efforts in Europe as well. They have focused their claims of Islamophobia on the French government's effort to ban outward displays of religion within government institutions. In 2004, France prohibited females from wearing the Islamic headscarf (*hijab*) in state schools and government offices; in 2010, it banned the wearing of the burqa and other full-length face coverings in public. Senior French officials justified the *hijab* ban as part of a broader campaign to preserve the secular principles of the French Republic by forbidding any outward displays of religion — including large crosses, Jewish skullcaps, and Sikh turbans as well as the Islamic headscarf — at schools and government offices. Jerome Rivière, the former deputy head of Sarkozy's ruling center-right UMP party, told the BBC that France's secular nature was being challenged by a small minority of hard-line Islamists, noting, "We don't have a problem with

and Islam [Washington, DC: Gallup, 2009], p. 4, available at: www.abudhabigallupcenter. com/File/144335/WorldReligion_Report_en-US_final.pdf [accessed January 30, 2011].)

67   United States Central Command Red Team, *Freedom of Speech in Jihad Analysis: Debunking the Myth of Offensive Words* (Tampa, FL: United States Central Command Red Team, 2008), available at: www.investigativeproject.org/documents/misc/198.pdf (accessed January 30, 2011).

68   Canadian Security Intelligence Service (CSIS), *From Radicalization to Jihadization*, Study 2007-7/07 (Ottawa: CSIS, 2006), available at: http://nefafoundation.org/miscellaneous/ FeaturedDocs/CSIS_RadicalizationJihadization.pdf (accessed January 30, 2011).

religion in France. We have a problem with the political use by a minority of religion."[69]

Rivière's observation reflects Islamists' attempt to compel women to wear the headscarf — which gives them a distinctive "Muslim" look — to promote among Muslims a sense of cultural separation from mainstream society. This goal is to an even greater extent behind the wearing of the burqa, a shapeless garment traditionally worn by Afghan women that covers them from head to toe, with even the eyes screened by a mesh covering. As British House of Commons leader Jack Straw noted while serving as foreign secretary, the burqa is a "visible statement of separation and difference" that is "bound to make better, positive relations between the two communities more difficult."[70] Many officials recognize the burqa as a cultural statement rather than a requirement of Islam, one that has been politicized by Islamists in their quest to obstruct Muslims' integration into European society.[71] They worry the burqa undermines social integration and security by severely restricting face-to-face communication. In the words of French lawmaker Andre Gerin, the burqa serves as a "walking prison" for women. French prime minister François Fillon declared in February 2010 that he would sign a decree denying French citizenship to a man who ordered his French wife to wear the full Islamic veil. "This case is about a religious radical. He imposes the burqa, he imposes the separation of men and women in his own home and he refuses to shake the hands of women," Fillon told the Europe 1 radio network. "If this man does not want to change his attitude, he has no place in our country. In any case, he does not deserve French nationality."[72]

Islamist propagandists jumped on the French government's limits on female head coverings. Ignoring the government's broader effort to prohibit all overt expressions of any religion in France's schools and government offices, the Islamists twisted the government ban on Islamic

69   Caroline Wyatt, "French Headscarf Ban Opens Rifts," *BBC News* (February 11, 2004), available at: http://news.bbc.co.uk/2/hi/3478895.stm (accessed January 30, 2011).

70   Jack Straw, "I Want to Unveil My Views on an Important Issue," *Lancashire Telegraph*, October 5, 2006, available at: www.telegraph.co.uk/news/1530718/I-want-to-unveil-my-views-on-an-important-issue.html (accessed February 13, 2011).

71   As a result of this politicization, the distinctions among traditional forms of covering such as the chador, the niqab, and the jilbab are being blurred; "burqa" is increasingly used as a catch-all term to describe any covering more extensive than a headscarf.

72   Steven Erlanger, "World Briefing Europe: France; Nationality to be Denied over Veil," *New York Times* (February 4, 2010), available at: http://query.nytimes.com/gst/fullpage.htm l?res=9504EEDA173FF937A35751C0A9669D8B63 (accessed January 30, 2011).

garb into attacks on Islam. According to Sir Iqbal Sacranie, France's *hijab* ban reflected

> an institutionalized Islamophobia that is unfortunately taking root in several parts of Europe ... Banning *hijab* will send a strong signal throughout the Muslim world that the French government is intent on revisiting its dark and brutal days in North and West Africa. We hope this is not the case.[73]

MCB Assistant Secretary General Refaat Drabu extended Sacranie's argument to the burqa ban in June 2009, declaring that "the French President appears to be initiating a policy which is set to create a fear and misunderstanding and may lead to Islamophobic reaction not just in France but in the rest of Europe too."[74] A similar response came from Islamist activists within France, such as Fouad Alaoui, president of the UOIF, who opined that the burqa ban "would only help Islamophobia."

Islamists have displayed a similarly aggressive pattern in response to Switzerland's ban on the construction of new minarets. In a national referendum held on November 29, 2009, 57 percent of voters endorsed the prohibition (which affected neither mosque construction nor existing minarets).[75] Many Swiss believed that the structures were altering their view of the traditional Swiss landscape, and that they represented the growing challenge to Swiss society presented by a politicized form of a minority religion. The referendum's organizers were inspired in part by a poem read in 1997 by Recep Tayyip Erdogan, then mayor of Istanbul (and currently Turkish prime minister) (resulting in his imprisonment for "provoking enmity and hatred"), which includes the passage: "The mosques are our barracks, the domes are our helmets, the minarets are our bayonets, and the faithful are our soldiers." Islamists twisted these reasonable concerns of Swiss voters into accusations that the referendum was an

---

73   Ahmad al-Azizy, "France's Hijab Ban Draws World Criticism," Islam Online (December 20, 2003), available at: http://www.mombu.com/religion/arabic/t-frances-hijab-ban-draws-world-criticism-numbers-faith-beliefs-religion-case-5452216.html (accessed February 13, 2011).

74   Murray Wardrop, "Muslim Leaders Condemn Sarkozy over Burqa Ban," *Telegraph* (June 24, 2009), available at: www.telegraph.co.uk/news/newstopics/religion/5616629/Muslim-leaders-condemn-Sarkozy-over-burqa-ban.html (accessed January 30, 2011).

75   Charles Bremner, "Swiss Voters Back Right-Wing Minaret Ban," *Times* (November 30, 2009), available at: www.timesonline.co.uk/tol/news/world/europe/article6936802.ece (accessed January 30, 2011).

attack on Islam. The chairman of the Federation of Islamic Organizations in Europe, Chakib Makhlouf, compared Switzerland's decision to the Nazi oppression of Jews, claiming that "the racist spirit that we as Muslims face is the same spirit that Adolf Hitler once harbored against the Jews." He suggested the persecution of Muslims was somehow more insidious because it was disguised as democracy, while Jews faced "direct persecution" by the Nazis.[76]

Many left-leaning commentators in Europe and the United States echoed the Islamists' attacks on Swiss voters. As Georgetown University professor John Esposito put it,

> Enlightened Switzerland has now become part of an "Enlightened Liberal Europe" that is increasingly not all that liberal. The stunning Swiss vote (57 percent) approving a referendum to ban minarets should not have been all that surprising, considering the growing power of Islamophobia. In both Europe and America right-wing politicians, political commentators, media personalities, and religious leaders continue to feed a growing suspicion of mainstream Muslims by fueling a fear that Islam, not just Muslim extremism, is a threat.[77]

Makhlouf's conflation of the minaret ban with the Holocaust actually reflects a shift in Islamist tactics. Though they often selectively cite Islamic scripture to condemn Jews, Islamists have now begun expressing a common cause with Jewish suffering for political purposes: they sought to put Swiss voters on the defensive and to aggravate Muslims' sense of victimization to accentuate their sense of separation from mainstream society. Other European Islamists have also exploited the example of the Holocaust. Shahid Malik, whom Gordon Brown made Britain's first Muslim cabinet minister (in the Department of International Development), attacked what he called the growing culture of hostility against Muslims in the UK:

> I think most people would agree that if you ask Muslims today what do they feel like, they feel like the Jews of Europe . . . I don't mean to equate

---

76 MEMRI Blog, trans.,"Muslim Leader in Europe: Anti-Muslim Racism Is Identical to Anti-Semitic Racism," MEMRI Blog (December 12, 2009), available at: www.thememriblog.org/blog_personal/en/22463.htm (accessed January 30, 2011).

77 John L. Esposito, "Are Swiss Alps Threatened by Minarets?" *Huffington Post* (December 2, 2009), available at: www.huffingtonpost.com/john-l-esposito/are-swiss-alps-threatened_b_376833.html (accessed January 30, 2011).

that with the Holocaust but in the way that it was legitimate almost —
and still is in some parts — to target Jews, many Muslims would say that
we feel the exact same way.[78]

Islamists have also used the negative legacy of McCarthyism to keep their
critics off balance while they consolidate a Muslim community. Recalling
the dark period during the Cold War when Senator Joseph McCarthy
ruined the professional and private lives of US officials and intellectuals
with unsubstantiated charges of treasonous sympathy for Communism,
some Islamists try to intimidate their opponents into silence by equat-
ing any criticism of Islamism with neo-McCarthyism. This is happening
both in the United States and in Europe. Reza Pankhurst, a postgraduate
teacher at the London School of Economics, was accused by students
(including Muslims) of spreading Islamism at the prestigious academic
institution by injecting political content into his sermons at Friday prayers.
Pankhurst, who served four years in Egyptian prisons for membership in
HT, responded by invoking McCarthy: such accusations were a "form of
McCarthyism directed against Muslims who speak out against UK foreign
policy . . . The innuendo, blacklisting, and McCarthyite witch-hunts are
very counter-productive."[79]

Another Islamist method of fostering accusations of Islamophobia
is to generate sympathetic media coverage by provoking outlandish and
attention-grabbing conflicts. One famous incident of this type involved
the "flying imams" in the United States. On November 20, 2006, six
Muslim clerics showed up at the departure gates of the Minneapolis–Saint
Paul airport and began praying very loudly. Upon boarding a US Airways
flight, they immediately engaged in suspicious behavior that alarmed passengers and crew: the imams reportedly refused to sit in their assigned
seats; fanned out in pairs to occupy the front, middle, and rear exit rows;
ordered unnecessary seat-belt extenders; loudly criticized President Bush
and the Iraq War; and noisily discussed al-Qaeda and Osama bin Laden.
The imams seemed intent on provoking a reaction with this excessive
and unnecessary behavior simply to justify a claim that Islamophobes had
victimized them. One of the imams already had experience mounting

---

78   Cahal Milmo, "Muslims Feel Like 'Jews of Europe,'" *Independent* (July 4, 2008),
available at: www.independent.co.uk/news/uk/home-news/muslims-feel-like-jews-of-
europe-859978.html (accessed January 30, 2011).
79   Owen Bowcott, "LSE Tutor Says He is Victim of McCarthyite Witch-Hunt over Hizb
ut-Tahrir Membership," *Guardian* (January 17, 2010), available at: www.guardian.co.uk/
uk/2010/jan/17/reza-pankhurst-mccarthyite-witchhunt (accessed January 30, 2011).

such claims (he served as legal counsel for a fellow member of his mosque who had tried to break into the cockpit on a 1999 flight and then sued the airline after being detained upon landing). Moreover, the six imams had just met with a group in Minneapolis that supported an anti-profiling bill pending in the US Congress, further suggesting they sought to provoke a public controversy. Indeed, after being forcibly removed from the aircraft and detained before takeoff, the clerics sued US Airways and the Minneapolis airport authority, as well as fearful passengers who had reported their suspicious activity. CAIR backed the lawsuit, which the airline settled out of court.[80]

As with the other tactics described in this chapter, the use of litigation to intimidate opponents into silence occurs on both sides of the Atlantic. Some Islamist activists search for courts in European countries that will claim jurisdiction in cases involving statements made elsewhere in the West that Islamists find offensive. In what has been called "libel tourism,"[81] they bring suit in the UK, where the law — and the courts — are the most cooperative. Another Islamist legal tactic is to push legislatures in Europe and in Muslim-majority countries to enact antiblasphemy laws, according to which any negative statement about Islam or the Prophet Muhammad is prohibited. The Organization of the Islamic Conference (OIC) is trying to go even further, lobbying the United Nations to issue a statement defining and condemning Islamic blasphemy, thereby applying Islamic doctrine to all people around the world regardless of their religion. The previously mentioned Dutch politician and filmmaker Geert Wilders faces hate speech litigation in the Netherlands from a radical imam who claims Wilders' film *Fitna* caused emotional suffering. Jordan has issued a request for Wilders' extradition to stand trial for violating the country's sharia-based blasphemy laws, an offense that is punishable by death.[82]

The most infamous case of Islamist intimidation through staged provocations is that of the "Danish cartoons." These depictions of the Prophet Muhammad, which do offend many Muslims, were largely

---

80 Madeleine Gruen and Edward Sloan, "Are Acts of Staged Controversy an Islamist Strategic Tactic?" *IPT News* (February 27, 2009), available at: www.investigativeproject. org/1002/are-acts-of-staged-controversy-an-islamist (accessed January 30, 2011).

81 The term was coined by the renowned Australian-born British human-rights lawyer Geoffrey Robertson, who handled the defense of Salman Rushdie as well as other high-profile cases.

82 Brooke Goldstein and Aaron Eitan Meyer, "How Islamist Lawfare Tactics Target Free Speech," Legal Project (April 29, 2009), available at: www.legal-project.org/article/294 (accessed January 30, 2011).

ignored when originally published in Copenhagen's *Jyllands-Posten* newspaper on September 30, 2005. The illustrations again prompted little reaction when republished (accompanied by an article critical of the cartoons) in Cairo's *El-Fagr* newsweekly on October 17. Months later, Danish Islamists decided to stage a confrontation with Denmark's mainstream, partnering with counterparts in the Middle East to launch a new campaign to publicize and condemn the then-forgotten cartoons as insulting to Islam. The Islamists staged violent rallies in several countries and disseminated the cartoons globally, with additional drawings that were never included in the original Danish collection. Moreover, the Islamists never criticized the publication of the cartoons in Egypt. As it turned out, Danish prime minister Anders Fogh Rasmussen (now secretary general of NATO) took a strong stand in defense of freedom of speech, upholding the Copenhagen newspaper's right to publish the cartoons.

Unfortunately, some of the most respected Western media outlets and publishers have taken a softer line in defending their rights than did the Danish government. For example, in 2007, accusations of Islamophobia and a threatened lawsuit intimidated PBS, a highly regarded American network, into canceling a documentary it had commissioned entitled *Islam versus Islamism*, which contrasted the views of Islamist activists and non-Islamists in the United States and Europe. Random House, one of the largest publishing houses in the United States, canceled the release of *The Jewel of Medina*, a novel about the life of Muhammad's wife, Aisha (including her engagement to the Prophet when she was six years old). Random House cited fears that the book "could incite acts of violence by a small, radical segment of the population."[83] Similarly, in 2009, Yale University Press decided not to include the infamous Danish caricatures of the Prophet Muhammad in a book on the incident by scholar Jytte Klausen.

Islamists have even tried to intimidate members of the US Congress into retracting their criticism of Islamism by accusing them of Islamophobia. In March 2009, CAIR accused Virginia Congressman Frank Wolf, co-chair of the Congressional Human Rights Caucus, of "abusing his office" when he sought background information on CAIR from the FBI.[84]

---

83   Alan Elsner, "Random House Pulls Novel on Islam, Fears Violence," Reuters (August 7, 2008), available at: www.reuters.com/article/idUSN0736008820080807 (accessed January 30, 2011).

84   CAIR, "GOP Rep Pressures FBI for 'Payback' against Muslim Civil Rights Group," CAIR (March 13, 2009), available at: www.cair.com/ArticleDetails.aspx?ArticleID=2576 9&&name=n&&currPage=1&&Active=1 (accessed January 30, 2011).

Congressman Wolf's concerns were not unfounded: the FBI cut its ties with CAIR in late 2008 after the Islamist organization was named an unindicted co-conspirator in a high-profile case involving the Holy Land Foundation's alleged ties to Hamas. CAIR has repeatedly assailed Congresswoman Sue Myrick of North Carolina, who in 2008 asked

> [w]hy would anyone allow a group, who the FBI says is tied to terrorism, to influence national security policy, or any policy for that matter? ... If the FBI has cut ties with CAIR, Congress should wake up and do the same.[85]

Islamist activists are particularly alarmed when fellow Muslims criticize Islamist ideology, especially those who see Islam and democracy as compatible and who favor secular rule of law over sharia. Such Muslim moderates become targets of harsh Islamist vitriol and other forms of abuse. Many American Muslims remain silent because they wish to avoid the ostracism suffered by M. Zuhdi Jasser, a Syrian American doctor specializing in internal medicine and nuclear cardiology and a former US Navy lieutenant commander. Jasser founded the American Islamic Forum for Democracy and serves on the board of the Arizona Interfaith Movement. In these civil society capacities, Jasser argues for the compatibility of Islam with American principles of democracy and pluralism in both politics and religion. Jasser accuses Islamists of distorting Islam through their insistence that a "true Muslim" must offer full allegiance only to God and sharia, and that secular laws promulgated by men, even in a democracy, do not carry genuine authority.[86] Recognizing Jasser's attempt to reconcile Islam and democracy as a serious threat to Islamist doctrine, CAIR and other Islamists have vilified this moderate as an extremist. CAIR spokesperson Ibrahim Hooper told the *Philadelphia Inquirer* that criticism from Muslims such as Jasser was "providing others with an opportunity to advance an agenda that is hostile to the American Muslim community."[87] The *Muslim Voice* newspaper in Phoenix, Arizona,

---

85   Jordy Yager, "Rep. Myrick Repeats Call to Cut CAIR Ties," *Hill* (October 17, 2009), available at: http://thehill.com/homenews/house/63571-rep-myrick-reiterates-call-to-cut-ties-with-cair (accessed January 30, 2011).

86   See M. Zuhdi Jasser's website, American Islamic Forum for Democracy, for his articles and speeches: www.aifdemocracy.org/ (accessed January 30, 2011); see also M. Zuhdi Jasser, "Americanism versus Islamism" in Zeyno Baran, ed., *The Other Muslims: Moderate and Secular* (London: Palgrave Macmillan, 2010), pp. 175–91.

87   Andrew Maykuth, "A Call for Moderation Sparks Tension: 'There is Civil War Going

accused Jasser of "putting his allegiance to the dominant culture ahead of his faith," and printed a cartoon depicting him as a rabid dog attacking other Muslims.[88] Such criticism of a pious Muslim who is also a proud US citizen underscores the Islamists' overarching goal: overturning the world's political order to replace democratic institutions with sharia rule.

Creeping Islamization and Homegrown Terror

The tactics described above are advancing the strategic goals of the Islamists' political-religious ideology. Polarization in Western societies is increasing, as Muslims identify more with their own religious community than with their countries of citizenship, and as more and more non-Muslims support anti-Islamic politicians like Geert Wilders. Since 2007, Western governments have begun to recognize these dangers, but have made only halting progress in the face of Islamists' political and legal counterattacks.

Islamist efforts to consolidate Western Muslims into segregated communities may be succeeding. Public opinion polling indicates that Muslims in the United States and Europe increasingly conceive their primary identity as "Muslim," with the identity of their country of citizenship as secondary. In 2007, it was reported that

> nearly half of Muslims in the U.S. (47 percent) say they think of themselves first as a Muslim, rather than as an American. But far more Muslims in three of the four Western European nations surveyed said they considered themselves first as Muslims rather than citizens of their countries.

This trend was even more pronounced among youth, with 60 percent of American Muslims aged 18 to 29 thinking of themselves first as Muslim, as opposed to 39 percent among Muslims aged 55 and older.[89] This trend toward "*umma*-ization" is even starker in Britain and Germany, where 81

On,'" *Philadelphia Inquirer* (January 3, 2006), available at: www.aifdemocracy.org/media-focus.php?id=1677 (accessed January 30, 2011).

88   Maykuth, "A Call for Moderation Sparks Tension." Many Muslims consider dogs to be unclean; thus, depicting someone as a dog is a serious insult.

89   Pew Research Center, *Muslim Americans: Middle Class and Mostly Mainstream* (Washington, DC: Pew Research Center, 2007), p. 3, available at: http://pewresearch.org/assets/pdf/muslim-americans.pdf (accessed January 25, 2011).

percent and 66 percent of Muslims (respectively) consider their primary identity as Muslim.[90]

The trend toward self-segregation by American Muslims has coincided with a growing feeling of discomfort toward Islam among non-Muslim Americans. At the start of President George W. Bush's administration, even immediately after September 11, a large majority of Americans did not associate Islam with violence. According to a November 2001 poll by the Pew Forum, only 17 percent of Americans associated Islam with violence. As the decade wore on, the percentage of Americans associating Islam with violence increased; in 2009, nearly 40 percent of Americans thought Islam was more likely than other religion to encourage violence among its believers. In his June 2009 speech in Cairo, President Obama acknowledged these growing tensions between Muslims and non-Muslims and warned they were aggravating anti-Muslim sentiment:

> Violent extremists have exploited these tensions in a small but potent minority of Muslims. The attacks of September 11, 2001 and the continued efforts of these extremists to engage in violence against civilians has led some in my country to view Islam as inevitably hostile not only to America and Western countries, but also to human rights. All this has bred more fear and more mistrust.[91]

Although extremists have yet to overthrow the legal and democratic institutions of Western society, they are undermining them in a process of creeping Islamization. Western efforts to foster Muslim integration and outreach have thus far failed to halt the Islamization of Western Muslim communities, since these initiatives ignore Islamism's role as the ideological conveyor belt to terrorist action.

A major consequence of these policy failures has been the growth of terrorism committed by Muslims born and/or raised in the West. This phenomenon first gained public attention in January 2005, when French authorities arrested three French-born citizens of Algerian descent for

---

90   The figure for France — 46 percent — is comparable to that in the United States. See Pew Global Attitudes Project, *Europe's Muslims More Moderate: The Great Divide; How Westerners and Muslims View Each Other* (Washington, DC: Pew Research Center, 2006), available at: http://pewglobal.org/reports/pdf/253.pdf (accessed January 30, 2011).

91   President Barack Obama, "Remarks by the President on a New Beginning," speech delivered at Cairo University, June 4, 2009, available at: www.whitehouse.gov/the-press-office/remarks-president-cairo-university-6-04-09 (accessed January 30, 2011).

plotting to blow up the Eiffel Tower.[92] The next major incident occurred in London on July 7, 2005, when bombers born and raised in the UK carried out an attack on the London public transport system. Britain's domestic intelligence chiefs estimated in 2008 that 2,000 people, mostly British citizens or residents, were involved in al-Qaeda–influenced terrorist activities in Britain; they claimed to be monitoring about 30 serious plots at any given moment.[93] In 2008, five men were arrested in central England for connections to a plot by al-Qaeda in Britain to assassinate Gordon Brown and Tony Blair.[94] At least one member of the organization has been described as a white British convert to Islam. In 2009, police in Amsterdam arrested seven individuals for planning to bomb an Ikea and several other large stores in Amsterdam. All suspects were Dutch nationals of Moroccan ancestry.[95] These are just a few of the numerous cases of homegrown terrorism seen across Europe over the last decade.

Even Muslim communities previously considered immune from radicalization are being attracted to Islamist terrorism. One such group is the Turkish community in Germany; the Turks have kept a low social profile since the arrival of the first guest workers in the 1960s, but they are now also radicalizing. A 2007 investigation by the German authorities identified a cell consisting of an ethnic Turkish citizen of Germany and two German converts to Islam who had traveled to Pakistan to receive training from an al-Qaeda ally, the Islamic Jihad Union (IJU). A number of Turks have subsequently been accused of terrorist collaboration in

---

92   Ian Sparks, "Terror Plot to Blow up Eiffel Tower Uncovered," *Daily Mail* (January 11, 2008), available at: www.dailymail.co.uk/news/article-507760/Terror-plot-blow-Eiffel-Tower-uncovered.html (accessed January 30, 2011).

93   Her Majesty's Government, *The Prevent Strategy: A Guide for Local Partners in England* (London: HM Government, June 2008), p. 5, available at: http://www.dcsf.gov.uk/violentextremism/downloads/Prevent%20Strategy%20A%20Guide%20for%20Local%20 Partners%203%20June%202008.pdf (accessed January 30, 2011); James Kirkup, "Terrorists in Pakistan Planning over 20 Attacks on Britain, Says Gordon Brown," *Telegraph* (December 14, 2008), available at: www.telegraph.co.uk/news/newstopics/politics/defence/3757357/Terrorists-in-Pakistan-planning-over-20-attacks-on-Britain-says-Gordon-Brown.html (accessed January 30, 2011).

94   Josh Hammer, "Analysis: Homegrown Terrorism in the U.S. and UK," Foreign Policy Association (September 11, 2008), available at: www.fpa.org/topics_info2414/topics_info_show.htm?doc_id=705094 (accessed January 30, 2011).

95   *Telegraph*, "Seven Held over Terror Plot to Bomb Dutch Ikea Shops," *Telegraph* (March 13, 2009), available at: www.telegraph.co.uk/news/worldnews/europe/netherlands/4982443/Seven-held-over-terror-plot-to-bomb-Dutch-Ikea-shops.html (accessed January 30, 2011).

Germany, including two men and a woman (all German citizens), who were arrested in February 2010 for sending money to the IJU.

The danger of homegrown terrorism attracted public attention in the United States only in late 2009 with Major Nidal Hasan's shooting rampage at Fort Hood, Texas. But for several years before that, pockets of radicalization were developing in the United States, especially among recent Muslim immigrants from conflict zones. Young immigrants often feel anger toward the United States for its perceived role in ongoing wars in their home countries and grow alienated from American society. Furthermore, in contrast to most other first-wave immigrants, many of these migrants come from countries where Islamism had supplanted traditional Islam before they departed. Somali Americans are a prime example. Many Somali immigrants are angry that the United States supported the Ethiopian forces that toppled Somalia's Islamist government in 2006. This anger is compounded by poverty rates reaching 51 percent among Somali immigrants.[96] The Somali terrorist group al-Shabaab takes advantage of this anger and alienation to indoctrinate young Somali Americans with Islamist ideology and then recruit them to fight for violent jihad in Somalia.

Islamist radicalization is also increasing within Pakistani American communities, even though they tend to be fairly well integrated in the United States (especially compared with Pakistani communities in the UK). Many Pakistani Americans choose to supplement their secular American educations by studying Islam in madrassas in Pakistan, where Islamism has replaced the religious traditions familiar to most families before they emigrated.[97] In the madrassas, the returnees are bombarded with Islamist rhetoric condemning US counterterrorism operations (such as drone attacks against al-Qaeda and Taliban targets in Pakistan's Federally Administered Tribal Areas bordering Afghanistan) as part of a US war

---

96   Spencer S. Hsu and Carrie Johnson, "Somali Americans Recruited by Extremists: U.S. Cites Case of Minnesotan Killed in Suicide Blast in Africa," *Washington Post* (March 11, 2009), available at: www.washingtonpost.com/wp-dyn/content/article/2009/03/10/AR2009031003901.html (accessed January 30, 2011).

97   In 2008, two American-born Pakistani American teenagers who had spent four years at a radical Islamist madrassa in Karachi returned to the United States, which prompted a call for hearings in the US Congress and a request by ten members of the US House of Representatives for Pakistan to deport to the United States the approximately 700 American citizens studying at Pakistani madrassas. (Stewart M. Powell, "Religious Learning in Pakistan: Antenna up on Islamic Schools; U.S. Officials Wary of Possible Al-Qaida Recruiting," *Houston Chronicle* [July 12, 2008], available at: www.chron.com/disp/story.mpl/world/5885181.html [accessed January 30, 2011].)

against Islam. Many other Pakistani Americans, like their counterparts in Britain, become radicalized without ever leaving their country of birth, as Islamist preachers recruit them on the internet, at local mosques, and at private gatherings; some of these people, who were born and raised in the United States, further radicalize to become potential terrorists. In December 2009, five US citizens from Alexandria, Virginia, were arrested near Pakistan's lawless tribal areas, where they hoped to join an al-Qaeda training camp. The five suspects are all US citizens of Pakistani and Ethiopian ethnicity in their 20s (including a dentistry student at Howard University in Washington, DC), who met at a youth group at the Islamic Circle of North America mosque in Alexandria, Virginia. Investigators believe the men were planning terrorist attacks in Pakistani cities and wanted to fight US soldiers in Afghanistan.[98]

The case of Jude Kenan Mohammad,[99] a 19-year-old Pakistani American from Raleigh, North Carolina, offers a blueprint of how Muslims born and raised in the West are radicalized by recruiters exploiting their spiritual alienation. Mohammad's father, Taj Muhammad, comes from a town of gunsmiths in Pakistan's lawless region south of Peshawar. His mother is a white American who converted from Christianity to Islam, moved to Pakistan, then returned to the United States in 1980 with her son, while her husband remained in Pakistan. As a teenager in Raleigh, Mohammad reportedly behaved like a typical teenager, drinking alcohol, dating girls, and hanging out with an eclectic mix of peers. According to one friend, "[h]e was very popular, cool as hell." In early 2008, according to the *Wall Street Journal*, Mohammad changed, as he apparently began to contemplate the Muslim component of his identity: "He began to play basketball outside the local mosque, and [increased] his visits to the mosque. He became a more observant Muslim. He quit partying." Mohammad left for Pakistan in October 2008. After visiting with members of his father's tribe, Mohammad was arrested when trying to enter Pakistan's North-West Frontier Province under suspicion of spying for the Taliban. He was released after a trial and payment of minor penalties. On August 8, 2009, Mohammad was again arrested, this time in the United States, after the FBI discovered that he was a member of

98   Zahid Hussain, Siobhan Gorman, and Neil King Jr., "Students Linked to Al Qaeda," *Wall Street Journal: Asia* (December 11, 2009), available at: http://online.wsj.com/article/SB126045800896585617.html (accessed January 30, 2011).
99   The discussion of the case in this paragraph draws on Hussain, et al., "Students Linked to Al Qaeda."

a gang of Americans from Raleigh planning to conduct violent jihad, including murder and kidnapping. The group was led by Daniel Boyd, a 39-year-old building contractor and convert to Islam who used his home "to stockpile weapons, spread extremist literature glorifying Osama bin Laden, and foster a cell of homegrown American *jihadi* terrorists."[100]

Jude Kenan Mohammad's case is not unique. Islamist radicalization is increasing in the United States, generating a small but dangerous pool of potential terrorist recruits, including those born and raised in the United States and integrated into mainstream society. Prominent examples of these American terrorists include Omar Hammami, whose case was described in Chapter 4, and John Walker Lindh, the California native and Islamic convert who was arrested in Afghanistan in late 2001 as a Taliban militant fighting US soldiers. A 2007 Pew Research survey found that a quarter of American Muslim men under 30 considered suicide bombings justifiable.[101] Increasing numbers of American-born converts to Islam, such as Mohammad's mother and his recruiter (Daniel Boyd), are helping to catalyze violent jihadism among US citizens. Adam Gadahn, another Californian convert to Islam, currently serves as al-Qaeda's spokesman. Since 2003, US authorities have thwarted several attempted terrorist attacks planned by US citizens who were radicalized in the United States, including a May 2003 plot to bomb a shopping mall in Columbus, Ohio; an August 2005 plan to attack US military, Jewish, and Israeli targets in Los Angeles; plots in June 2007 to bomb federal buildings in Miami and the Sears Tower in Chicago; and the May 2007 plan to attack the US military base at Fort Dix, New Jersey.

Perhaps the most prominent case of homegrown terrorism in the United States is that of Nidal Hasan, the US Army major who murdered 13 and injured 30 of his fellow soldiers at Fort Hood, Texas, on November 5, 2009. Born and raised in Virginia to Palestinian parents originally from a town near Jerusalem, Hasan was raised both as an American and as a Muslim. Hasan seemed to be fully integrated into mainstream American society. After finishing high school, he joined the US Army, which financed his university and medical school education. However, warning signs remained that Hasan was radicalizing spiritually

---

100   See also Declan Walsh and Daniel Nasaw, "American Jihad or FBI Blunder? The Riddle of the 'North Carolina Taliban,'" *Guardian* (September 3, 2009), available at: www.guardian. co.uk/world/2009/sep/03/carolina-taliban-jude-mohammad (accessed January 30, 2011); WRAL.com, "Johnston Man Pleads Guilty in Terrorist Conspiracy" (February 9, 2011), available at: www.wral.com/news/state/story/9081721/ (accessed February 21, 2011).
101   Pew Research Center, *Muslim Americans*, pp. 6, 54.

and politically. While presenting a medical lecture to other psychiatrists at the Walter Reed Army Medical Center in Washington, DC, in 2007, Hasan preached about Islam, warning that unbelievers would be sent to hell, and arguing that suicide bombings were justified.[102] In keeping with Islamist doctrine, Hasan avoided contact with female colleagues and eventually isolated himself from all non-Islamist Muslims. The business card he distributed just before the Fort Hood shootings described his professional title as "S.O.A.," meaning "Soldier of Allah."

A key agent in Hasan's radicalization appears to have been Anwar al-Awlaki, a US-born cleric with Yemeni parents. Hasan sought political-religious guidance from al-Awlaki at the aforementioned Dar al-Hijrah Mosque in Virginia, just outside Washington, DC, on subjects such as when jihad is appropriate and whether killing innocents in a suicide attack is permissible. Hasan told al-Awlaki in an email that he "could not wait to join" al-Awlaki in the afterlife.

Al-Awlaki was born in New Mexico, but at age seven he returned with his parents to Yemen. He attended college in the United States, receiving a BS in civil engineering from Colorado State University in 1994 and an MA in education leadership from San Diego State University. While in San Diego, he served as an imam at the Rabat Mosque. Throughout 2001, while pursuing a PhD in human resource development at George Washington University, al-Awlaki also served as an imam at Dar al-Hijrah. Al-Awlaki's associates at the center attest that his behavior indicated he was moderate. Given the center's Islamist outlook, this response is perhaps not surprising; according to Dar al-Hijrah's outreach director, Imam Johari Abdul Malik,

> when Anwar al-Awlaki was [here], he was articulating the same message that I articulate today in Dar Al-Hijrah, a very open, a very engaging, a very . . . contemporary understanding of the faith within the framework of its traditionalism.[103]

---

102 Dana Priest, "Fort Hood Suspect Warned of Threats within the Ranks," *Washington Post* (November 10, 2009), available at: www.washingtonpost.com/wp-dyn/content/article/2009/11/09/AR2009110903618.html (accessed January 30, 2011).

103 Johari Abdul Malik, interview by Michel Martin, "Devout Muslims Sometimes Split On Beliefs," *Tell Me More*, National Public Radio (NPR) (November 12, 2009), transcript available at: www.npr.org/templates/story/story.php?storyId=120344756 (accessed January 30, 2011); for Imam Johari Abdul Malik's Islamism, see *IPT News*, "Virginia House Opens to Radical Cleric," *IPT News* (March 11, 2010), available at: www.investigative project.org/1850/virginia-house-opens-to-radical-cleric (accessed January 30, 2011).

It is unclear when or how al-Awlaki was radicalized into an Islamist activist. Some speculate he may have "snapped" after being arrested in San Diego for soliciting prostitutes, or was perhaps recruited by Islamists in Yemen and hid his radicalism while at the Islamic Center. What is clear is that at some point, al-Awlaki became an adherent of the radical Wahhabi sect of Islam, and reportedly delivered pro-jihad and anti-Israel sermons. In February 2010, al-Awlaki told *Al Jazeera*, "We advocate for Islam that which Allah brought upon Muhammad, prayer and peace upon him: the Islam of *jihad* and *sharia* establishment."[104] Al-Awlaki's pro-jihad sermon, *Constants on the Path of Jihad*,[105] is regarded as the "virtual Bible" for self-radicalized Islamists, according to Evan Kohlmann, a prominent US terrorism expert. The sermon is based on an Arabic-language text penned by the founder of al-Qaeda's network in Saudi Arabia, Yousef al-Ayyiri, and states:

> *Jihad* does not end with the disappearance of a person. *Jihad* must continue regardless because it does not depend on any particular leader or individual . . . *Jihad* does not depend on any particular land. It is global. When the Muslim is in his land, he performs *jihad* . . . No borders or barriers stop it. The message cannot be conveyed without *jihad*. If a particular people or nation is classified as . . . "the people of war" in the *sharia*, the classification applies to them all over the earth. Islam cannot be customized to suit the condition where you are, for instance Europe."[106]

Witnesses told the FBI that while living in San Diego in 2000, al-Awlaki had close relationships with two of the September 11 hijackers, Nawaf al-Hazmi and Khalid al-Midhar, and served as their spiritual advisor. Authorities say the two hijackers regularly attended the Rabat

---

104   He also stated that "we advocate for Islam that which Allah brought upon Muhammad, prayer and peace upon him: the Islam of Jihad and Sharia establishment." Al-Awlaki's inter-view by *Al Jazeera*, *Al-Jazeera Interview with American Yemeni Cleric Sheikh Anwar al-Awlaki: "I Support the Attempt of Bombing Detroit,"* NEFA, trans. (NEFA Foundation, February 2, 2010), is available at: www.nefafoundation.org/miscellaneous/nefaAwlaki0210.pdf (accessed January 30, 2011).

105   Anwar al-Awlaki, *Thawaabit 'ala darb al Jihad* [*Constants on the Path of Jihad*] by *Shaykh Yusuf al 'Uyayree*, Mujahid Fe Sabeelillah, transcriber and ed. (n.d.), available at www.hoor-al-ayn.com/Books/constants.pdf (accessed January 30, 2011).

106   Evan Kohlmann, "Investigating Ft. Hood: Anwar al-Awlaki's 'Constants on the Path of Jihad,'" Counterterrorism Blog (November 9, 2009), available at: http://counter terrorismblog.org/2009/11/investigating_ft_hood_anwar_al.php (accessed January 30, 2011).

Mosque that al-Awlaki led in San Diego. Another would-be Islamist terrorist, Umar Farouk Abdulmutallab, reportedly sought spiritual advice from al-Awlaki in Yemen after being radicalized in the UK and before attempting to blow up a Delta Airlines flight from Amsterdam to Detroit on Christmas Day 2009.[107]

Thus, after adopting Wahhabi Islamist beliefs himself, al-Awlaki facilitated the development of other Islamists, drawing on his knowledge of both American culture and Islamist ideology to radicalize them, even to the point of their becoming terrorists. For a decade, al-Awlaki apparently deflected US law enforcement officials' scrutiny because he did not espouse violence. Though many of his Islamist colleagues initially claimed he was a "moderate," al-Awlaki burnished his Islamist credentials when he announced from Yemen on March 18, 2010, that all Muslims have a duty to fight violent *jihad* against the United States.[108]

Nidal Hasan, therefore, appears to be just one in a series of Muslims whose search for meaning and spiritual guidance brought them into contact with Islamist activists. Jihadist sermons like al-Awlaki's can provide the ideological pressure that solidifies a radicalizing Islamist's view — that the West is irreconcilably opposed to Islam and must be attacked. Hasan's path to radicalization followed an increasingly common pattern: a devout Muslim American seemingly at home in the mainstream flirts with Islamist ideology via the internet, attends a mosque with a charismatic Islamist imam, then withdraws from mainstream society in accordance with Islamist doctrine. Hasan went one terrible step further, translating the Islamist message of jihadism into brutal action: he reportedly jumped onto a desk at Fort Hood on November 5, 2009, shouted "Allahu Akbar [God is great]!" and fired more than 100 rounds at his US Army colleagues, whom, he believed, were waging war on Islam.

Islamist organizations initially rejected any connection between Hasan's religion and his "alleged" crimes. ISNA and four other Muslim and Arab organizations held a press conference the day after the Fort Hood shootings at ISNA's Washington office on Capitol Hill to condemn the shootings and to urge the public to view the attack as an isolated action by an individual criminal:

---

107   CBS News, "Abdulmutallab: Cleric Told Me to Bomb Jet," *CBS News* (February 5, 2010), available at: www.cbsnews.com/stories/2010/02/04/national/main6174780.shtml (accessed January 30, 2011).

108   M. Zuhdi Jasser, "American Muslims Respond to Al-Awlaki's Call for Jihad," *Daily Caller* (March 18, 2010), available at: http://dailycaller.com/2010/03/18/american-muslims-respond-to-al-awlakis-call-for-jihad/ (accessed January 30, 2011).

We don't know the motives or the state of mind of the perpetrator of this heinous crime, but we want our fellow Americans to know that Muslim Americans condemn this horrific attack and see it as a complete violation of Islamic values and norms. As with Timothy McVeigh, the sniper, we focused on the person, not their religion. You wouldn't take a Christian or a Jewish soldier who did something like this and look at other Christians and Jews and say, "Can we trust them?"[109]

ISNA's attempt to compare Hasan and his Islamist ideology to Timothy McVeigh and his Christianity is a classic Islamist tactic. ISNA's leaders know McVeigh did not invoke religion when he blew up the Murrow Federal Building in Oklahoma City, whereas Hasan *did* as he murdered his colleagues. Moreover, in cases where religious doctrine did play a role in mass violence, US media and officials readily acknowledged this point. One of the most famous such cases was the April 1993 clash between David Koresh's Branch Davidian religious cult and US law enforcement officials. The standoff ended in a fire that destroyed the organization's compound in Waco, Texas, resulting in the death of Koresh and dozens of his followers. The fact that Koresh led a Christian cult was a prominent element of all news coverage. Given Hasan's own admission that he was motivated by his religion to kill his Fort Hood comrades, ISNA's public claims about Muslim "victimization" were notably lacking in credibility, even by Islamist standards. The arrests of five young Muslim American men in Pakistan shortly after Hasan's attack placed further pressure on US Islamist organizations to soften their reflexive denial of any link between Islamist doctrine and violence.

CAIR and other US Islamist organizations long denied any link between Islamist ideology and terrorism and rejected claims that their narrow interpretation of Islam was radical. When asked about CAIR's adherence to Wahhabism, CAIR spokesman Ibrahim Hooper replied that Wahhabism

is one of those terms which is invented to scare people about Muslim bogeymen. It's just all part of the extremely powerful right wing and

---

109   ISNA, "Muslim Organizations Urge the Media and Public to View Ft Hood Attack as Criminal Act," ISNA (November 6, 2009), available at: www.isna.net/articles/News/Muslim-Organizations-Urge-the-Media-and-Public-to-View-Ft-Hood-Attack-as-Criminal-Act.aspx (accessed January 30, 2011).

their agenda right now to demonize Saudi Arabia and demonize anything associated with Saudi Arabia.[110]

Such views were expressed by CAIR legal director Arsalan Iftikhar in his 2004 opinion editorial in the *Dallas Morning News*: "The term 'Islamist terrorism' is nothing more than an oversimplification of our complex and kaleidoscopic national security paradigm."[111]

Since 2009, CAIR has gradually changed its rhetoric — especially after the Fort Hood attacks at the end of the year. On December 9, 2009, CAIR publicly admitted for the first time that radicalization was a growing problem in American Muslim communities; CAIR Executive Director Nihad Awad conceded:

> We also as a community realize and recognize that there is a problem. This problem we believe is not widespread. But . . . as a community, we acknowledge that there is a problem, and we are going to deal with it effectively. We are going to launch a major campaign of education to refute the misuse of verses in the Koran or the misuse of certain grievances in the Muslim World.[112]

However, as of this writing, the organization has yet to take even the most tentative step toward combating Islamism.

Mainstream media sources in the United States continue to echo the propaganda line pushed by Islamist organizations — that each terrorist incident is motivated exclusively by personal factors and has nothing to do with religion. One of the *New York Times'* initial reports on the Fort Hood shootings, entitled "Little Evidence of Terror Plot in Base Killings," stressed that Hasan "might have long suffered from emotional problems that were exacerbated by the tensions of his work with veterans of the wars in Iraq and Afghanistan who returned home with serious psychiatric problems." The story further argued that Hasan's (secular) counselling

---

110   David Staples, "Local Mosque Denies Links with Controversial Group," *Edmonton Journal* (July 8, 2003).

111   Arsalan Iftikhar, "Constant Use of 'Islamist' Overlooks Real Threats," *Dallas Morning News* (August 3, 2004), available at: www.ghazali.net/amp/html/constant_use_of.html (accessed January 30, 2011).

112   Nihad Awad's remarks at the CAIR press conference on Muslim community assisting FBI in finding five missing Muslim youth, December 9, 2009, Washington, DC, "CAIR News Conference on Missing Youth (Part 1)," Youtube, available at: www.youtube.com/watch?v=2w8jSrYDVTk&feature=player_embedded (accessed January 30, 2011).

activities with veterans "may have further fuelled his anger and hardened his increasingly militant views as he was seeming to move toward more extremist religious beliefs — all of which boiled over as he faced being shipped overseas, an assignment he bitterly opposed." The story concludes with the observation that "so far, investigators have unearthed no evidence that he was directed or steered into violence or ever travelled overseas to meet with extremist groups, as defendants in some recent terrorism cases are accused of doing."[113] Like the vast majority of media accounts, this story stopped short of looking into the impact of Islamist ideology as a catalyst of Major Hasan's terror.

Such sentiment, stoked by Islamist victimization rhetoric, has deterred US officials from publicly discussing the role of Islamist ideology in inspiring the massacre. Hasan's peers and superiors — some of whom sensed his religious radicalization — never spoke up before the shootings, apparently fearful of being accused of Islamophobia. The official analysis of the Fort Hood massacre prepared by the US Department of Defense in January 2010 failed to transcend this climate of political correctness; it does not mention Islam, Islamism, or Islamist radicalization anywhere in the text, concluding that Hasan was just another disgruntled workplace shooter.[114]

Belated Western Awakening to the Threat of Islamist Ideology?

Before the Hasan case, few officials in local or national government had accepted the 9/11 Commission's conclusion in 2004 that the key to defeating terrorism was to defeat Islamist ideology. Even when the Bush administration tried to produce a counterextremism strategy on the basis of this finding, its efforts were stifled by bureaucratic inertia.

A rare exception was the New York City Police Department (NYPD) under Chief of Police Ray Kelly. In August 2007, the NYPD issued an insightful and courageous report that broke new analytical ground by

---

113   David Johnston and Eric Schmitt, "Little Evidence of Terror Plot in Base Killings," *New York Times* (November 7, 2009), available at: www.nytimes.com/2009/11/08/us/08investigate.html (accessed January 30, 2011).

114   US Department of Defense Independent Review, *Protecting the Force: Lessons from Fort Hood* (Washington, DC: Department of Defense, 2010), available at: www.defense.gov/pubs/pdfs/DOD-ProtectingTheForce-Web_Security_HR_13Jan10.pdf (accessed January 30, 2011).

identifying Islamist ideology as the key driving factor behind a frightening new phenomenon: homegrown terrorism in the United States and Europe. The report, entitled *Radicalization in the West: The Homegrown Threat*,[115] described how Islamist radicalization was occurring and expanding within Muslim communities in the United States and Europe. Islamist organizations assailed the NYPD report as an attack on Muslims, but did not take issue with specific elements of the report's analysis. A coalition of Islamist organizations led by CAIR and MPAC tried to divert attention from the report's warnings — about links between Islamist ideology and terrorist action — through incendiary claims that Muslims had been victimized by the NYPD report: "The study of violent extremism . . . should decouple religion from terror to safeguard civil liberties on free speech and equal protection grounds as a matter of strong public policy."[116] CAIR board chairman Parvez Ahmed further noted, "Whatever one thinks of the analysis contained in the report, its sweeping generalizations and mixing of unrelated elements may serve to cast a pall of suspicion over the entire American Muslim community."[117]

Another cogent analysis was released in 2007 by the Netherlands General Intelligence and Security Service (AIVD). The report, entitled *The Radical Dawa in Transition: The Rise of Islamic Neo-Radicalism in the Netherlands*, identified Islamist ideology as both a root cause of terrorism and a threat to Europe's democratic order. It warned that Islamist groups such as the Muslim Brotherhood and HT sought to undermine "the Western democratic legal order . . . without resorting to, appealing for, or glorifying violence." The AIVD explained that Islamist groups use "clandestine tactics designed to actively oppose and disrupt the process of the democratic order . . . and clandestine efforts to gain strategic influence over local government policy-making and to secretly enter mainstream social organizations." Such efforts, the AIVD warned, "could gradually

---

115   Mitchell D. Silber and Arvin Bhatt, *Radicalization in the West: The Homegrown Threat* (New York: New York City Police Department, 2007), available at: www.nypdshield.org/public/SiteFiles/documents/NYPD_Report-Radicalization_in_the_West.pdf (accessed January 30, 2011).

116   Muslim American Civil Liberties Coalition (MACLC), "Counterterrorism Policy: MACLC's Critique of the NYPD's Report on Homegrown Radicalism," MACLC (November 20, 2008), available at: http://maclcnypdcritique.wordpress.com/ (accessed January 30, 2011).

117   PR Newswire, "CAIR: NYPD Terror Report Casts Suspicion on All U.S. Muslims," PR Newswire, news release (August 15, 2007), available at: www.prnewswire.com/news-releases/cair-nypd-terror-report-casts-suspicion-on-all-us-muslims-58251287.html (accessed January 30, 2011).

harm social cohesion and solidarity and undermine certain fundamental human rights."[118] In a separate effort, the Municipality of Amsterdam similarly warned governments and private citizens of the growing societal threat of Islamist radicalism, which it defined as "the growing preparedness to wish to or to support fundamental changes . . . in society that do not fit within our democratic system of law."[119]

Later that year, the Dutch government launched its own *Polarisation and Radicalisation: Action Plan 2007–2011*, which sought to prevent Islamist radicalization through programs that intervened with individual Muslims "at risk of slipping away or turning away from Dutch society and the democratic legal order."[120] These groundbreaking reports and initiatives deeply worried Islamist activists, who counterattacked with political pressure on the Netherlands government to reject the AIVD findings as anti-Muslim. For some time, the Islamists' pressure tactics worked, and Dutch authorities maintained their focus on countering "violent extremism" rather than Islamist ideology. But by early 2010, growing segments of Dutch society were rejecting their government's continuing acquiescence to Islamists' hardball tactics and self-segregation.

The British government has perhaps gone further than any other in Europe in identifying the ideological threat posed by Islamism, having developed a comprehensive strategy to blunt violent extremism and having to a large degree suspended politically correct tactics such as "engagement" with "nonviolent extremists." However, such progress has

118 AIVD, *The Radical Dawa in Transition: The Rise of Islamic Neo-Radicalism in the Netherlands* (Zoetermeer: AVID, 2007), pp. 9–10, available at: www.investigativeproject.org/documents/testimony/341.pdf (accessed January 30, 2011). Two other important AIVD reports are: Netherlands Ministry of the Interior and Kingdom Relations, *From Dawa to Jihad: The Various Threats from Radical Islam to the Democratic Legal Order* (The Hague: Ministry of the Interior and Kingdom Relations, 2004), available at: www.minbzk.nl/contents/pages/42345/fromdawatojihad.pdf (accessed January 30, 2011), and Netherlands Ministry of the Interior and Kingdom Relations, *Violent Jihad in the Netherlands* (The Hague: Ministry of the Interior and Kingdom Relations, 2006), available at: www.investigativeproject.org/documents/testimony/50.pdf (accessed January 30, 2011).

119 Municipality of Amsterdam, *Amsterdam Against Radicalisation* (Amsterdam: Municipality of Amsterdam, 2007), p. 5, cited in Vidino, "Europe's New Security Dilemma," p. 64, available at: http://www.eenveiligamsterdam.nl/publish/pages/164993/amsterdam_against_radicalisation.pdf (accessed January 30, 2011).

120 Netherlands Ministry of the Interior and Kingdom Relations, *Polarisation and Radicalisation: Action Plan 2007–2011* (The Hague: Interior and Kingdom Relations, n.d.), available at: http://english.minbzk.nl/aspx/download.aspx?file=/contents/pages/89799/minbiz007_actieplanuk-v3.pdf (accessed January 30, 2011).

moved in fits and starts due to Islamist pressure, political timidity, and bureaucratic inertia. Prime Minister Tony Blair's statement following the July 7, 2005, bombings in London — that there is danger in terrorists' beliefs as well as their actions — spurred elements of his government to action. The Home Office launched a new counterterrorism strategy dubbed "CONTEST," consisting of four pillars: pursue, protect, prepare, and prevent. The $225 million "prevent" component, only implemented in 2008, was comprised of six elements:

1. Challenging Islamist ideology and supporting mainstream voices (through education, media training, and support for civic organizations of moderate Muslims who seek to resist Islamist recruiters).
2. Disrupting those who promote violent extremist ideology (by deporting or barring the entry of foreign radicals).
3. Supporting individuals who are vulnerable to recruitment by violent extremists.
4. Increasing "community resilience" (i.e., training non-Islamists how to identify and resist Islamist recruiters).
5. Addressing Muslims' social grievances.
6. Developing strategic communications to counter violent extremism.[121]

The Home Office steered clear of working solely with its previous Islamist partners and chose a "let a thousand flowers bloom" approach: thus, it cooperated with a non-Islamist think tank, the Quilliam Foundation, as well as with non-Islamist groups like the Sufi Muslim Council.

The UK government has nonetheless continued to work with and provide funding to "nonviolent Islamists" who disseminate their views throughout British society via a subinitiative dubbed the "Radical Middle Way." This project includes prominent "soft Islamists," like UK's Tariq Ramadan and American Islamist leader Jamal Badawi, as speakers; women speakers wear the *hijab*.[122] In promotional materials, British officials have wrongly referred to the Islamist participants in the Radical Middle Way as "mainstream Islamic voices in the UK." Respected journalist and Islamism expert Martin Bright has concluded that the fundamental approach of the Radical Middle Way is based on the ideas of Yusuf al-Qaradawi, the

---

121   Mark Williams, remarks at "Terrorist Dropouts: Learning from Those Who Have Left," research conference, Washington Institute for Near East Policy, January 21, 2010.
122   For more information on the group, see its website, www.radicalmiddleway.co.uk/about (accessed January 30, 2011).

spiritual leader of the Muslim Brotherhood.[123] In other words, while it theoretically could push British Muslims away from committing violent acts — at least on British soil — the project still instills a Muslim-first identity that requires the adoption of sharia norms.

Notwithstanding this and other setbacks in which British officials continue to partner with "nonviolent Islamists," other top officials have recognized the threat Islamism poses to British society and advocated a change in policy. In October 2008, when advocating fundamental changes in the criteria used to disburse public funding for counterradicalization programs, Ruth Kelly, then secretary of state for the Department of Communities and Local Government, argued, "It is only by defending our values that we will prevent extremists [from] radicalising future generations of terrorists."[124] Jacqui Smith similarly warned in December 2008 when Home Secretary that Islamist groups that condemn violence but promote values incompatible with those of the UK are not worthy partners: "They may not explicitly promote violence, but they can create a climate of fear and distrust where violence becomes more likely."[125] Smith's Home Office announced a new counterradicalization strategy in March 2009 known as "Contest 2":

> Our strategy to prevent people becoming terrorists is not simply about tackling violent extremism. It is also about tackling those who espouse extremist views that are inconsistent with our shared values. Decisions on which organisations to fund are taken very carefully and are subject to robust scrutiny. We are clear that we will not continue to fund groups where we have evidence of them encouraging discrimination, undermining democracy and being ambiguous toward terrorism.[126]

Under Contest 2, the British government is "branding as extremists those

---

123   Martin Bright, *When Progressives Treat with Reactionaries: The British State's Flirtation with Radical Islamism* (London: Policy Exchange, 2006), available at: www.policyexchange. org.uk/images/publications/pdfs/When_Prog.pdf (accessed January 30, 2011).

124   Philippe Naughton, "Funding Cut-off Threat by Minister Angers Muslim Groups," *Times* (October 11, 2006), available at: http://www.timesonline.co.uk/tol/news/politics/ article668544.ece (accessed March 3, 2011).

125   Alan Travis, "Time to Tackle the Non-Violent Extremists, Says Smith," *Guardian* (December 11, 2008), available at: www.guardian.co.uk/uk/2008/dec/11/counter-terrorism-strategy-extremists (accessed January 30, 2011).

126   BBC, "Home Office Statement on Muslim First, British Second," *Panorama*, BBC (February 13, 2009), available at: http://news.bbc.co.uk/panorama/hi/front_page/ newsid_7888000/7888793.stm (accessed January 30, 2011).

conservative Muslims who, while eschewing violence, maintain that Islam is incompatible with British democracy, call for the creation of a caliphate, promote *sharia*, and argue in favor of an Islamic ban on homosexuality."[127] By launching Contest 2 from this perspective, the British government has identified more clearly than any other government the strategic threat posed by Islamist ideology to the democratic, political, and legal order of Western civilization. Islamists replied with a harsh political and media counterattack, calling Contest 2 a "modern day witch-hunt."[128] Inayat Bunglawala of the MCB warned that the new strategy's focus on countering Islamist ideology "would alienate the majority of the British Muslim public" (inadvertently revealing his view that most British Muslims hold Islamist views that do, in fact, contradict British values). This Islamist pressure has slowed implementation of Contest 2, but the overall strategy remains on track.

Whitehall followed a similar pattern of advance and retreat in its relations with the MCB. In March 2009, the government suspended its official relations with the Islamist organization because MCB director Daoud Abdullah had joined 90 other Islamist leaders in signing a pro-Hamas declaration at the January 2009 Shura Council conference in Istanbul. The declaration celebrated Hamas' victory against "Zionist Jewish occupiers" and urged Muslim nations to regard any foreign warships in their territorial waters (such as British and US ships believed to be aiding Israel) "as a declaration of war, a new occupation, sinful aggression, and a clear violation of the sovereignty of their nation . . . [which] must be rejected and fought by all means and ways."[129] As in so many other cases, the Islamist response was one of loud criticism. On January 10, relations were restored after the MCB declared its opposition to violence.[130] Abdullah received an appointment to the University of London's

127   David Sapsted, "UK to Isolate Hardline Preachers," *Abu Dhabi National* (February 19, 2009).

128   Fahad Ansari, *British Anti-Terrorism: A Modern-Day Witch-Hunt* (Wembley: Islamic Human Rights Commission, 2006), available at: www.ihrc.org.uk/file/2006Terrorreport.pdf (accessed January 30, 2011).

129   Richard Kerbaj, "Government Moves to Isolate Muslim Council of Britain with Cash for Mosques," *Times* (March 30, 2009), available at: www.timesonline.co.uk/tol/news/uk/article6004850.ece (accessed January 30, 2011).

130   James Slack, "Labour Restores Official Ties to Muslim Council of Britain Despite Their Refusal to Remove Deputy Accused of Supporting Hamas," *Daily Mail* (January 15, 2010), available at: www.dailymail.co.uk/news/article-1243588/Labour-restores-official-ties-Muslim-Council-Britain-despite-refusal-remove-deputy-accused-supporting-Hamas.html (accessed January 30, 2011).

Birkbeck College to teach a 22-week course entitled "Introduction to Islam." Houriya Ahmed, a non-Islamist Muslim researcher at the Centre for Social Cohesion think tank, called the appointment "deeply worrying." In his view,

> [i]t is bad enough when hardline preachers are invited on campus; but to have someone actually lecturing on behalf of the university is far worse. It is shocking they think that this man is suitable to introduce students to Islam.[131]

For the moment, the British government seems to be ahead of the US government in recognizing the societal threat posed by Islamist ideology. In his landmark speech in Cairo, President Barak Obama did warn that "violent extremists" are seen in some quarters of US society as undermining democracy and human rights, but did not include himself among those concerned Americans. Instead, he called for reconciliation between the United States and the "Muslim world," lumping all Muslims into a single community in keeping with Islamist doctrine. Nor did President Obama echo the British Home Office and move beyond the worn formula of condemning "violent extremism" to identify Islamist ideology as a threat to the fundamental values of democracy. Finally, the president repeatedly mentioned a Muslim woman's "right" to wear the headscarf in his Cairo speech, while failing to also mention her right to *refuse* to wear an Islamic head covering.[132]

Reluctance to confront Islamist ideology is prevalent elsewhere in the Obama administration, at least as of this writing. Dalia Mogahed, advisor to President Obama's Council on Faith-Based and Neighborhood Partnerships (and executive director of the Gallup Center for Muslim Studies) has spoken in favor of sharia for all Muslims. She explained to the *Telegraph* newspaper that sharia "is not well understood" and that Muslim women support "universal values of justice and equality" but reject "Western values," which she said they associate with "promiscuity."[133]

---

131   Andrew Gilligan, "Hamas Supporter Teaching at London University," *Telegraph* (January 21, 2010), available at: www.telegraph.co.uk/news/uknews/7037659/Hamas-supporter-teaching-at-London-university.html (accessed January 30, 2011).

132   President Obama, "Remarks by the President on a New Beginning."

133   Andrew Gilligan and Alex Spillius, "Barack Obama Adviser Says Sharia Law is Misunderstood," *Telegraph* (October 8, 2009), available at: www.telegraph.co.uk/news/worldnews/northamerica/usa/barackobama/6274387/Obama-adviser-says-Sharia-Law-is-misunderstood.html (accessed January 30, 2011).

When Mogahed appeared on a program hosted by an HT member on the Islam Channel, the Muslim Brotherhood's global English language television station, she did not speak up when the host and her HT co-panelist repeatedly attacked secular law and proposed sharia law instead. Instead, she said:

> I'm sure there are people out there — and in fact they are not all Muslim — who believe that this is something that the United States and Britain and other countries should be open to — the concept of integrating shari'ah into laws in Muslim-majority societies. And of course, most Muslim-majority societies do have shari'ah as a part of their laws already.[134]

Washington's aversion to scrutinizing Islamist ideology extends beyond the White House. In January 2010, the Department of State reversed the Bush administration's decision to deny an entry visa to Tariq Ramadan, explaining, "[b]oth the president and the secretary of state have made it clear that the U.S. Government is pursuing a new relationship with Muslim communities based on mutual interest and mutual respect."[135] At the Department of Homeland Security, Secretary Janet Napolitano initially made no mention that the would-be bomber of an airplane heading from Amsterdam to Detroit on Christmas Day 2009 was either Muslim or Islamist. With public attention still heavily focused on the failed Christmas Day attack, Napolitano met in January 2010 with the Islamist organization ISNA in conjunction with her department's "counterradicalization" efforts, offering this bland explanation:

> In times of crisis, leaders of faith-based communities and other grassroots organizations often play a critical role in the broad and timely dissemination of accurate information. Strengthening our partnerships with

---

134   A transcript of Dalia Mogahed's interview by Ibtihal Bsis Ismail on the Islam Channel's *Muslimah Dilemma*, October 4, 2009, is available at: www.counterterrorismnews. com/home/index.php?option=com_content&view=article&id=1467:transcript-of-dalia-mogahed-on-islam-channels-muslimah-dilemma-program&Itemid=37 (accessed January 30, 2011).

135   *Washington Times*, "Clinton Clears 2 Muslims for Entry," *Washington Times* (January 21, 2010), available at: www.washingtontimes.com/news/2010/jan/21/clinton-clears-2-muslims-for-entry/ (accessed January 30, 2011). US immigration authorities first withheld Ramadan's visa in July 2004, after he had been offered a tenured teaching position at the University of Notre Dame in Indiana. In 2006, Ramadan was denied a new visa due to his $1,300 contribution to a Swiss-based charity, the Association de Secours Palestinien, which is believed to be allied with Hamas, Muslim Brotherhood's political/military wing.

faith- and community-based groups will allow improved information sharing and better coordination in preparing for, assessing and responding to threats.[136]

Secretary Napolitano, with prodding from Senator Joseph Lieberman of Connecticut, eventually acknowledged the possibility that democracy might actually protect itself against Islamist efforts to undermine it. During a hearing in the US Senate on February 24, 2010, Senator Lieberman, chairman of the Homeland Security Committee, complained about the administration's reluctance to use terms such as "Islamist extremism" or "Muslim terrorist," especially in the Department of Defense report on the Fort Hood shootings. Secretary Napolitano eventually acknowledged that Islamist ideology was connected with Hasan's attack and other cases of terrorism:

> "Violent Islamic terrorism" is something that we fight and deal with every day at the Department of Homeland Security. There is no doubt about that. It was the motivation [for the failed Christmas Day bombing], it was part and parcel of the Ft. Hood killings and other incidents we have seen this year within the United States."[137]

It remains to be seen whether Secretary Napolitano's statement will mark a shift in US policy from countering "violent extremism" to confronting the political-religious ideology that seeks to undermine the values and institutions of American democracy. Bureaucratic inertia still drives policymakers to seek engagement with "nonviolent Islamists" rather than to differentiate between Islam and Islamism. But popular anger generated by cases of homegrown terrorists such as Colleen R. LaRose, a blonde-haired and blue-eyed American woman living in Pennsylvania who was radicalized into a prospective murderer by Islamist recruiters and called herself "Jihad Jane," is driving US officials to search for better ways to identify and stop potential terrorists. Profiling on the basis of physical appearance is no longer effective. The only factor that links all Muslims considering terrorist action is the political-religious ideology of Islamism.

---

136   Department of Homeland Security, "Readout of Secretary Napolitano's Meeting with Faith-Based and Community Leaders," press release (January 28, 2010), available at: www.dhs.gov/ynews/releases/pr_1264712375316.shtm (accessed January 30, 2011).

137   Mike Levine, "Ft. Hood Attack Publicly Called 'Terrorism,'" LiveShots blog, *Fox News* (February 24, 2010), available at: http://liveshots.blogs.foxnews.com/2010/02/24/ft-hood-attack-publicly called-terrorism/ (accessed January 30, 2011).

Islamist terrorists are the ideological kin of millions of nonviolent Islamists around the globe who seek the same objectives: universal imposition of their draconian social and legal norms in a struggle for the heart and soul of Islam and the subsequent restructuring of the global political order.

CHAPTER 6

Conclusion and Policy Prescriptions

From Islamism's early beginnings in the postwar era to the present day, the United States and Europe have been largely oblivious to its rise as a political ideology bent on overturning the modern world's political and legal order. As Western leaders focused on defeating Nazism and Communism, Islamic fundamentalists refined their ideology and honed their tactics according to the example of both totalitarian movements; they then consolidated their financial strength and embedded themselves in Western societies. Today, Western concepts of religious freedom make government leaders, civil society activists, and academic and media experts uncomfortable with directly confronting Islamists' utopianist rejection of democracy and universal human rights. Islamists have learned how to use the strictures of political correctness to their advantage, employing liberal-sounding slogans to deflect scrutiny of their ideological goals while ruthlessly silencing their critics. Islamists have thus succeeded in masking a frightening truth: nonviolent Islamists seek the same strategic goals as the Islamist terrorists who struck on September 11, 2001. The West is traveling down a path to defeat, with Islamists gaining ground as they push Muslims and non-Muslims further apart in their long-term effort to consolidate Muslim support and segregate Muslim communities from mainstream society. In this way, they come closer each day toward their objective of a global *umma* ruled by sharia. To reverse this trajectory and win the hearts and minds of Muslims, Western governments need to make fundamental policy changes. They can accomplish these desperately needed reforms by:

1. Accurately diagnosing the threat confronting modern civilization.
2. Choosing the right partners to discredit that threat.
3. Discrediting and defeating Islamist ideology.
4. Helping Muslim moderates launch an Islamic renaissance.

1. Diagnosing the Threat: Islamism not Islam

So far, Western governments and societies have not clearly defined the problem that they have been trying in earnest to address since September 11, 2001. This lack of clarity has led to ineffective and even counterproductive policies. The West has focused on countering the tactical threats of terrorism and "violent extremism," but has rarely recognized the strategic threat posed by Islamism. Islamism is a political-religious ideology that is related but not identical to Islam. Islamism seeks to impose on the rest of the world an intolerant interpretation of Islam rooted in medieval Arabia, and to harness that vision of Islam to fulfill a political agenda — namely, the replacement of the world's political institutions and values with its own legal norms and social customs. Islamist ideologues and tacticians have learned how to deflect Western scrutiny of their underlying goals, conflating their political religious ideology with the religion of Islam by cloaking their rhetoric in the very principles of democracy and human rights they seek to undermine.

To appreciate the danger posed by Islamism, Western governments and societies must first deepen their understanding of Islam and the diversity of religious thought among Muslims. Islamists derive their ideology primarily from a single strain of Islamic jurisprudence dating to ninth-century Arabia. Dozens of other branches of Islamic thought flourished at the time when the "gates of *ijtihad* were closed." These varied strains of Islamic thinking were subsequently refined and adapted to cultural conditions in the lands far beyond Arabia where Islam was adopted. Islamists reject this rich diversity and claim a monopoly on interpreting the Qur'an and defining Islamic doctrine. As with Christianity, interpretations of Islam range from fundamentalist to liberal, and include the deep divide between Sunnis and Shiites. Despite Islamists' claims to the contrary, no single "correct" interpretation of Islam exists; nor is there one accepted set of rules of behavior that any "true Muslim" must adopt. Liberal and reformist Muslims who blend local culture and scientific learning with their religious faith have as legitimate an Islamic outlook as conservatives who insist that their faith is the very same as the "original" Islam of the seventh century. Unlike Christianity with its popes, patriarchs, bishops, and priests, Islam lacks a system of religious authority; there is no intercession between the individual believer and God.[1] Islam instead stresses the centrality of the individual's personal relationship with God. Imams deliver sermons and lead prayers, but in other respects are not considered different from the rest of the congregation. Moreover, there is no clerical hierarchy that determines Islam's theological doctrines. This direct connection between the believer and God has for centuries allowed individual Muslims to interpret the key tenets of their faith in accordance with the traditions and practices of the diverse societies in which they have lived. This adaptability is in fact a key reason why Islam has spread so widely around the world. Yet, Islamists reject the notion of Islam's adaptability and seek to eliminate those who disagree.

Non-Muslims cannot determine the outcome of this debate within Islam. However, they have a deep interest in ensuring that the winner of this ideological struggle is an Islam compatible with the universal values of democracy, freedom, tolerance, and human rights that form the foundation of modern pluralistic societies. Muslims, like members of other faith groups, should be free to interpret and practice their religion; but Islamist practices that derive from medieval Arabic traditions and contradict secular democracy and universal human rights (e.g., a separate legal system, gender segregation, mandatory covering for women) need not be accepted by modern Western societies, nor by the 80 percent of the world's Muslims who live outside the Arab Middle East.

This is not just an issue for the governments and people of the West. Millions of Muslims beyond Europe, the United States, and other parts of the West have an equally strong interest in insulating Islam from corruption by Islamist ideology. In countries where Islamists have secured political power, they have imposed their political, social, and religious views on Muslim populations. The theocratic regimes that they have established and supported reject alternative interpretations of Islam, thereby violating human rights and threatening international stability. This

---

1   The Sufi belief in intercession is an exception.

trend began in the 1920s in the Arabian Peninsula, where the reach of Wahhabism expanded together with the political authority of the House of Saud. Severe restrictions on individual liberty have been in place ever since, with particularly severe burdens on women — who are forced to live lives of complete segregation. In Iran, the Islamic Revolution of 1979 established the world's first Islamist republic, with clerical "guardians" in complete control of the country's politics as well as its religious life. Not only did these clerics curtail political freedom and civil liberties at home; abroad, they committed acts of terrorism and spread Islamist ideology among both Shiites (through Hezbollah) and Sunnis (through Hamas). In neighboring Afghanistan, the Movement of the Students — better known by the Arabic name of Taliban — seized power in 1995 and promptly imposed a severe interpretation of sharia on that country's diverse ethnic and religious groups.

The Taliban government became one of the world's most repressive regimes, as it sequestered women from the rest of society, destroyed artistic and archaeological treasures (like the ancient Buddha statues of Bamyan), offered refuge to al-Qaeda, and publicly executed anyone who disagreed with its policies. The story has been much the same in other regions where Islamists have risen to power, such as Hamas-led Gaza and pockets of Sudan, Yemen, Somalia, and Pakistan. In these areas, Islamist groups kill other Muslims — including moderate clerics and tribal leaders — while eliminating institutions and practices they deem "un-Islamic," including music radio stations, movie theaters, soccer matches, and the education of girls and women. In areas of Somalia controlled by the Islamist sepa-ratist group al-Shabaab, these brutal extremists have imposed draconian measures on fellow Muslims to ensure they conform to the militia's harsh and narrow interpretation of sharia, which have completely altered everyday life. Al-Shabaab has even banned playing soccer and watching it on television and using ringtones on cell phones with anything but "Qur'anic" sounds (i.e., a recording of a Qur'an passage or the call to prayer). Women are forced to cover themselves from head to toe in thick cloth robes known as *abayas*, cannot wear bras, must ride in the back of segregated buses, and are permitted to ride only female donkeys. Al-Shabaab morality police roam the areas controlled by the militia, stoning presumed adulterers and amputating the limbs of presumed thieves.

The virus of Islamism has also spread to the West, although the symptoms there are not yet as severe. Islamists are active among Muslims — whose alienation they exacerbate — and among the institutions of society at large, whose openness and tolerance they exploit to introduce elements of sharia into the daily lives of Muslims and non-Muslims alike. Western policymakers, civic activists, and experts remain surprisingly unaware of this strategic threat, as their discomfort with discussing specifically "religious" issues prevents them from differentiating between Islamism and Islam. Their efforts to tackle the problem that is misdiagnosed as "violent extremism" have managed to alleviate many symptoms, but unless the underlying Islamist infection is also addressed, recovery is highly unlikely.

The West is making moral and operational errors in its dealing with Islam. Morally, Western leaders' acceptance of Islamists as spokespersons for all "mainstream Muslims" contradicts their embrace of diversity as a core value of their society. Operationally, when Western governments and societies partner with Islamists against "violent extremism," they are empowering ideologues in pursuit of the same utopian goals as terrorists. And by failing to condemn Islamists' hateful and seditious speech, Western leaders undercut their own efforts to mitigate extremism, both in its violent and its political form.

Western governments and societies therefore must change course: they must end their tolerance of Islamists' intolerance and instead embrace the diversity of religious thought among the world's Muslim societies. By differentiating Islam from Islamism, Western leaders can attract and retain the support of the majority of Muslims who want the chance to enjoy rights for themselves, not "rights" for their religion as the Islamists define it.

2. Empowering the Right Partners: Moderates, Not Islamists

Since 9/11, Western governments and societies have far too often partnered in their counterterrorism efforts with Islamists who renounce violence, rather than with moderate Muslims who reject Islamism. Not surprisingly, this approach has failed both to reduce radicalization and to facilitate the integration of Muslims into Western societies. Islamists have thus had success in consolidating many Western Muslims into discrete communities that (uneasily) exist alongside — rather than within — society as a whole. Furthermore, Islamist ideology radicalizes a small but far from negligible number of these isolated Muslims into dangerous terrorists. Western leaders will be unable to integrate Muslims into mainstream society, strengthen social cohesion, or stem the flow of potential terrorist recruits until the Islamists' "ideology factory" is shut down. This process can begin only if government officials, journalists, and academics stop granting legitimacy to Islamists as partners and spokespersons for all Muslims.

Changing long-established patterns of engagement with Muslims will require political courage on the part of Western governments. Years of close interaction with Islamist groups, such as CAIR and ISNA in the United States and the MCB in the UK, have generated so much political momentum that these partnerships cannot be discontinued quickly. Due to their flexible organizational structures, considerable financial resources, and enormous political clout, these groups are able to adeptly focus on suppressing their opponents within both the broader Muslim community and the political arena. Most politicians and government bureaucrats are unwilling to brave these groups' reflexive accusations of Islamophobia in response to scrutiny of their activities, and have chosen inertia over confrontation. Moreover, many Western law enforcement officials continue to misperceive these organizations as "moderate" and "inclusive" umbrella organizations that represent "the Muslim perspective" within their countries. Ensuring that Muslim voices are represented in the policymaking process is appropriate; but as Islamist groups are still seen as the reliable eyes and ears of government and law enforcement within Muslim communities, most Muslim voices remain unheard. The need to keep channels to the Muslim community open explains why the FBI refused to curtail relations with CAIR and ISNA, even as evidence flowed into FBI field offices that these groups were pursuing subversive goals and had close ties with terrorist groups in the Middle East. The FBI ceased official cooperation with CAIR only in November 2008, when a US federal court named CAIR, ISNA, and a dozen other Islamist organizations as unindicted coconspirators in the Holy Land Foundation case.

Since September 11, 2001, most European governments have followed the United States in engaging Islamists who renounce violence in the hope of preventing further terrorism. But in the latter half of the last decade, policies began to shift for the better, first in the Netherlands and then in the UK, as officials in The Hague and London perceived the threat of Islamist ideology to societies' democratic institutions and fundamental values. In the Netherlands, intelligence analysts and law enforcement personnel led the way in recognizing that counterterrorism efforts alone would not protect Dutch society from the strategic threat of Islamism and its ideology. In the UK, progress toward this crucial realization has come in fits and starts. In 2005, Prime Minister Tony Blair warned of the danger to British society of Islamist thinking, but he was shouted down both by Islamist activists and by left-wing elements within his own party. However, thanks to courageous efforts in the Home Office to expand Britain's "Muslim engagement" effort beyond a narrow circle of Islamist organizations, British officials have begun to hear more diverse views, including those of Muslim moderates. After years of partnering solely with groups like the MCB, the UK launched a new counterterrorism strategy in March 2009 in consultation with non-Islamist groups. The government declared that it would no longer support views that "fall short of supporting violence and are within the law, but which reject and undermine our shared values and jeopardize community cohesion."[2] The MCB and other Islamist groups continued to denounce such assertions as "Islamophobic," and have had some success at slowing implementation of the new strategy; nevertheless, the strategic tide may be turning in the UK.

The West as a whole can right its strategic drift by following the course of the Netherlands and the UK in partnering with non-Islamist Muslims, the true believers in moderation and nonviolence. Of course, it is not always easy to identify true non-Islamist partners. Islamists cloak their extremism in Western-friendly rhetoric, claiming to be fully committed to democracy, human rights, and respect for cultural and religious diversity. Rather than mentioning their goal of sharia explicitly, Islamists in the United States and Europe conceal this objective behind coded phrases like "a more ethical and just society."

But it is possible to identify non-Islamist potential partners in the West on the basis of four key distinguishing characteristics:

1. Non-Islamists do not insist on a single interpretation of Islam, and acknowledge that God alone knows the Truth, and tend to focus on the spiritual essence of religion (which unites not only Sunnis and Shiites, but those who follow other faiths as well), rather than superficial differences (as reflected in dogma).
2. Non-Islamists embrace the rule of secular law as the foundation of legal authority in the modern public sphere, with sharia relevant only in their private lives.
3. Moderates respect universal human rights and gender equality, and do

---

2   HM Government, *Pursue, Prevent, Protect, Prepare: The United Kingdom's Strategy for Countering International Terrorism* (London: The Home Office of the United Kingdom, 2009), p. 15, available at: http://merln.ndu.edu/whitepapers/UnitedKingdom2009.pdf (accessed January 30, 2011).

so without qualifying them as valid only providing they do not conflict with sharia.

4. Non-Islamists accept diversity as a core value of the modern West (as opposed to Islamists, who seek to create a uniform society with no gays, no uncovered women, and no religion equal to Islam). Accordingly, for non-Islamist Muslims, a "true" Muslim can choose not to eat pork in accordance with Islamic cultural traditions, but has no right to demand that pork not be served in restaurants or that other people (including other Muslims) also refrain from eating pork.

Non-Islamist activists are often lone wolves, struggling without the advantages of sophisticated organizational structures, financial resources, or political support. They are often ostracized by fellow Muslims who fear becoming Islamist targets themselves. Moreover, non-Islamists lack a single ideology to unite them, as they represent a wide range of religious and cultural traditions. This diversity has the advantage of making them *truly* representative of the rich variety of Islam, but it also inhibits the formation of umbrella organizations of sufficient scale and influence to counter Islamist mega-groups like CAIR, ISNA, and the MCB. Instead, when non-Islamist Muslims do organize themselves, they do so into small groups that focus on discrete issues (e.g., women's rights, social integration, education, employment). Non-Islamists may differ with each other on policy priorities or even on the relative weight sharia should carry in modern life; but all agree that Islamism is a serious threat to their individual rights, especially the freedom to practice their religion as their consciences dictate. Cultivating small and disparate non-Islamist organizations and weaving them into a coalition of activist Muslim moderates requires greater effort than partnering with Islamist umbrella organizations. However, there is no other way for governments to develop a meaningful policy of "Muslim engagement" to replace their current self-destructive partnerships with Islamists.

Western governments should keep in mind that non-Islamist partners can also be found in organizations that form along cultural, ethnic, or national lines rather than religious ones. European and American cities abound with Moroccan, Turkish, and Pakistani associations that seek to sustain their distinct culture and traditions in their adopted countries. Often, these associations directly reject Islamist teachings and practices; it is not unusual, for example, for Turkish business associations or Bosnian sporting clubs to serve alcohol. It is precisely the diversity of culture and faith reflected in national differences that Islamists seek to destroy, because they realize such pluralism is the greatest threat to their vision of a monolithic *umma*.

Once Western leaders have identified and cultivated non-Islamists on a broad scale, their work will not be completed; they must lend financial and organizational support to moderates, whose Islamist opponents have enjoyed a 30-year head start. Over the course of a few decades, Islamists have attracted billions of dollars in funding, established extensive organizational networks, and developed a clear sense of mission; these advantages grow more pronounced every day, as Islamists continue to receive enormous financial support from Saudi Arabia and Gulf countries. US officials in particular have typically hesitated to provide funding to non-Islamist organizations out of concern that such assistance might violate the principle of the separation of church and state. However, this argument is rather late in coming, since US government agencies have helped fund Islamist organizations for years, from Afghan mujahedeen in the 1980s to Pakistani madrassas today. The true reason why US officials have avoided supporting Muslim moderates is that they have mistakenly considered Islamist organizations such as CAIR and ISNA to be representative of American Muslims.

Fortunately, some European officials are becoming more active than their American counterparts in supporting non-Islamist groups and including them in programs aimed at promoting social integration and de-radicalization. Efforts by the Dutch and British governments to reach out to Muslim moderates have already been mentioned. Other governments seem to be taking similar steps. The German government ignored protests by Turkey's Islamist Milli Görüş movement and included staunch non-Islamists, such as the Turkish German lawyer Seyran Ateş (who argues for sexual revolution in Islam), in its dialogue with Muslims in Germany. The French government banned the wearing of the burqa and other full-face coverings in public and has continued to assert France's secular norms in partnership with non-Islamist Muslims.

When reaching out to Muslim moderates outside their own borders, the United States and Europe need to calibrate their assistance to avoid discrediting their new partners as Western "agents." The United States and its allies have suffered from a growing credibility deficit in many Muslim societies, thanks to the increasing popularity of the Islamist perspective on historical and current events, from the Crusades and colonialism to relations with Israel and the wars in Afghanistan and Iraq. Nevertheless, even those non-Islamists who dislike the West can partner with it in countering the strategic threat of Islamist ideology, provided that overt Western support does not increase their vulnerability to domestic attacks from Islamists and from authoritarian regimes that fear Western intervention.

The most effective tactic that Western governments can use to empower non-Islamist activists outside the West is to extend their assistance via third parties, especially local business and civil society leaders, who can operate independently, without detailed government oversight. In addition to avoiding the dangers of micromanagement, this approach also has the advantage of bolstering civil society groups working to sustain religious pluralism, gender equality, and respect for human rights in the region.

Western governments should also seek to work with governments of Muslim-majority countries to empower Muslim moderates. After all, these regimes have a selfish interest in ensuring their secular authority is not undermined by Islamist ideology. In the Middle East and Pakistan, where political tension continues to increase rapidly due to Islamist activism and government repression, Western leaders should proceed prudently. This means focusing on general issues such as religious freedom and pluralism without aggravating fears that the West is imposing its values, undermining local regimes, or supporting the political repression these regimes may be guilty of. Outside the Middle East, especially in countries and regions with traditions of religious pluralism (including North Africa, Central Asia, Azerbaijan, South Asia, and Southeast Asia), local governments may be more willing to support Muslim moderates actively and directly.

3. Countering the Strategic Threat of Islamist Ideology

Identifying and empowering the right partners will enable the West to focus on what ought to be its strategic goal: preventing Islamist extremists (whether political or violent) from winning the struggle for Islam. The key actors in this struggle must be Muslims themselves, but the West can make a significant contribution from the margins by helping Muslim moderates achieve three operational goals:

i. Expose and discredit Islamism for what it is — a utopian political ideology rooted in an intolerant interpretation of Islam that aspires to global dominance and a return to medieval social norms.

ii. Resist Islamist efforts in the West to consolidate and segregate Muslim communities from mainstream society.

iii. Encourage religious pluralism and cultural diversity among Muslims around the world.

These three goals hinge on a fourth goal for the West itself:

iv. Work with the governments of Muslim-majority countries to combat Islamism.

These operational goals are interrelated: as Islamists become less capable of imposing their political-religious views on other Muslims, diverse religious and cultural traditions will flourish; and as pluralism returns to Muslim communities around the world, Islamism will then be weakened as a global force. Finally, as Islamism weakens, fewer Muslims will be radicalized into political extremists and terrorists.

i. Discrediting Islamism as a Political Ideology Rooted in Religion

The West can help achieve the first operational goal, discrediting and defeating Islamism, in several key steps. First, Western officials and civil society leaders must stop legitimizing Islamists. Choosing the right Muslim partners for engagement and counterterrorism, as described above, is a prerequisite for success. The next step in avoiding legitimization of Islamism is for Western governments to stop protecting hateful and seditious preaching by Islamist activists. In particular, prosecutors need to recognize the balance that exists in Western constitutional law, on one hand between the protections of freedom of speech and assembly, and, on the other, the prohibitions against incitement to violence and sedition. Fearful of career-ending accusations of Islamophobia, officials currently tend to assume that all Islamist statements are protected speech; the laws against incitement and sedition need to be applied rigorously and evenly to Islamists as well as to other domestic extremists.

Second, Western governments and civil society leaders should draw popular attention to the ways in which Islamism harnesses religion for radical political ends. The general public must understand two key facts: Islamists represent a minority of Muslims who seek to undermine the secular democracy, human rights, and diversity that form the foundation of modern society; and the majority of the world's Muslims value political, legal, and social freedoms as much as their religious faith. Western leaders, especially in local governments, can no longer acquiesce to Islamists' creeping demands for the introduction of sharia norms in the West, such as gender segregation in doctors' offices and public swimming pools, mandatory covering of women (in whatever form, from the simple headscarf to the burqa, chador, and *jilbab*), polygamy, and obligatory conversion of non-Muslims who marry Muslims. These practices challenge the very core values of modern Western society. Moreover, they also contradict the belief of many traditional Muslims that immigrants to new lands are obliged to obey the laws and respect the customs of their adopted countries, and that sharia should apply only to personal matters. US and European leaders should insist that Muslims abide by all secular laws, and furthermore that they eschew self-segregating behavior such as covering women's faces. In short, the West must stop tolerating intolerance.

Third, Western governments should publicly refute incendiary Islamist propaganda that sows discord between Muslims and non-Muslims, and should expose their radicalization campaigns to public criticism and scrutiny. Law enforcement agencies must rebut claims by Islamist organizations such as CAIR in the United States and the MCB in Europe that investigations into jihadist networks in the West reflect a deliberate "war on Islam." They should also highlight Islamists' hypocritical double standard, according to which they demand equal access to employment and social benefits for Muslims while simultaneously denying equal access to basic freedoms to Muslim women and minorities.

ii. Defeating Islamists' Quest for Segregated Muslim Communities in the West

Discrediting Islamism for what it is — a political ideology cloaked in the language of religion — is by itself still not sufficient to ensure a Western strategic victory. It must be accompanied by an active effort to prevent Islamists from segregating Muslims in the West into separate communities whose members' primary identity is "Muslim" rather than "citizen." The West's traditional social integration policies have helped to reduce social alienation by ameliorating social disparities (e.g., in education, employment, and income); but such programs are not enough, and must be expanded to include mitigation of prejudices mutually held by non-Muslims and Muslims. Negative stereotyping — and the societal tensions it heightens — only plays into the hands of Islamist activists as they separate the Muslim community from society as a whole. One approach that could help would be to educate European publics more fully about the successful efforts in the United States to overcome the legacies of racism and social injustice, recounting the historical experiences of slavery, the Civil War, Reconstruction, the civil rights movement, and the election of President Barack Obama, while also acknowledging the economic disparities and social tensions that persist to this day. This and analogous historical examples can help assure Europeans that an integrated and cohesive multicultural society is a possibility, can help keep their justifiable anti-Islamism from degenerating into an unjustifiable anti-Islam, and can also make clear to European Muslims that, for the vast majority of black Americans, "separate but equal" is a reviled concept.[3]

The West must also broaden the focus of its secular integration efforts to include private Islamic schools. Many of these are run by Islamists who teach children that their primary loyalty is to Islam rather than to their countries of citizenship, and who inculcate attitudes toward females, gays, and members of other religions that reflect premodern norms. As David Bell, then chief inspector of schools in England (and later appointed Permanent Secretary of the Department of Education), has warned, these schools give their students "little appreciation of their wider responsibilities and obligations" to society.[4] Other European officials have expressed similar concerns about Islamic schools in their countries. Western governments must move away from their hands-off approach to the content being taught in Islamic schools; otherwise, they should not be surprised when these children grow up to be loyal citizens of the *umma* and not their countries. Religious schools should be encouraged to teach civics, history, philosophy, and critical thinking skills as well as the tenets of their faith. Moreover, they ought to provide their students with the opportunity to discover art, music, theater, and sports, all of which are frequently forbidden to students, especially girls, on the grounds that they are "un-Islamic." Governments should not provide financial assistance to any school that fails to meet these basic standards.

---

3   "Separate but equal" served for nearly a century as the rationale behind the racist Jim Crow laws; it was explicitly upheld by the Supreme Court in its infamous 1896 decision in *Plessy vs. Ferguson*. The goal of the civil rights movement was to overturn this doctrine and enable African Americans to become an equal part of society.

4   Tony Halpin, "Islamic Schools Are Threat to National Identity, Says Ofsted," *Times* (January 18, 2005), available at: www.timesonline.co.uk/tol/life_and_style/education/article413752.ece (accessed January 30, 2011).

Western governments cannot succeed alone in overcoming Islamists' opposition to secular integration; they need help from Muslim families as well. Local governments should encourage parents to study the language of the country where they live, and ensure that women in particular get the chance to attend language classes; since they often do not work outside the home, female immigrants tend to have fewer opportunities to learn. Parents are also key in countering spiritual alienation, which extremist recruiters exploit to spread Islamism and to radicalize some young Muslims into terrorists. Spiritual alienation arises most often when young Muslims lose touch with their families' traditions and begin to wonder about what it means to be a Muslim. Parents need to teach their children the non-Islamist traditions of their countries of origin so Islamist recruiters are less easily able to sell their doctrines on young Muslims searching for a religious identity. Carefully trained imams (see below) can help parents avoid passing on home-country practices that date back only to the recent spread of Islamism, notably those that marginalize or harm women or perpetuate intolerance and prejudice against non-Muslims. Muslim parents can also mitigate spiritual alienation by remaining engaged in their children's lives, in particular keeping track of who their friends are, what those friends say about Islam, what their children read about Islam on the internet, and who is teaching their children about Islam. Governments can help by providing parents training in how to recognize early indicators of Islamization (such as children's distancing themselves from non-Muslim and non-Islamist friends, challenging the family's religious traditions, and becoming markedly more introverted) and in how to stop the radicalization process once it has begun.

Indeed, government assistance is critical in reinforcing parents' efforts to prevent Islamists from exploiting and radicalizing spiritually alienated children. By themselves, parents cannot compete with Islamist recruiters, but government aid could help non-Islamists establish platforms offering religious advice to young Muslims searching for their Muslim identity. Such platforms should include websites that answer questions about Islam and Muslim identity from the perspective of non-Islamist thought and that counter the Islamist narrative. Governments should also work with non-Islamists to train imams who can reach out to individual Muslims and help them rediscover the compatibility of their families' Islamic traditions with secular democracy and universal human rights. Well-intentioned European policymakers often require that such "homegrown" imams preach only in the state's official language, so as to facilitate secular integration of Muslim immigrants. But this requirement is shortsighted, since many first-generation Muslim immigrants — especially women, as earlier noted — fail to learn the language of their adopted country; even those who are fluent in Western languages are less likely to attend a mosque or to feel connected to their families' Islamic traditions if an imam does not speak the language of their country of origin. European governments should therefore help train a new generation of imams who speak and will preach exclusively in South Asian languages, Arabic, and other key languages.

Regardless of the language in which they preach, *all* imams should be monitored by governments for any illegal incitement to sedition or violence. Monitoring — which need not be done surreptitiously — can also give governments advance warning of any tendencies that could undermine social cohesion and facilitate Islamist radicalization. Understandably, government monitoring of imams' sermons is a sensitive and controversial topic. For many Americans and Europeans, such scrutiny can appear to violate the principle of freedom of religion. A useful model of how to conduct such monitoring without violating civil liberties is provided by Turkey and its Directorate of Religious Affairs (in Turkish, Diyanet). As employees of the Diyanet, Turkish imams are professional civil servants; as imams, however, they enjoy considerable freedom to preach on Islamic morals and ethics. They are enjoined only from preaching in ways that directly undermine secular democracy. European governments have been reluctant to consider the Diyanet model for their own societies due to their general discomfort with regulating religion and their perception that Diyanet imams encourage Turks in Europe to maintain their primary loyalty to Turkey. Despite these concerns, the governments of the Netherlands and Germany have begun working with the Diyanet on imam training due to their rising concerns about Islamist recruitment.

iii. Reviving Religious and Cultural Diversity as Antidotes to Extremism

Another way that the West can slow or even reverse the spread of Islamist extremism is by helping Muslims around the world resurrect non-Islamist teachings and traditions. For nearly 15 centuries, Islam has been enriched by diverse religious and cultural traditions, which often contrast positively with Islamism's draconian interpretation of Islam. Rekindling ties to these varied traditions can provide a viable alternative to Islamist preaching, especially in the West and former Soviet Union, where spiritual alienation has emerged as a direct consequence of the loss of contact with older, more tolerant customs.

While Western governments do lack the expertise and credibility among Muslims to lead such an effort, they can provide financial, political, and moral support to non-Islamist scholars. Such assistance can focus on helping Muslim moderates form discussion networks, convene conferences, and popularize lesser-known hadiths and Qur'anic interpretations that stress the tolerance and innovation that characterized mainstream Islamic thought prior to "the closing of the gates of *ijtihad*." For example, non-Islamist scholars need financial assistance to preserve, restore, translate, and disseminate religious manuscripts that were lost to the world in forgotten warehouses, especially in Uzbekistan and the other Central Asian states that emerged from the wreckage of the Soviet Union. Academic exchanges should emphasize the universal contributions to global scholarship by Islamic thinkers such as Avicenna, Ibn Tufayl, and Averroës (whose influence and importance are described in Chapter 2) as well as the Iranian poet Rumi (whose mystical expression of the love of God is unmatched in its emotion and lyricism). By helping to reacquaint Muslims everywhere with these monumental and diverse expressions of Islamic thought, the West can provide a potent antidote to the hatred, subversion, and totalitarianism preached by al-Qaradawi and bin Laden.

Governments can also help Muslims restore a measure of religious pluralism and cultural diversity to their communities by preserving elements of national heritage in Muslim-majority countries. These elements include the religious (shrines and archeological sites of Islamic saints) as well as the secular (traditional music, crafts, and other arts); all of these are rejected, and eliminated, by Islamists, who view them as contrary to the norms of "true Islam." Wahhabi sects, in particular, have systematically destroyed tombs, houses, and other historical sites pertaining to some of Islam's greatest figures, including the homes of the Prophet Muhammad's family. The West can both discredit Islamist extremism and improve its own image among the world's Muslims by publicizing acts of cultural vandalism committed by Islamists, and by showing that the Islamists, not the West, are the ones who are in fact "anti-Islamic."

iv. Working with Governments of Muslim-Majority Countries against Islamism

It bears repeating that the struggle for what Islam will and should be is mainly a struggle involving Muslims themselves. At the same time, if Western governments are to assist Muslim moderates in turning back the advance of Islamism — chiefly by the measures just described — they will need help from governments of Muslim-majority countries. To date, rather than partnering with the West against their common Islamist enemy, many Middle Eastern governments have encouraged anti-Western and anti-Semitic sentiments at home, thereby diverting popular criticism away from the failings of their rulers. Other governments have ignored or even cultivated Islamism within their countries. In Pakistan, President Muhammad Zia ul-Haq supported and partnered with Islamist extremists in the 1980s to consolidate his political legitimacy and strengthen the country's military position vis-à-vis India (especially in the disputed territory of Kashmir). In Afghanistan, the United States supplied anti-aircraft missiles and other critical military supplies to violent Islamist mujahedeen against the Soviet Army. In Saudi Arabia, King Abdullah has acknowledged the strategic threat Wahhabi extremists pose to his kingdom, but Wahhabism remains entrenched as the kingdom's official ideology; even an absolute ruler cannot ignore the tremendous political and societal influence Islamists wield in the country. And in Turkey, a NATO member and EU candidate country, top government leaders refuse to discuss Islamism as a political ideology and reject the notion that Islamism plays any role in radicalizing Muslims toward violence.

US and European leaders have largely turned a blind eye to anti-Western indoctrination and Islamism in these countries so long as their governments cooperated on geopolitically important issues, such as the Israeli–Arab peace process, counterterrorism, and energy security. But neither the West nor these governments can afford to continue this short-sighted policy of "reciprocity." After their conquest of the Swat Valley in 2009, Pakistan's Islamist militants were on the verge of taking Islamabad itself; only after a bloody series of counterattacks was the Pakistani Army able to push the extremists back to the Afghanistan–Pakistan border region to which they had been previously confined. At the same time, Islamist terrorists in Saudi Arabia were preparing to unleash a massive wave of attacks crippling the country's oil and gas industries; this danger was only narrowly averted by the plotters' apprehension in March 2010. These near misses in two key countries may have created an opening for

Western leaders to press for reform; they should seize it. Specifically, they should press for school and university curricula and textbooks to purge hateful elements while emphasizing religious pluralism, cultural diversity, and critical thinking — for both genders. Western governments also need to insist on reciprocity from governments of Muslim-majority countries on issues of religious freedom; while Western governments readily grant Muslims permission to proselytize and to build new houses of worship, most Muslim-majority countries strongly prohibit these same activities for other religious groups — often under penalty of death. Western governments should also acknowledge (and give additional support to) those governments that are taking steps in the right direction. One example is Morocco, which, since the 2003 terrorist bombings in Casablanca, has sponsored numerous conferences and issued publications that highlight both the country's traditions of tolerance and pluralism, and the role of Sufism as a counterweight to Wahhabism and other extremist interpretations of Islam.

Western countries should also insist on the universal nature of human rights in their relations with Muslim-majority countries. This means, in particular, the firm rejection of efforts by the 56-member OIC to move international law into "compliance" with the Islamist version of sharia. Western leaders should categorically reject the claims by several OIC member states that they are not bound by any aspect of international law that contradicts their interpretation of sharia. The West should not fool itself into thinking it is showing "respect" to Muslims by acquiescing to the OIC's revisionist and intolerant approach to fundamental texts like the 1948 Universal Declaration of Human Rights; on the contrary, it would be more respectful to defend those Muslims currently denied such rights.

Governments of Muslim-majority countries clearly have much to do at home to hold back the tide of Islamism, in particular by reducing political repression and upholding human rights. As *The 9/11 Commission Report* concluded, a modern society based on democratic freedom and respect for human rights can provide a hopeful alternative to the hatred and medieval norms of Islamism. But as Western governments press for progress on democracy and human rights, they must be cognizant of political realities on the ground, especially the way Islamists use Western rhetoric and democratic processes to advance sharia at the expense of secular law. The Islamist terrorist group Hamas, which has long been dedicated not just to wiping Israel off the map but also to upholding sharia, exploited the process of democratic elections strongly favored by the United States to gain political power in the Gaza Strip. Western leaders must therefore help societies conduct prudent planning to prepare for elections and prevent Islamist extremists from misusing democratic processes to undermine democracy itself.

Finally, Western governments need to improve their cooperation with governments of Muslim-majority countries in rehabilitating Islamist radicals. Most counterradicalization programs, especially in the Middle East, focus on dissuading violent Islamists from continuing their violent behavior. A key tactic of such programs is to "rehabilitate" violent Islamists by convincing them to renounce violence in pursuit of their political objectives. From a strategic perspective, this approach is completely self-defeating, as the political goals — and thus the danger to Western societies — remain exactly the same. Moreover, many violent Islamists who have been "rehabilitated" in this way have returned to violence.[5] Recidivism among "former" Islamist terrorists and jihadists has been especially high in Yemen, where the government makes no attempt at ideologically deprogramming its Islamist extremists. Saudi Arabia's rehabilitation program has been more successful, because it offers money and jobs to those who complete the course. But even some graduates of Saudi Arabia's program — which similarly fails to address Islamists' political ideology — have returned to violent jihad.[6] The key to successfully rehabilitating violent Islamists is to address their underlying motivation; that is, their Islamist ideology. Once indoctrinated into Islamism, a person will not desist from the ideological objective of global domination just because he is convinced to reject violent tactics. Only after abandoning the political ideology of Islamism can a person move beyond the movement's intolerance and hatred.

4. Catalyzing an Islamic Renaissance

Even if the above policies are implemented immediately, the West remains at a disadvantage because it has awakened so late to the strategic threat

---

5   See, for example, the *60 Minutes* report about 11 of the 117 Guantanamo returnees who, after enrolling in the Saudi Arabian rehabilitation program, have since appeared on the country's most wanted list: *60 Minutes*, "Reeducating Osama Bin Laden's Disciples," *60 Minutes*, *CBSNews.com* (May 3, 2009), available at: www.cbsnews.com/stories/2009/04/30/60minutes/main4980766.shtml (accessed January 30, 2011).

6   See, for example, Robert F. Worth, "Freed by the U.S., Saudi Becomes a Qaeda Chief," *New York Times* (January 22, 2009), available at: www.nytimes.com/2009/01/23/world/middleeast/23yemen.html (accessed January 30, 2011).

posed by Islamism. As this political-religious ideology has spread around the world in recent decades, its narrow and harsh interpretation of Islam has crept into mainstream thinking among Muslims in Europe, the United States, and around the globe. This reality makes the measures described above all the more urgent. But even these steps are unlikely to suffice in redirecting the momentum of Islamic thought toward the religious pluralism, cultural diversity, and rationality that once prevailed in mainstream Islamic thinking. Preventing the spread of Islamism in both its violent and political forms may require a renaissance in Islamic thought itself.

In 2010, Islam began its fifteenth century, as measured from the year 610, when Muhammad first began receiving the revelations that became the Qur'an. By comparison, as Christianity began its fifteenth century, it was only gradually emerging from the Middle Ages. Humanist scholars were rediscovering the "pagan" Greek and Roman classics; *The Ninety-Five Theses* of Martin Luther that began the Reformation were still 22 years in the future; and in the future, too, were the resulting centuries of struggle for the "mainstream" of Christian thought. The ideas that religion might not be the key to human understanding, and that it was an entity separate from both literature *and* politics — in sum, the ideas of the Enlightenment — would not take root for a further three centuries. Indeed, as historians Peter Gay and Robert K. Webb have argued, in the Europe of this period, "economics and politics were not yet separated from religion, [not] even in thought."[7]

Seen from the perspective of Christianity's own history, it is less surprising that Islamist ideology insists that politics, economics, and all other aspects of life be regulated by God's divine law. It should not be inconceivable that during its fifteenth century, Islam could experience its own renaissance, perhaps leading to periods of reformation and enlightenment according to the pattern of Christianity's experience. After all, hundreds of millions of Muslims seek to preserve the political, economic, and cultural freedoms they currently enjoy in diverse societies around the world even as they struggle to comprehend the appropriate role for sharia in their private and public lives. Given the chance, the vast majority of the world's Muslims, like Renaissance Christians before them, would want to make the individual's relationship with God the central focus of their religion. But Islamists are hard at work to prevent this from happening.

It is those Muslims who have suffered acutely from Islamist pressure

---

7   Peter Gay and Robert Kiefer Webb, *Modern Europe to 1815* (New York: Harper & Row, 1973), p. 127.

who most seek a return of humanism in Islam. These include large seg-ments of Iran's population, who for three decades have argued they should not be denied the universal human rights and democratic freedom Westerners cherish simply because of their politics and religion. They also include the members of "differentiated communities," discussed in Chapter 3, who for reasons of theology or ethnicity have for centuries been oppressed by fellow Muslims. Moreover, millions of other Muslims, whether in Muslim-majority or Western countries, are fully commit-ted both to Islam and to the universal human rights proclaimed during Europe's Enlightenment. Such advocates are regularly (and often vio-lently) silenced by Islamists (who see them as apostates) and ignored by Westerners (who fear taking sides in an internal religious debate). Worse, many Westerners do not believe such a humanist movement in Islam could succeed given the serious opposition it faces (and given their own societies' timidity in confronting Islamist ideologues). As a result, non-Islamists are stuck in a vicious cycle, in which their lack of insufficient financial, political, and moral support leads to further losses of financial, political, and moral support. If they remain trapped in this virtual black hole, moderates will never be able to disseminate their ideas, organize themselves, or project their voices with any real impact.

Muslim humanists can help their own cause by refocusing the inter-nal Muslim scholarly debate away from the zero-sum approach to the question of why Islam declined relative to Christianity, and toward the problem of *how* to ensure the realization of each individual Muslim's full human potential. Many leading Muslim thinkers have fixated on explain-ing "what went wrong" from the sixteenth century onward, as Europe's scientific, technological, philosophical, and literary achievements began to eclipse those of previously dominant Muslim scholars. This obsession with the fall of Islam has generated a victimization complex and a sense that "Islam is under siege." The main result of this sense of victimization, as this book suggests, is the rise of militant Islamism as a source of renewed confidence. The sense of victimization is responsible for Islamists' call to "purify" Islam by returning to a period when the West was a weakened nonentity: to the first century *anno Hegirae*; that is, the first century of the Islamic era. It does not seem to concern them that they are viewing this "pure" era through the distorting lenses of revisionist fundamental-ism (i.e., the teachings of Ibn Abd al-Wahhab and Ibn Taymiyyah) and of revolutionary idealism (i.e., the teachings of Marx and Lenin). What matters is the *hope* that this stark fundamentalism provides: all is not lost, as the *umma*'s "defeat" at the hands of the West can be avenged.

Fortunately, this bleak political vision represents just one strain among many in Islamic thought. There are dozens of other schools that have accepted the compatibility of Islam and humanistic reason, even after *ijtihad*'s gates allegedly clanged shut some 11 centuries ago. An Islamic renaissance would involve the further development of Islamic humanism, perhaps even in new directions; what it *does not* mean is the spread of the fossilized, frozen fundamentalism of the Wahhabis. This new humanism can and should remain inclusive, though there is one strain it must reject: the Arabian tribal norms and totalitarian ideological tendencies that are Islamism's poisoned gift to Islamic philosophy. The underlying goal of this effort would be to restore the individual and his or her personal relationship with God as the central focus of Islam. Both Jesus and Muhammad preached against religious hierarchies and their legalistic, rigid understandings of God; Christianity has overwhelmingly returned to its founder's vision, and Islam must do the same.

In addition to this large-scale reexamination of fundamentalist and Islamist legacy, Muslim scholars must clarify two particular aspects of the current mainstream understanding of sharia that are utterly at odds with the modern concept of human rights: the mistreatment of women, and the condemnation of apostates.

The return of humanism to Islam would indeed offer vast improvements in the lives of Muslim women, and could invigorate Muslim societies as a whole. The current predominant interpretation of sharia permits Muslim men to escape responsibility in making arduous moral choices by imposing restrictions on the freedom of women. For example, the covering of women in theory reduces sexual temptation for men in daily life; the sanctioning of polygamy eliminates the dilemmas surrounding adultery; and the institution known as *nikah al-mutah* ("temporary marriage") often provides men with a religiously justified equivalent to prostitution. These medieval interpretations of sharia discourage Muslim men from developing respect for women as individuals, and therefore from resolving conflicts through compromise within their households, societies, and the international community. Such thinking aggravates the divide between "us" and "the other," which makes it harder to view Jews or Americans in any way other than as enemies. Thus, a key starting point for an Islamic renaissance would be to modernize the understanding of sharia to ensure Muslim women's human rights and full equality with Muslim men.

Sharia need not be an all-encompassing legal system based on medieval legal codes. Today, the dominant interpretation holds that Muslims who convert from Islam to another faith — as well as those who merely disagree with the tenets of Islamism — are apostates. In the minds of Islamists, apostasy can have only one punishment: death. Yet countless Muslim theologians and intellectuals over the centuries have maintained that only individual Muslims — and not, say, sharia courts — can determine for themselves their standing with God and God's laws. Similarly, the separation of state and religion, which is anathema for Islamists, is possible in Islam. (It was only recently that this separation took hold among Christian nations.) The key to initiating such a rebirth and reform of Islam is to separate medieval Arab cultural norms from Islam's universal messages, and to denounce any practice that is repressive toward women (such as honor killings, female genital mutilation, and forced covering) as incompatible with Islamic ethics.

While Muslim moderates must bear the primary burden in restoring humanism to Islam, the West can contribute to this effort in three key ways. First, the West can help lay the intellectual and psychological foundation for humanism's reemergence in Islamic thought. Specifically, instead of focusing Muslim outreach programs on interfaith dialogue in which individuals from varying religions identify common views, Western officials and activists can facilitate conversations among secular as well as religious leaders to explore the interrelation among the concepts of Islam, democracy, and universal human rights. Western governments can promote the writings of non-Islamist Muslim theologians who advocate for the compatibility of Islam and universal human rights and who are often attacked in their own countries as apostates. Rather than referring to "the Muslim world" or treating American or European Muslims as if they somehow speak for the billion others who share their faith, Western governments need instead to treat Muslims as individuals, with the same rights — and responsibilities — as any other individuals and citizens. Outreach programs should not focus only on religion, but should include — and target — a much broader range of social and cultural activities, such as music, fine arts, and sports, while also involving gender mixing across religions and ethnicities. Not every Muslim citizen can be reached at a mosque; after all, a government outreach effort directed toward Jews would be hopelessly incomplete if it included only those worshiping at a synagogue. In the contemporary Western context, individuals choose many ways to express their spirituality; not all of them do so via participation in organized religious activity.

A second way Western governments can help catalyze an Islamic renaissance is by focusing education and exchange programs on historical and intellectual connections between Muslim thinkers and European humanists during the Renaissance and by extension the Enlightenment. Such programs would highlight the influence on the Renaissance of Islamic philosophers, scientists, and mathematicians, who blended tolerant faith and scientific learning and who valued reason as a tool understanding God's divine law and the external world. We know, for example, that Avicenna's medical studies formed a key element of Renaissance medical curricula, while Averroës was considered "the Commentator" on Aristotle. These and many other Islamic thinkers did not believe society should be organized around a specific interpretation of sharia; they neither rejected reason as a means of ascertaining divine truth, nor kept silent about the destruction of manuscripts and slaughter of scholars that accompanied the shutting of *ijtihad*'s gates in the tenth century. Furthermore, tolerant and pluralistic interpretations of sharia and Islam live on in the present day, especially in the areas beyond the Arab Middle East where more than 80 percent of the world's Muslims live. These interpretations are found among the followers of al-Maturidi and the Mu'tazili, and are present as well in some Sufi movements that embrace humanism and religious tolerance.

A third way Western governments can help catalyze an Islamic renaissance is to support understandings of Islam that accept gender equality. While it remains the task of Islamic scholars to develop interpretations of sharia that would accord women equal treatment, the West can stop allowing Islamist men to carve out "religious" exemptions for Muslim women from the universal application of human rights. In the West, women won their civil and human rights through centuries of struggle against entrenched social customs and religious authorities; gender equality is now a fundamental principle of Western law. This acquiescence to so-called Islamic sensitivities — in reality Islamist sensitivities — casts doubt on the West's insistence that all human beings enjoy the same fundamental rights and smacks of a double standard.

Even some Western feminists are reluctant to support Muslim women who fight physical and psychological abuse, deeming their Muslim counterparts as "Westernized" and therefore disrespectful of their own Islamic culture. They often justify repressive practices within Islam by pointing to examples of them in Western cultures, for example the wearing of head coverings among devout Christian and Jewish women.[8] However,

---

8   See, for example, Phyllis Chesler, "How My Eyes Were Opened to the Barbarity of Islam: Is it Racist to Condemn Fanaticism?" *Times Online* (March 7, 2007), available at: www.timesonline.co.uk/tol/comment/columnists/guest_contributors/article1480090.ece

such comparisons are at best inaccurate, since the practice of wearing a headscarf is not widespread among non-Muslims and is evident today only within smaller Christian or Jewish communities, such as Maronite Catholics, Amish Protestants, or Hasidic Jews. Western feminists cannot legitimately justify their tolerance of Islamist intolerance, given its serious and sometimes tragic consequences — including beatings and honor killings — for Muslim women. Western feminists and others can help mitigate such abuse against women through a process of dialogue that highlights Islam's own history, such as the Prophet Muhammad prohibiting forced marriages. Western engagement initiatives can also call attention to writings by Muslim women about their personal experiences, especially those who once suffered physical abuse justified by family members on religious grounds, but who eventually realized such behavior had no place in Islam.

Ultimately, an Islamic renaissance is unlikely to emerge anytime in the near future. Muslim moderates who espouse the values it would usher in are doubly rejected: by Islamists as apostates who betray their faith, and by the West as naifs of marginal influence. Yet the seeds are already planted deep in the soil of the Muslim community, in the form of the philosophies of classical Islam and the aspirations of hundreds of millions who want lives that include both the liberties of modern life and a time-honored spirituality. Western governments and societies face a fundamental choice: they can make the prospect of an Islamic renaissance more remote by continuing to partner with Islamist ideologues, or they can help hundreds of millions of Muslims sustain the compatibility of their modern lives and Islam.

Like Christianity, which has evolved over time, Islam can and must adapt to the changing norms of modern society. As Islam completes its fourteenth century, it remains caught in a struggle between Islamist fundamentalists and modern Muslim moderates for its heart and soul. Perhaps this is the beginning of an era of profound reform within Islam, during which democracy and human rights will flourish. Perhaps instead it is the end of an era, when Islam's richly diverse traditions of tolerance and moderation will be consigned to the history books. What can be said for certain, however, is that the outcome of this struggle should leave no one indifferent — especially Muslims, whose destiny is being decided at this very moment.

(accessed January 30, 2011); and Kay S. Hymowitz, "Why Feminism is AWOL on Islam," *City Journal* (Winter 2003), available at: www.city-journal.org/html/13_1_why_feminism. html (accessed January 30, 2011).